"A superb read! Im
everyone interestec
turn greater safety.

—**Joe Navarro**, author of the international bestseller, *What Every BODY is Saying*

"Sam is the ultimate warrior, both mentally and physically. He understands we have to invest today to both protect and shape the future of tomorrow. I could not recommend *Live Ready* more highly."

—**James Scalo**, CEO Burns & Scalo Real Estate, and Author of *Work them to Life*

"I've known Sam as one of the world's leading authorities on personal security for nearly 20 years, and *Live Ready* is the first book of its kind to provide real, comprehensive solutions for everyday people for living in a predatory world. Buy this book, and give copies to everyone you love."

—**Karen Eden**, Martial Arts Master Instructor

"Take it from a guy who has taught street safety and situational awareness since 1969, including 29 years as a police officer: *Live Ready* is a vitally important book for everyone—pacifist and warrior alike. Sam Rosenberg's writing is clear, straight to the point, and information-rich. His innovative approach to 'protecting yourself in an uncertain world' made me sit up and go, 'This is great. Why haven't I thought of this?' This book will change your life."

—**Loren Christensen**, bestselling author of over 70 books, including *On Combat*, *Deadly Force Encounters*, and *Surviving a School Shooting*

"Blending a mastery of human behavior and a warrior ethos, *Live Ready* is a gripping and invaluable resource that will change the way you view personal safety. With powerful personal anecdotes and practical lessons, Rosenberg equips readers with the skills needed to protect themselves and their loved ones in these turbulent times. This essential guide offers a lifeline in a world plagued by violence, urging readers to embrace a life of readiness and live life to the fullest."

—**Robin Dreeke**, retired FBI agent, USMC Veteran, author of *Sizing People Up: A Veteran FBI Agent's User Manual for Behavior Prediction*

"How do you minimize the likelihood of becoming an unprepared victim of violence? Read this book! *Live Ready* is an excellent guide to assessing, reacting, and responding to perceived threats. As the author states, 'In the swimming pool of life, there are no lifeguards.' Each person is inherently responsible for their own safety as well as their family. Sam Rosenberg takes the reader through an A-to-Z examination of how to be prepared for and to recognize a threat, while utilizing techniques in avoiding a violent encounter. This an essential read for anyone interested in executive protection or personal safety and vigilance."

—**Mike Roche**, retired U.S. Secret Service, and author of *Mass Killers: How You Can Identify Workplace, School, or Public Killers Before They Strike.*

"Early in Sam's book, *Live Ready*, I came across this statement: 'Knowing how to protect yourself from danger is much more than just a skill; it comes with a special brand of confidence, one that fulfills a fundamental human need.' That fundamental itch, once experienced, remains with you and becomes who you are. I've used it to protect myself, those dear to me, and others throughout my life. Reading his book and paying attention to both the written word and its context will impart confirmation of areas that you may need to improve. Sam writes, 'The reality is that you control the most important situational factors. You have to understand those factors and consciously never relinquish control of them. By understanding and accepting your own power, deterrence is not only possible; it's probable.' From Sam's mouth to God's ear. I've known Sam for a very long time. He walks the walk. *Live Ready* is highly recommended."

—LCDR **Larry B. Lambert** USNR (Operational SEAL Teams)/ Supervising Investigator and Task Force Commander/Clandestine Service Officer

"*Live Ready* is an enlightened read for both the average Joe and seasoned fighter. It reminds us all how vulnerable we are in today's society, and it helps us navigate the little things that are often the important things: Awareness, diffusing situations, and common-sense practices for being safe and living ready!"

—**Rick Steigerwald**, Pennsylvania State Athletic Commissioner

"*Live Ready* is an owner's manual for personal security, a must read for anyone interested in learning how to protect themselves and their loved ones. The timing is critical considering the increased incidence of violence in our world.

The book is well-written, related in an accessible and easy-to-understand style that uses the power of real-world situations to help the reader better understand and apply critical principles. Importantly, *Live Ready* integrates scientific and verified third-party statistics to support the author's expertise and experience."

—**Sandra Gramling**, Behavioral Healthcare Professional

"*Live Ready* could literally save your life! I've been fortunate to have known Sam for over 20 years, and he is dedicated to helping us be prepared for an event we all hope will never happen in our lifetime. Sam worked with me, my family, everyone else in my life that could be helped by Sam's teachings. He is an Angel!"

—**Bob Ford**, Former PGA Professional at Oakmont Country Club and Seminole Golf Club

"In this dangerous world, *Live Ready* could save your life. Read it, read it again, and then share it with those who are most important to you. *Live Ready* provides a roadmap for those seeking to take accountability for their personal protection."

—**Elaine Conte**, President & CEO, Alston Machine Company

"Oh, this is such a great book, a vitally important book. Written by a master's master in his field, Sam Rosenberg's easy-to-understand, conversational approach will make it seem like he is right there next to you as you read his words. His teachings and methods will absolutely save lives. Yours might be one of them.

So please, read it slowly and carefully to fully understand all the techniques and information. I promise you that this book will change your life for the better, and make you a safer person in a very unsafe world. My great wish is that I could snap my fingers and magically get *Live Ready* into the hands of every single American in our great country."

—**Richard Busch**, JPFO Ambassador, Jews for the Preservation of Firearms Ownership

"I saw combat during my 20 years in the Marine Corps, and I've had countless confrontations in bars, traffic, and other random situations (despite the fact I am not a hothead). This book both clarified things I have experienced and filled in critical gaps in my knowledge base. If I had access to these concepts when I was 20, I could have faced life with greater confidence and had far less 'discovery learning' in dangerous situations. Now, I can empower my family with these vital skills, at a time it will serve them for life! Thank you for writing it, Sam."

—**Dan Rubel**, USMC, Retired

"As a proud military veteran, someone with an accomplished law enforcement and academic career, and as the founder of CSI, Corporate Security and Investigations, I take recommendations very seriously simply because they are a reflection of my name and reputation. In this case, not only do I not hesitate to recommend Sam Rosenberg's book, *Live Ready*, I am proud and honored to do so. I can personally attest to the fact that *Live Ready* is a manifestation of Sam's life's work not only in the military but in the venues of law enforcement, academia, and business, where I have personally relied on Sam's expertise in every venue to deliver to our clients the very essence of the material in this work that everyone should read and absorb.

Sam, I thank you for making this product available to the general public."

—**Lou Gentile**, Founder of CSI

"Violent crime has a profound effect on society. There is no doubt that we are seeing more of it now than we have in decades. Yet when someone is in imminent danger, it is mind boggling how many bystanders do absolutely nothing to help, not even to call 911 … And the police most often cannot be there in time to help anybody. So, we must all be our own first responders.

None of this is meant to frighten you into hiding under your bed. Rather, it is an invitation to empower yourself to learn to live your life more fully and freely, safely and resourcefully.

*Live Ready* teaches us that each individual has a responsibility, a social compact, to better protect themselves. We are not helpless. We can learn new skills and how to utilize them. With a thoughtful reading of this book, you will be better equipped to stop (as Sam calls them) 'the Bad Guys.' It just may save your life, and the lives of those you love."

—**Cynthia Busch**, Pittsburgh Symphony Orchestra Musician, Retired

# LIVE READY

ISBN 978-1-960378-13-2 (hardcover)
ISBN 978-1-960378-14-9 (paperback)
ISBN 978-1-960378-15-6 (eBook)

1st edition
Pittsburgh, PA

Design by Anna Hall

*For Chrissy, Ruby, and Samson*

# LIVE READY

---

## A GUIDE TO PROTECTING YOURSELF IN AN UNCERTAIN WORLD

---

by Sam Rosenberg

# Contents

# AUTHOR'S NOTE

I HAVE WORKED for more than twenty years in close protection services, an industry that holds client confidentiality in extremely high regard. As such, while the stories and anecdotes contained in this book are all true, I have altered the names of my clients and other identifying details to protect their confidentiality and better ensure their safety and the safety of their families.

You will also find that I have taken the liberty of using the term "Bad Guy" to describe the people who commit the kinds of violent crime addressed in this book. A few caveats for this catch-all term:

1. Though it contains the word "Bad," this does not mean that everyone who commits an act of violence is a bad person. People commit violence for many reasons, and certainly not all violent acts are committed by bad people. I use this term for simplicity's sake to generally define those who would commit predatory or targeted violence against the innocent.

2. Just because the term contains the word "Guy," it certainly does not mean that every perpetrator of violence is a "guy," as you will see in some of

the case studies explored in this book. As with "Bad," I use this word for simplicity's sake, as the majority of violent perpetrators, both nationally and internationally, are in fact men.

3. In keeping with the above, this book often uses masculine pronouns to describe those perpetrators. This is for simplicity, convenience, and consistency. Sometimes the more general "they" or "them" fits the context of the discussion, but other times, singular pronouns are more efficient.

In the end, the term simply refers to someone who would attempt to harm you, whether they are a professional criminal or a first-time offender, and no matter what their gender. The central goal of this book is to teach you everything you need to know to identify these Bad Guys so that you can avoid them, or defend yourself against them, in any setting and scenario you might encounter in this dangerous world.

Lastly, it's true that notoriety is the fuel that feeds the fire for those who commit mass homicide. That said, the decision to use the perpetrators' real names in this book was a deliberate one. It is a decision I struggled with, as I have always been a proponent of never mentioning these names and feeding this fire. Ultimately, I decided to do so here as I believe that the risks are outweighed by the learning value gained through a frank discussion of these incidents, both in terms of accuracy and as a matter of record.

# FOREWORD

By Lt. Col. Dave Grossman

SAM ROSENBERG'S *Live Ready* is the best book I have read in many, many years. And I read a *lot* of books. I usually read very quickly, but every once in a while, I encounter the rare book that requires me to go back and read it again, slowly and carefully. *Live Ready* was one of those. It is a vital, valid, and invaluable resource for those who desire to protect themselves and their loved ones in these violent times.

At one level, *Live Ready* is a powerful personal tale—a coming-of-age story, a warrior's journey as gripping and well written as any novel. From the first few pages, when our protagonist has a gun shoved in his face, you can't help but find yourself identifying with the narrator. But unlike a work of fiction, this story is true!

Most importantly, on another level, this book delivers a treasure trove of essential and immediately applicable lessons on how to live a life of readiness, and how to survive and thrive in a violent world. These lessons are masterfully communicated by Sam Rosenberg, a world-class warrior, trainer, protector, and in his words, "a fanatical student of the craft." (And we can now add "master warrior-word-smith" to the list!)

Sam's observation about the fear and insecurity we can observe among even the rich and powerful is simply superb:

> *I came to realize that this uncertainty originated from a sense of insecurity in their ability to protect themselves and their families on a primal level. They had achieved financial security long ago. Most lived in safe neighborhoods and for the most part were well protected by society and the people around them. But there was that nagging sensation in the back of their minds that, physically, someone could take it all away from them in a heartbeat.*

*This* is the sheep vs. the sheepdog, the predator vs. the prey, in a way that I have never seen it put before. A life of full contentment is indeed about being able to "Live Ready" so that you can live fully and completely.

Much as we think of the heroes and lawmen of the Wild West, future generations will look back in awe upon the warriors who rose to the challenges of this era. Yet, while the violence of those bygone days is mostly a Hollywood myth, the violence of today is very real. I call these violent times we live in a "Warrior Renaissance," and with *Live Ready*, Sam Rosenberg proves that he is one of the great minds to usher us through.

Now more than ever, we all need this book. But before we dive deeper into why I believe this is true, you must first understand some critical concepts related to what feels like (and in fact *is*) a huge uptick in violence, both in the US and globally. It's easy to read or watch the news and feel as if the situation is grim. When we examine the raw numbers, we see that it is in fact much, much worse than it looks.

## *Medical Technology Is Holding Down the Murder Rate*

The annual increase in homicides is a key factor in assessing the degree of violence in our society. At the micro level of an individual attack, or even at the macro level of national homicide rates, the "number of dead people" is the measurement by which we typically judge the problem.

But there's a major flaw in this data: the murder rate underrepresents the rate of violent crime simply because *medical technology is saving more lives than ever before.*[1]

In 2002, Anthony Harris, along with a team of scholars from the University of Massachusetts and Harvard, published their landmark research in the journal *Homicide Studies.* They concluded that advances in medical technology between 1960 and 1999 *cut the reported murder rate to*

---

1    In response to this flaw, there is a temptation to use the "aggravated assault" data instead of the murder data, but it is too easy to fudge the figures on ag assault. Any seasoned cop will tell you that we can make the ag assault rate say whatever we want it to say, simply by shifting that magic line between ag assault and simple assault. It's very much like grade inflation in our schools. Murder offers far better data to draw from because there is no imaginary line. Dead is dead, and it's harder to fudge those numbers.

*a third—and in some instances, even to a quarter—of what it would have been otherwise.* The leaps and bounds of lifesaving technology that have emerged in the decades since have had a similar impact on the ability of first responders, medical professionals, and even everyday citizens to save the lives of victims of violence, thus preventing ever more murders.

Consider, for instance, that almost all first responders (and many civilians) now carry tourniquets, while twenty years ago, this was unheard of. If a cop slaps on a tourniquet and saves a crime victim's life, they have prevented a murder. Some medical experts believe that tourniquets alone may have cut the murder rate in half in just the past decade. And that's only one small piece of the astounding medical technology being applied every day, saving lives and holding down the body count while also concealing just how violent and destructive our nation has become.

Everyone understands the concept of inflation-adjusted dollars. When we finally start reporting "medically adjusted murders," then we will begin to appreciate just how desperately, tragically *bad* the situation has become. For every murder we report, *an ever-increasing number of our citizens might have had their lives saved, and yet they remain* physically maimed and scarred, emotionally crippled and traumatized by the violence they experienced. These are the many crimes that don't cross the threshold into murder simply because medical technology saved the victim's life.

So what are the real numbers? By Harris's findings, we can deduce that we must multiply reported homicides in the 1990s by a factor of about 3.5 if we hope to compare the numbers accurately with those reported during the

1960s. A similar dynamic is in play between the 1990s and the 2020s.

Even before we consider the medically adjusted murder rate, the recent annual increase in homicides in the United States is unsettling. In 2020, it was over *30 percent*. The worst we had ever seen previously happened way back in the 1960s, when we saw a 12 percent annual increase. But that comparison completely breaks down when you remember the factor of 3.5 between reported homicides and medically prevented homicides during the period between 1960 and 1990. If we can assume a similar factor between 1990 and today, then what happened in 2020 was nearly ten times more violent than anything we have ever seen before, and 2021 (up another 4 percent) was even worse.

When we think of the matter in these terms, it's clear that we all need to learn how to Live Ready; it's a dangerous, violent world out there. Today, that need is demonstrably, irrefutably, orders-of-magnitude greater than the reported homicide rate would have you believe.

## *We Are Getting Good at Stopping These Crimes!*

Across America, as I train law enforcement and school safety professionals, I hear a consistent message: "You never hear about the ones we stop." Our society in general, and our law enforcement community in particular, have become very good at stopping many of these horrific mass murders. In schools and workplaces, we are no longer in denial (with some notable, tragic exceptions), and we often take effective action before the crime occurs. (What kind of action is "effective?" Funny you should ask, because the answers are in large part what this wonderful book is all about!)

I believe that today the odds are *very good* that the Littleton, Colorado, school shooters would have been caught before they committed their massacre at Columbine High School.

This much is clear: we are getting better at spotting and stopping these killers ahead of time. And when attempted mass murders do occur, rapid and effective response by police (and, increasingly, by citizens) has been a key dynamic in the equation of life and death.

Even still, school homicide rates are exploding. And the number of attacks is also increasing.

The National Center for Education Statistics' "2021 Violent Deaths at School" report[2] tells us that after a modern low of eleven reported school shootings in the 2009–10 school year,[3] the rate trended upward to thirty-six in 2016–17 before climbing rapidly to an astonishing seventy-five separate shooting incidents in both 2018–19 and 2019–20. The final year is particularly troubling because schools were closed for a large portion of that year due to the pandemic.

---

2  National Center for Education Statistics. (2022). Violent Deaths at School and Away from School and School Shootings. Condition of Education. U.S. Department of Education, Institute of Education Sciences.

3  Roughly half of these reported incidents were to people who presented with "injuries only," while the rest were categorized as "shootings with deaths."

## This Is Not Normal. It Is Not "Business as Usual"

Yes, there have always been mass murders. Historically, they were most often motivated by war, religious or tribal conflict, or ideology. But the "lone wolf" massacres like those we hear about almost every day in the news are profoundly rare by historical comparison.

In my own research, I have tracked mass murders committed by juveniles in their schools. Until recently, such an event was unprecedented in human history. In my book *Assassination Generation*,[4] I compiled a list of school massacres committed by juveniles (up through 2014), and a few things immediately stood out.

First, over the course of 5,000 years of recorded history, 500 years of gunpowder weapons, and 150 years of repeating firearms, the first time a juvenile committed a mass murder in their school was in 1975. Today, massacres and the threat of such crimes are a reality more than once per week in the United States. But the other startling discovery to emerge from my research is that they occur in nearly every nation on the planet.

During the period studied, these murders occurred in Argentina, Canada, Finland, Germany, Russia, and Thailand. The first (again, the very first that I can find in human history) occurred in Canada, while a

---

4   *Assassination Generation: Video Games, Aggression, and the Psychology of Killing.* Lt. Col. Dave Grossman, Kristine Paulsen, and Katie Miserany. Little, Brown and Company. November 15, 2016.

seventeen-year-old student in Germany set the all-time
record number of murders for a mass-killing juvenile (and
not just in a school, but anywhere). The two Columbine
killers murdered thirteen people between them, but the
killer in Germany gunned down fifteen by himself. [5]
In 2018, in Russia, twenty were murdered and seventy wounded
by an eighteen-year-old perpetrator on a college campus.
In China, we have seen a series of knife massacres across
the years, with horrendous body counts in schools, kinder-
gartens, and even nurseries.

Thus, this book and Sam Rosenberg's work are not just
vital information for America. Around the world, people
are asking the question that Sam answers in the pages to
come: How can we be safe in these violent times?

This breakdown of law and order, the systematic erosion
of the fabric of our civilization, is the single most important
issue facing us today. And the most horrific part is that most
people don't even know what is happening!

As Sam so superbly puts it,

> *In a dangerous world, you have two choices. You can*
> *either pull the veils of denial back over your eyes and*

---

5    None of these totals include the killers when they commit suicide as
     part of the act. Also, in 2002, a nineteen-year-old, expelled high school
     student murdered sixteen people at his former school in Erfurt, Germany,
     and an eighteen-year-old student murdered nine in his school in Tuusula,
     Finland, in 2007. Because these killers were over the age of eighteen,
     however, they don't qualify for the juvenile mass murder hit parade.

*return to the myths of helplessness and randomness,*
*or you can choose to become dangerous yourself, own*
*your personal security, master this step on the hier-*
*archy of self-actualization, and Live Ready.*

## *What Are the New Factors?*

If we're going to figure out why these disturbing trends
are occurring, we must think like a scientist, think like a
detective, and ask the vital question, "What are the *new*
factors that were never there before?"

Here, too, Sam has made a singularly vital contribution
to our understanding. His work tracing the societal transi-
tion from serial killers to spree killers covers ground I have
never seen touched upon before. And his explanation as to
the new factors is brilliant:

> *This is not to suggest that you can't have some rotten*
> *apples; rather, it is to illuminate that the cases where*
> *a seemingly normal kid devolves into a monstrous*
> *mass killer always come from a place where that*
> *sense of personal responsibility and morality is*
> *absent, usually in their early upbringing. Kids*
> *who are allowed to play [violent video games] and*
> *submit to this culture without moral and personal*
> *oversight have the potential to develop violent*
> *tendencies, and even then, those tendencies are not*
> *enough on their own to make them killers. There*
> *is a massive difference between being systemati-*
> *cally desensitized to violence and being capable of*

*murder. The latter requires intense underdevelopment, character disorder, narcissism, paranoia, and a malignant lack of personal responsibility.*

*So yes, conditions in our society and culture are making it more possible for people to evolve into killers of this nature, but what makes them killers is a (thankfully) rare psychological cocktail dominated by intense paranoia and this specific brand of narcissism.*

*Put this way, the profile of a mass killer starts to sound similar in many ways to the profile of a serial killer. Both are mission oriented. Both take pleasure in violence. Both are ultimately seeking notoriety from a society that they believe has ignored or mistreated them. They are mad, and they want everyone to know why. Just as importantly, they are so narcissistic that they actually believe everyone in the world will care.*

To this, I can respond with the ultimate compliment from one author to another: I wish I had written those words!

In my books, encyclopedia entries, and scholarly journal articles, I have repeatedly written that violent media, video game "mass murder simulators," and the fame given to killers by our media are just the *new* factors. No matter what we do about them, all the *old* problems *are still there.* And those problems extend beyond just the body count; they have an immeasurable impact on society at large.

## The Psychological Trauma of Violence

A monstrous mass murder by a single individual can create more psychosocial trauma than countless deaths by disease. In its section on PTSD, the *DSM-5* (the bible of psychology and psychiatry) tells us that, whenever the cause of trauma is "human in nature" (such as assault, torture, or rape) the degree of trauma is usually "more severe and long lasting."

I often say to my audiences, "You tell me: Is there a difference between a tornado hitting your house and putting your family in the hospital, and criminals breaking into your house and beating your family into a hospital stay?"

Most people would say that there is all the difference in the world.

Millions die from disease every day, and it has little impact on our behavior. But one serial killer or serial rapist can paralyze a city. And one horrendous mass murder can stun a nation.

On 9/11, terrorists murdered 3,000 of our citizens. Our stock market crashed, our way of life changed, and we invaded two nations in response. That same year, over 30,000 Americans died in traffic accidents, and nothing changed—*because they were accidents.*

The overall societal harm of violent crime can be far greater than the harm caused by disease or other deaths by natural causes.

To whatever degree you were concerned about the impact of violence upon you and your loved ones, today, that concern should be amplified, focused, and equipped with an understanding of the psychologically corrosive and destructive impact that a violent incident can force upon you and your loved ones.

Which brings us back to the book you hold in your hand. I know of no other book like it! Amazingly well written, informative, and empowering, *this* is essential reading for every citizen in these violent times.

*Live Ready* is the natural successor to my book *On Combat*.[6] It truly delves into the science of this vital subject, focusing from the general (the psychology and physiology of combat) to the specific (the sharing of this essential information in order to Live Ready, to survive and thrive in a violent world).

In Sam's words, it is about,

> . . . *developing that powerful, resilient, confident psychology that will carry over to every aspect of your life. But ultimately, what this book is really about is making you a more complete person; it is about forging you into someone stronger, more resilient, more capable, and better equipped to live your best life. This has very little to do with the actual, physical act of self-defense; rather, it has very much to do with the idea that humans fundamentally need to feel secure, and that genuine sense of security*

6    *On Combat: The Psychology and Physiology of Deadly Conflict in War and in Peace.* Lt. Col. Dave Grossman, Loren W. Christensen. Warrior Science Publications. October 1, 2008.

*cannot come from outside forces. That genuine sense of security is entirely up to you. It is literally in your hands . . .*

Even in the realm of Sam's guidance on finding a martial art or a training system (with his advice to seek a "vertical system" rather than a "horizontal system"), this work is brilliant, spot-on, and based on solid science.

## *For Such a Time as This*

A virus of violence, a cancer of crime is exploding in our streets and in our lives. This explosion of violence and mass murders is real, and it has enormous potential to inflict horrendous harm upon our citizens and our civilization. And yet, in the midst of these tragic times, Sam Rosenberg offers great hope:

> *To me, this is the essence of Living Ready. To be peaceful is not to be helpless; it is to have the capacity to do violence if need be, but to never do so inappropriately . . .*
>
> *Life is not about waiting for the lifeguards. It's not about constructing bunkers and living in fear. When you accept that the world is not without danger, that anything worth doing is not without risk, and that you can be your own lifeguard, that is when you conquer fear and live beyond uncertainty.*
>
> *Ultimately, you become certain not in the outcomes but in your ability to meet whatever challenge*

*may present itself. You become dangerous yourself and learn to Live Ready.*

To which I can only say, "Amen."

With all my heart, I encourage you—I *exhort* you—to read, study, and apply this book into your own life. As we love our families, as we love our nation, as we love our way of life, we must rise to the challenge of the Warrior Renaissance.

Apply this book and make your part of the world a better and safer place. Then buy copies and send them to your friends and loved ones. In doing so, you can help save lives and join Sam Rosenberg in leading us home from the dark and tragic place to which we have traveled.

—Lt. Col. Dave Grossman (US Army, ret.), award-winning author of *On Killing, On Combat, On Spiritual Combat*, and *Assassination Generation.*

# LIVE READY

Part 1:

# THE MYTH OF HELPLESSNESS

# CHAPTER 1

# The Gun

I SIGNED UP for the job to make a little money and maybe meet some girls. No one told me I would soon find myself on the wrong side of a gun.

Back in the early '90s, as a twenty-year-old kid attending the University of Pittsburgh, I had just started work as a bouncer in a college bar. The sum total of the training for this position was a five-minute discussion with the manager, who explained the "sophisticated" crisis response plan of this establishment like so: if there was trouble in the bar, the bartenders would flash the lights in the vestibule where the bouncers hung out checking IDs, and we were supposed to run in and figure it out.

Back then, I thought of myself as a tough guy. I'd been fanatical about martial arts since I was a little kid; I'd been in more than my share of fights in school and on the streets over the years; and I was a Division 1 wrestler at the University of Pittsburgh. So, naturally, when the lights flashed during my second shift on the job, I had to be the first through the door.

The place was so packed that we had to shove our way

through the crowd to get to the fight taking place near the bar. In the couple seconds it took to reach the fight, something about the situation struck me as odd. Someone didn't belong here. In my twenty-year-old mind, the man who had the upper hand in the fight looked like "an older guy." He was probably about forty, which nowadays sounds pretty young to me, but back then, given the context of a college bar, his age raised a red flag in my mind.

The older guy had grabbed a college kid and was slamming him against the bar. I rushed over to break them up, shoving the older guy aside and pinning the college kid against the bar to keep him from coming back swinging. My assumption was that my fellow bouncer John, who was right behind me, would jump in and grab the older guy.

But John hesitated.

The older guy didn't.

He bounced off the crowd a couple feet away, pulled a gun from his waistband, and stuck it in my face.

"Now I'm gonna kill you," he said.

You know how they say that in a life-or-death situation your life flashes before your eyes? Well, I've been in numerous situations that qualify—this one among them—but I can tell you from experience that my life has never flashed before my eyes.

What did happen was that my brain flashed back to a time when I was about twelve years old and practicing Karate. I had just asked my dad what to do if a Bad Guy had a gun. Now, I could see clear as day my dad telling me (in a very well-meaning but ultimately unhelpful way), "Do whatever the guy with the gun tells you."

The problem in my present predicament was that the Bad Guy wasn't telling me to do anything. He'd simply threatened to kill me.

Like a computer with faulty programming, my mind began searching for a solution that simply wasn't there. So what did I do?

I froze.

Then, a surge of adrenaline hit me on a level I'd never experienced before, even with all my competitive wrestling, martial arts bouts, and schoolyard fights. My heart rate went through the roof. Time seemed to slow down. Everything melted from my field of view except the barrel of the gun, and even though the place was packed, all I could hear was my own heartbeat.

After what felt like minutes, but was realistically only a few seconds, my brain came to the conclusion that doing nothing would be thoroughly unproductive. So I gathered myself, looked around the gun so I could see the Bad Guy's face, and realized that his body language indicated he didn't actually intend to shoot me. He looked like a man who had overreacted and had immediately regretted his decision.

Something about that expression allowed me to snap out of my paralysis, grab the gun, and redirect it to the safest trajectory I could think of at the time, which happened to be down at the floor. What happened next surprised me: as I took action, the Bad Guy seemed to freeze, offering virtually no resistance, with an incredulous look on his face that I'll never forget. It was at this moment that my fellow bouncer John jumped in, and the two of us "negotiated" the situation to a safe conclusion.

## *A Reasonable Risk Assessment*

A little while later, John and I were back in the vestibule, doing what most guys do as they decompress from a dangerous situation: we played it cool, as if nothing out of the ordinary had happened.

But then John turned to me and said, "You know, Sam, they're paying us like thirty-five bucks a night for this job, before taxes. This shit isn't worth it." He quit that night and never came back.

That risk assessment struck me as completely reasonable, but for whatever reason, my mind didn't follow that direction. Instead, it got stuck on a series of questions:

1. What just happened?
2. How is it possible that everything I thought I knew about violence and its management was demonstrated to be false in just a matter of seconds?
3. With all my training and experience, why did I freeze?

As I contemplated these questions, my first realization was that it wasn't my body that had failed me; it was my mind.

I was bigger, stronger, faster, and younger than the Bad Guy. I was an experienced martial artist, a high-level competitive wrestler, and certainly no stranger to interpersonal aggression and the stress that comes with it—or so I had thought. But none of that mattered, because my plan (or lack thereof) to manage an armed opponent had proven meaningless.

I remember thinking how I'd read stories and seen movies about people who could act heroically and perform in the face of life-or-death stress, and I wondered: what quality did these people have that I apparently did not? More importantly, was it something that could be learned? And if it could be learned, was it something that could be taught?

I quickly became obsessed with understanding the nature of real violence and its management—so much so that I decided to pivot away from my college plan to become a schoolteacher and instead spend the time necessary to figure all this out. I decided to go where I thought the toughest people on the planet could be found. So I joined the Marines.

My enlistment took me through Officer Candidate School (OCS), after which I became a Marine officer. It was enlightening to experience firsthand lessons drawn from thousands of years of military science on how to train a young person to become psychologically and physically capable of handling combat. But it wasn't long into my post-Gulf War active duty that I realized how allergic I was to the bureaucracy and lack of personal independence that (at least in my view) defined the peacetime Marines in those days.

So, in 1996, I took the first exit that presented itself, abandoning my visions of leading troops courageously into battle. I took a job for a few weeks in a silicon caulk factory (the "glue factory," as I called it). As I spent each day repetitively loading caulking tubes into boxes, I contemplated going to law school or becoming a cop. Then a friend introduced me to my first real mentor, a man named Kevin Pegnato. Kevin was a world class personal security trainer and protection specialist who was so ahead of his time that I still consider him today to be one of the top thought leaders in the field. With Kevin, I landed squarely in the private sector, teaching self-defense to executives and doing close protection—a fancy way of saying bodyguarding.

The experience represented my first exposure to truly sophisticated personal protection methodologies and tactics designed to combat real violence, which I soaked up like a sponge. It also provided me with opportunities to work with other truly exceptional professionals in the personal security industry, along with many high-profile clients, including heads of state, A-list actors, business luminaries, and many others who found themselves in real and genuine trouble. Protecting high-profile people is exciting, but protecting people who are actively being targeted is another matter entirely. It is like a chess match with life-and-death consequences and zero safety nets. You're on your own.

I loved it, to the point that I became a fanatical student of the craft.

When I wasn't actively protecting people, I was practicing and teaching martial arts and competing in tactical firearms competitions—honing my own skillsets. But in 2003, I had an epiphany: it's good to have a lifeguard, but ultimately, it's better to know how to swim. So, I decided to pivot my career once again, this time from protecting people and organizations to teaching people how to protect themselves with the same tools and skills I used to protect public figures and those whose lives were in danger.

This shift in focus opened my eyes to a new reality: knowing how to protect yourself from danger is much more than just a skill; it comes with a special brand of confidence, one that fulfills a fundamental human need.

## *Advancing the Hierarchy*

Food, clothing, and shelter are fundamental human needs, but many don't know where the notion of "human needs" originated. The concept stems from Abraham Maslow's Hierarchy of Needs, first published in 1943.[1] Maslow was an American psychologist and sociologist who, rather than studying disorder, chose to study how and why some people are able to live a truly optimized life—or what he termed *self-actualization*.

SELF-
ACTUALIZATION
ESTEEM
LOVE &
BELONGING
SAFETY
PHYSIOLOGICAL

---

1    "A Theory of Human Motivation." *Psychological Review*. 1943.

In Maslow's hierarchy, people progress vertically up the tiers of a pyramid of fundamental needs, beginning with our most basic physiological needs—those of food, clothing, and shelter—at the base of the pyramid. This is followed by subsequent tiers such as safety, love and belonging, and esteem, eventually ascending to a state he called self-actualization. According to Maslow, one cannot master higher needs while lower, more fundamental needs are left unmet or lacking.

Throughout my career as a trainer, I've had the privilege of working with many wildly successful individuals. From the outside, most of these folks seemed to have it all—financial independence, freedom, influence, recognition—and most were by all accounts exceptional people. But as I got to know them, I came to recognize an underlying and often unspoken sense of uncertainty or doubt, one that kept them from feeling like they had truly mastered their lives.

After a fair amount of investigation, and from witnessing the same pattern in many people over many years, I came to realize that this uncertainty originated from a sense of insecurity in their ability to protect themselves and their families on a primal level. They had achieved financial security long ago. Most lived in safe neighborhoods and for the most part were well protected by society and the people around them. But there was that nagging sensation in the back of their minds that, physically, someone could take it all away from them in a heartbeat. They were protected, but all that protection only made them feel less secure.

While they had mastered other aspects of Maslow's

tier of safety and security, they had not mastered personal security, at least not in the primal sense. What they really wanted was to know that they could take care of themselves no matter what the situation; that they would know what to do and how to do it, without needing to rely on someone else to save them. My close protection clients themselves—every single one of them, in fact—wanted some level of training, usually for their families as well as themselves. These are people with the means to engage a team of bodyguards 24/7, and even with all those highly trained people watching their backs, they still wanted to know how to take matters into their own hands should the situation arise.

Interestingly, overcoming this sense of insecurity did not require my training clients or my close protection clients to become Jiu Jitsu black belts or MMA fighters, nor did it require them to test themselves in the crucible of competitive violence. All it took was the right knowledge. They simply needed to know what to do and how to do it.

Without the primal *knowing* that you can manage your personal security, it's almost impossible to conquer the doubt and take that final step into self-actualization. It's like trying to climb a ladder while missing a giant rung. This book provides that missing rung—it removes the void of uncertainty that leaches the confidence you need to live life to its fullest. With the mental skills and the practical tools this book will provide you, you will have the ability to protect yourself and be a protector to those you love. You will gain the confidence that comes with this knowledge, confidence that will help you live life on your own terms;

do what you want to do; have the moral courage to say no to the things you don't want to do; and have the physical courage to live the life you've dreamed of living.

Too many people are afraid to take chances, afraid of conflict, or afraid of pursuing their actual dreams. Some of this fear comes from being afraid of what people will think of them or afraid of what will happen if they fail. But that fear is all rooted in the same sense, or lack of sense, of personal security. It is that same brand of security, that same level of confidence, that allows you to walk down any street at any time of day or night knowing you can handle yourself, that you're not dependent on the police to protect you, that you don't always need your environment and your situation to be perfectly mapped out and planned in advance, because you know you can adapt to whatever comes your way.

In this respect, this book is not simply about teaching you the skills of personal protection that few understand (and even fewer teach); it is about developing that powerful, resilient, confident psychology that will carry over to every aspect of your life. But ultimately, what this book is really about is making you a more complete person; it is about forging you into someone stronger, more resilient, more capable, and better equipped to live your best life. This has very little to do with the actual, physical act of self-defense; rather, it has very much to do with the idea that humans fundamentally need to feel secure, and that genuine sense of security cannot come from outside forces. That genuine sense of security is entirely up to you. It is literally in your hands...

## *It's Good to Have a Lifeguard,*
## *but It's Better to Know How to Swim*

This book is not just a distillation of my own lessons, but also the lessons of my thousands of clients, from CEOs, to celebrities, to members of Congress, to professional athletes, to moms, dads, and kids. As I taught these clients, they equally taught me.

Starting from my soul searching in the vestibule of that bar so many years ago, I have dedicated my life to answering the most important and often most frightening questions related to the human factor of personal protection:

- ▸ Why do you freeze or panic under life-or-death stress, and how do you override these instinctual reactions?
- ▸ What are the best strategies to keep yourself and your family safe and to manage real-world violence?
- ▸ What must you understand about personal security to survive and thrive in today's often uncertain and dangerous world?
- ▸ What kinds of Bad Guys are out there, how do they select their targets, and why?
- ▸ Are there discernable warning signs that you may be being targeted, and if so, how do you spot them, even if the Bad Guy is skilled at masking

his or her intent?

▸ How do you recognize and manage the interview process that typically precedes an attack?

▸ How do you know—definitively—when you need to go from "talking" to "touching" in your efforts to escape a situation?

▸ Which physical self-defense skills and tools work, and which ones might get you killed?

▸ Ultimately, what is the collective science you need to protect yourself, your loved ones, or your organization, even if someone has made it their mission to harm you?

This book answers all these questions and more. It reveals the tactics of the personal protection trade so that you can protect yourself and be a protector for your loved ones with the same skills and tools we use to safeguard public figures. It synthesizes these insights in a way that is useful to anyone, no matter your background, your size, your physical ability, or your experience with personal protection.

More importantly, this book will go beyond teaching you how to recognize, avoid, and manage danger; it will empower you in ways you never thought possible, allowing you to live more confidently and independently in this dangerous world. Ultimately, we can never fully control our circumstances, only our responses to them. My objective on this journey is to enable you to respond, rather than react; to help you learn how to think under pressure and make the right decisions even in the face of the most extreme circumstances; to equip you to Live Ready.

# CHAPTER 2

# Learned Helplessness

A soft drizzle of rain falls on a muddy field. In the distance, a dozen workers in overalls unpack a train brimming with colorful panels, canvas, signage, and the bells and lights of a carnival and circus. A dozen more engage with a series of heavy ropes, working in concert to position the center pole of what will become a giant big-top tent.

Here and there, the three rings that will compartmentalize the performances stand in varied states of completion. In one, a tiger trainer rehearses. The crack of her whip alerts that you're standing closer to a live, uncontained tiger than you ever have in your life. Your heart races in time with the sounds of steel hammers pounding stakes into the soft earth, carnival barkers hollering after the workers, and the roars of exotic animals echoing from all directions.

Through the noise comes the shrill trumpeting of a circus elephant. The massive animal eclipses your line of sight from the right. Her sheer size would terrify you, especially since she passes no more than ten yards from where you stand. But you remain at ease because her trainer seems to have her under control at the end of a rope.

In any logical scenario, this rope should not put you at ease. If that elephant were to lose her temper and decide that she would rather trample you than follow her trainer, neither her handler nor that slender piece of rope would stand a chance of stopping her. But there's a story about why this elephant, even as the world's largest and most powerful land mammal, makes no effort to resist, and I'm afraid it's not a happy story.

Another elephant, this one a baby, illustrates why. There in the muck alongside the train tracks, the baby's behavior serves a stark contrast to his mother's. He struggles ferociously against the rope binding him to a long stake driven into the ground. The trainer has left the baby alone to dig and pull and wrench against his bindings. Clearly, the little elephant's efforts are futile, but still he fights.

This is how they train circus elephants to abide the trainer's rope. They take the babies away from their mothers and they tie them to a stake. When bound in this way, a baby elephant commits to a natural reaction. He tries everything he can to free himself. Eventually, the effort having proven useless time and again, he gives up.

This lesson dominates the rest of his life. Even after he reaches his full, intimidating size—even as the world's largest and most powerful land mammal—he follows obediently behind his trainer, believing himself unable to resist the rope on which he is led. In this way, the elephant spends his life surrendering to the myth of his own helplessness.

## *You Are Similarly Conditioned*

Though human beings are not bound to a stake like the elephant, the forces that convince us of our own helplessness—particularly against violence—are every bit as relentless. A compelling array of cultural influences slowly and meticulously conditions us to believe that the act of defending ourselves is unethical, unsafe, or even impossible.

In schools, students are told that if they stand up to a bully and fight back, they will be punished equally alongside the bully. Meet violence with any physical effort at self-defense, and you will be suspended or expelled. Your only choice is to run, beg for an authority figure to protect you, or worse, simply roll over and take it. This is not to suggest that fighting back is the only, or even the immediate solution to bullying—far from it. The problem is that punishing self-protective behavior does not teach students to be more peaceful, but rather, to feel helpless. It teaches them to be victims.

Most law-enforcement agencies, well intentioned though they may be, tend to perpetuate this mentality. The message that you should never try to protect yourself, that you should just call 911 and let the police handle it, indoctrinates us into the erroneous notion that average citizens are incapable of protecting themselves, and that the professional lifeguards of society are the only people with the capacity to manage violence. As a result, far too many people are victimized in situations where fighting back would have led to a better outcome.

The notion is never more insidious than when women are taught that fighting back against sexual assault only increases the chance that they will be more seriously injured or killed. This misguided message—one based on zero evidence—is particularly damaging because it encourages women to give up on the prospect of doing the one thing that might actually save them from assault. Even in a society where one in five women will be raped within their lifetimes,[2] fighting back against sexual assault has been shown to curtail or prevent more than two thirds of attacks.[3]

These are particularly harrowing statistics, given that the prevailing alternative—"Don't fight back; just endure it and then let the police handle it"—so rarely leads to justice. According to the Rape, Abuse, and Incest National Network (RAINN), "Perpetrators of sexual violence are less likely to go to jail or prison than other criminals." Out of every 1,000 sexual assaults, only 230 are reported to police, only 46 of those reports lead to arrest, only 9 of those cases are referred to prosecutors, and a paltry 5 of those cases result in a felony conviction. All told, for every 1,000 sexual assaults, 995 perpetrators walk free.[4]

---

2    National Sexual Violence Resource Center. "Statistics About Sexual Violence." 2015.

3    Erin Anderssen. "Teaching women to fight back an effective way to reduce sexual assaults: study." The Globe and Mail. October 24, 2017.

4    Rape, Abuse, and Incest National Network. "Criminal Justice System: Statistics."

These realities give rise to a fear that further conditions us into the myth of helplessness. And here, we can always count on the news media to fan the flames. If it bleeds, it leads. No matter where you get your news, it's going to be packed with stories about violence and disaster. It will marinate you in the prospect of something terrible happening to you or someone you love, even if the events depicted in these stories are rare and patently unlikely to happen to the vast majority of us.

The net effect of all these influences is to instill a sense that the world is an extremely dangerous place—so dangerous that there is nothing an individual can do to avoid or prevent violence. Many people respond to this myth of helplessness by metaphorically throwing their hands up and collectively abdicating responsibility for their own personal defense to the perceived lifeguards of society. In so doing, they submit to a particularly dangerous illusion.

## *The Illusion of Security*

In response to our conditioning into the belief that all violence, even in self-defense, is wrong, and that ordinary people are incapable of defending themselves, the logical conclusion is that we must instead rely on others to keep us safe. Unfortunately, the ability of private security, technology, law enforcement, the government, or society in general to keep every individual safe from harm is an illusion.

Let's start with private security. In my training classes about how to respond and stay safe during an active shooter situation, I often show a video that opens with a uniformed security guard standing and talking with a bouncer seated near the entrance to a bar. When a man enters and pulls out a gun, the uniformed guard immediately bolts, high-tailing it off screen. In the same instant, the bouncer gets on his feet and starts talking to the gunman. There is a brief exchange, and then, as soon as the gunman raises his weapon, the bouncer springs into action, disarms him, and takes him down.

The first thing I ask my training classes after the video ends is, "What would you say about the security guard's reaction?"

Almost everyone says the same thing: "She's a coward. She's supposed to be protecting everyone, but she just runs away to save her own skin. She panicked…"

This is certainly one assessment, but I don't think it's accurate. I'm sure the guard in this video was scared by the sight of the gun, but from my perspective, she's not panicking; she's moving with purpose. She's doing exactly what she was told to do: run and call someone who could help—or in other words, call 911.

The problem is, when we see a uniformed security officer, most of us immediately think we are therefore "safe." But the reality is entirely different. Think about it: what role can an unarmed uniformed guard really play in the context of security? Certainly, they can deter bad behavior such as vandalism or theft, but when it comes to preventing or responding to violence, not only are they generally untrained or unprepared, their employers expressly prohibit them from doing so. The last thing any security guard company wants is a minimally trained, minimally paid guard making critical use-of-force decisions and touching people in ways that would almost certainly result in a lawsuit.

There are exceptions to the limitations of hired security, of course. Trained close protection services, not unlike the Secret Service, will know how to keep people safe. But unless you have the resources to hire professional body-guards to watch over you 24/7, the security you see around you each day is less about keeping everyone safe and more about providing the illusion of security (otherwise known as "security theater").

In almost every respect, uniformed security is incapable of doing anything more than observing and reporting or calling 911. But of course, *you* could do that. So could I or anyone else, for that matter. We all have phones. What, then, is the purpose of a security guard? The purpose is simple: to create an illusion of security that makes people *feel* safe… to give you the sense that "something is being done" to protect you from the Bad Guys of society.

## *Spectator Syndrome*

Among the most common protection recommendations made by security professionals is to travel in groups, and when in trouble, seek crowded places for safety. This is a simple and logical suggestion born from the basic belief that there is safety in numbers, and that for Bad Guys to victimize, they need a degree of privacy. Most people believe that if others are around, someone will come to their aid in an emergency. And while I am of the mindset that certainly there are people out there like myself, and perhaps like you, who are of a protector's mindset and who will step up in the face of danger, the matter is a bit more complicated.

On March 13, 1964, a twenty-eight-year-old bartender named Kitty Genovese was on her way home from work when she was attacked outside her apartment building in Queens. The story, at least according to *The New York Times*, was that as many as thirty-eight people in the building either saw or heard the attack, and no one tried to help or even called the police.

Though there were some inaccuracies in the initial story, the tragic incident remains illustrative of a startling component of human psychology. The phenomenon is known as "spectator syndrome," or "the bystander effect," and it has only become more prevalent in today's world, where generations of people have grown up watching violence as entertainment. When I review and evaluate incidences of violence caught on film, all too often, the bystanders present will display one of three behaviors: a few may help, most will run, while others will pull out their phones and film what's happening so they can post it to their social media pages. The latter behavior is unfortunately becoming more typical all the time.

Many high-profile incidents of this type have been documented at festivals, at grocery stores, on subways, on the street, and in many other public settings. Whether the tendency not to get involved comes from "it's not my responsibility," or the natural fear of facing violence oneself, or from a voyeuristic form of entertainment, the bystander effect is real.

Unfortunately, what this means is that we can never outsource our safety to strangers. People have been conditioned, by and large, not to help each other, but rather, to watch.

## *The Illusion of Technology*

On the subject of "something being done," another common reaction to the threat or occurrence of violence is to assume that more advanced technology will keep us safe. "Let's put up more cameras. Let's give everyone panic buttons. Let's make everyone stand in line and pass through metal detectors."

In the immediate aftermath of a high-profile school shooting like Sandy Hook or Parkland, concerned parents will aggressively demand that something be done to prevent such atrocities from occurring in their school district. Very often, school boards respond by proudly spending millions of dollars on sophisticated camera systems, often linked to 911 call centers, as a decisive display that something is being done. This despite the fact that camera systems cannot and do not prevent—or even help to mitigate—an attack, nor have they ever been shown to speed response time by law enforcement. Not to mention that, frighteningly, school shooters often meticulously plan to commit their attacks in the very areas where the school has placed cameras, so that they can be caught on film and have their actions preserved into perpetuity.

Similar knee-jerk responses tend to follow deadly attacks in places of worship. Even after the 2018 massacre at the Tree of Life Synagogue in Pittsburgh—a horrific event in which a white supremacist killed eleven people and wounded six more (including four responding police officers); an event that occurred in the otherwise peaceful neighborhood of Squirrel Hill, where I grew up—the illusion of security remained pervasive. In the wake of the incident, money was spent on technologies to alert and speed law enforcement to the scene. These technologies included active shooter "pull-stations" much like fire alarms, and panic buttons the rabbis could wear during services. These were excellent security enhancements, but when I discussed the idea of providing training to enable staff, volunteers, and congregants to be able to fight back if need be, the idea was scoffed at by the then director of security for the community, a former federal law enforcement officer.

"The only solution is to get gun carriers into the building sooner," came the reply that I will never forget. To him, "gun carriers" meant law enforcement. Implicit in his statement: unless you're an armed and armored cop, you're helpless in the face of violence.

The sentiment that ordinary people don't have the ability to protect themselves, that the best you can hope for is to get the professional lifeguards there faster, is the very definition of the myth of helplessness. With or without access to panic buttons, "gun carriers" would not have arrived in time to prevent the deaths of all those peaceful people that day. But had those people been taught and empowered to protect themselves, perhaps the story might have been very different.

Panic buttons, security cameras, locked doors—these technologies can help keep people safe, but they are merely tools. Relying on them as your exclusive strategy for defending against violence is to put your faith in the *hope* or the *chance* that they will be effective in the event of the unthinkable. Rather than leaving your fate to hope and chance, it is far better to learn how to protect yourself so that something like this never happens to you, your loved ones, your classmates, or your fellow worshippers. We are fundamentally never helpless. We just need to be taught how to respond to violent threats.

Unfortunately, the technologies can seem like such attractive panaceas. After mass shootings, particularly in schools, people often say, "We should install metal detectors. If people can't get guns into the building, then we don't have to worry about guns." At first glance, this is perfectly logical—so logical, in fact, that many districts began doing this after some of the higher profile school shootings over the past two-plus decades. But as too many examples prove, metal detectors don't always deter the violent act; they simply force the Bad Guy to change his strategy.

Recall the Red Lake Massacre of March 21, 2005, which was at the time the deadliest attack on a high school since Columbine. Red Lake Senior High School in Red Lake, Minnesota, had installed a metal detector at the primary entrance to the school. This did not stop sixteen-year-old killer Jeff Weise from entering the school, killing seven people, and wounding five others. In fact, he walked straight into the school through the entrance with the metal detector and made one of the two security guards monitoring the door his first victim. The other security guard fled, escaping without injury, while Weise continued his spree unabated.

The presence of metal detectors does not by itself prevent shootings. It simply causes some shooters to shoot rather than sneak their way in.

This is not to say that sneaking in doesn't still happen. If you look at most school environments, they are incredibly porous. Even if a district installs metal detectors and requires all students to file in through the same few doors at the start of each day, most schools are wide open in the afternoons and evenings for after-school programs, sporting events, and so on. It is not difficult for someone with a working knowledge of a building this size, with so many windows and doors and so much activity in any given day, to smuggle a cache of weapons into a locker to be used the following day.

Please don't misunderstand me; technology is a vital component of any security infrastructure. But we cannot rely on it exclusively to keep us safe. The reality is that it's the human element, not technology, that often serves as the weak link in the chain. Those same school districts and places of worship rarely spend the time or money needed to properly teach their staff what to do in the event of an active shooter. Often, they simply give it lip service by sending an email or publishing a memo on the subject. Sending an email or creating a policy that says, "In the event of an active shooter, you should run, hide, or fight" is not the same as actual training and preparedness.

Now it is important to note that I am not advocating for everyone to carry a firearm at all times, nor for the arming of teachers, the staff at places of worship, and employees.

Teachers should be teaching, spiritual leaders should be preaching, and employees should be able to comfortably focus on doing their jobs. Rather than engaging in the ideological debate related to guns, we should be focusing on logical strategy. People waste too much time arguing ideologically when we should be thinking tactically.

Take, for instance, the armed Flight Deck Officer program. In response to 9/11, this program encourages pilots to endure remarkably challenging firearms qualification programs so they can carry a gun in the cockpit. But if we're thinking tactically, we have to ask the question: "Okay, now what happens if there's a problem in the passenger compartment of the plane?" Does the pilot now leave the cockpit to address the issue with his gun? Wouldn't this then leave the cockpit vulnerable to attack? Wouldn't this put tremendous strain on the lone remaining pilot in the cockpit?

If we think tactically, the answer is not to rely on an armed pilot; it is to equip the cockpit with a ballistic door, then rely on well-trained flight attendants or air marshals, and to trust that passengers will help to manage the situation—which, post 9/11, many absolutely will.

In schools, asking teachers to arm themselves similarly lacks tactical consideration. Say you have a school building with fifty classrooms. Are you going to ask all fifty teachers to undergo extensive firearms training? Even if you did this, you might wind up with only two who actually followed through. The tactical problem is that those teachers cannot abandon their classrooms to run to the sound of the guns to hunt down a killer in the event of an attack, which once again makes this measure good as a wildcard deterrent, but ultimately just another example of the illusion of security.

Okay, so maybe we should arm the administrators. Here, we are still relying on people who might not have the background or even the desire to learn how to use a firearm. Even if a school manages to train a handful of administrators, who is to say they will be willing or able to use deadly force if the situation ever arises?

The same is true of hired security. Tactically speaking, school security should be entrusted to professionals, such as school resource officers, but even districts that follow this logic almost always fail to invest in the necessary manpower to do it right, often leaving a lone officer to manage multiple campuses. This nearly defeats the purpose. Beyond the overextension of that officer's time and attention, it confines responsibility for protecting all those lives on all those different campuses to a single person.

## To Serve and Protect (the State)

Okay, so private security and technology do not guarantee our safety from harm. Aren't the police here to protect us?

Technically, No.

Law enforcement's ability (or for that matter, their mandate) to ensure your safety is also little more than an illusion. Despite the "to Serve and Protect" motto on the side of most police vehicles, they are not here to prevent Bad Guys from committing violence against you, the individual. Their primary duty is to step in after the violence has already occurred so that they might investigate the crime and then represent the state or federal government in any criminal case that results.

Now to be clear, most of the police I know would do literally anything to be there to protect the innocent from those who would harm them, and by that token, if they are present during the moment of the crime, they can and typically will help you. But they are in no way meant to serve as your personal protective service. If a Bad Guy wants to do harm to you, unless there is an officer standing immediately nearby, the police simply won't be there to protect you during the moment of truth.

But isn't the government here to protect us—that whole "cradle to grave" thing? Isn't that why we pay taxes?

Certainly, the government and the society it oversees attempt to provide an infrastructure of security. But let's look at that infrastructure with a critical eye. Functionally speaking, the government and law enforcement view *all* violence in a negative light. If a Bad Guy attacks me and I defend myself, the law institutionally assumes that both of us have committed a crime. This universal condemnation of violence supposedly encourages every individual to remain peaceful. But just as with schools, the unintended lesson is that all use of force is bad, and that none of us has the right to protect ourselves.

What many people think of as "self-defense" is actually more accurately defined as "justification of force." If a Bad Guy tries to attack me, then my violent response may be *justified* because I was using force in the defense of myself or others. For hundreds of years, western countries have viewed self-defense as justifiable; that this power must ultimately reside in the hands of the individual. And yet, in this modern society, too many people are convinced that it is the government and society's job to provide the ultimate protection and security for the individual, as if somehow this were even possible.

For others, there is a profound realization that even if we had created a utopian society with the true mission to protect every citizen from harm, we still can't count on the lifeguards to always be there to keep us safe. Far more often than not, there is no Superman to stop the gunman who barges into your workplace or place of worship. Far more often than not, there is no police officer there to stop the rapist from pinning you down in that dark alley.

Now, does this mean that I am advocating for ignoring the presence of government and law enforcement and just arming ourselves to the teeth? Absolutely not. Again, to me, a firearm is nothing more than a tool. By nature, a tool allows you to do more with less effort. A firearm is a force multiplier, and it can be a very powerful force multiplier and force-projection tool, provided you know how, and are willing, to use it. There again, your ability to protect yourself has less to do with the tool than with the skill of the hands wielding it. There are circumstances where a firearm would certainly be the best tool for defense, but it can't be the one and only deterrent a responsible person leans on for protection.

We live in a country with a stable legal system, a government that is ever improving toward greater equality, and strong social support for those who need it; a place with high-quality civil services and infrastructure like law enforcement and the military; but at the same time, we cannot allow ourselves to become dependent on these entities or abdicate our personal responsibilities toward security. Nor can we allow ourselves to become entirely dependent on technology, and that includes firearms.

We need to find that space where we respect the institutions designed to defend us, and we prepare our homes, schools, and public spaces with the right technology, but more important than any of that, we each must accept responsibility for protecting ourselves. This shouldn't be a controversial position to take. It's in many ways the ethos on which America was founded—that rugged and patriotic brand of individualism.

In that spirit, it is time to stop pointing fingers about what is to blame for the epidemic of violence in our country and around the world. We need to quit allowing fear to set us in opposition. Turning on each other in panic is as dangerous to us as the Bad Guys themselves.

There are no unilateral solutions to this incredibly complex, multifaceted problem. Solving this epidemic of violence is up to us. If each of us, as individuals, takes responsibility for our own safety, then not only do we improve our own chances of staying safe; we contribute to the security of everyone.

## *An Individual Responsibility*

Over the years, I have found that many people approach learning how to protect themselves with similar types of skepticism:

How do I protect myself from someone much bigger than me? Or stronger? Or younger? How does a woman stop a man twice her size? What if the Bad Guy has a gun? Or a knife? Or what if there's more than one Bad Guy? What if it's an active shooter or terrorist? What if I've never been in a fight in my life?

Concern over the physical dynamics of violence is logical, and any self-defense trainer who says that size doesn't matter is lying to you. But here's the reality: just as I experienced firsthand in that bar so many years ago, it doesn't matter how big or tough you are if you freeze and lose the ability to think during the moment of truth.

Conversely, it doesn't matter how big, strong, or crazy that Bad Guy is if you can cause him to freeze. You could be a 100-pound woman going against a 300-pound man with a gun, and if you cause him to freeze, then you have gained decisive control over the next few moments, and that is typically all you need to gain control over the next few moments after that, and so on.

The key is knowing how to prevent yourself from falling back into learned helplessness; how to keep yourself from freezing in the face of danger; how to avoid losing control of your mind; and just as importantly, how to exploit this predictable weakness in an adversary.

No matter who you are or what your background, you can learn techniques to recognize danger, avoid trouble, or ward off the predators of the modern world. You don't have to be bigger or stronger than anyone to effect this outcome. Most of the time, you don't even have to be a better fighter. You simply have to be willing to protect yourself, willing to control your fear and turn it against your attacker, and willing to accept that personal security is a fundamental human need, but ultimately an individual responsibility.

The time has come to accept that you are never helpless. The time has come to stand up, take responsibility for your own safety, and recognize that even in a society full of lifeguards, it is better to know how to swim.

## CHAPTER 3

# Staying SAFE

ON MARCH 15, 2019, Naeem Rashid arrived to a Friday prayer service at the Al Noor Mosque in Riccarton, a peaceful suburb of Christchurch, New Zealand. Having attended these services regularly for the nearly ten years since he and his family immigrated from Pakistan, Rashid had become a well-respected member of the mosque—the kind of man who volunteered to prepare meals for needy families in the community.

The beloved husband and father of three progressed through the crowd, offering warm greetings to all. This was to be a particularly special afternoon, as he intended to meet with worship leaders after the service to make plans for the upcoming wedding of his twenty-one-year-old son Talha, who had accompanied him that day. Neither man could have known that these would be their last few minutes alive.

Just outside the doors of the building, as Rashid, Talha, and their fellow worshippers prepared for the service to begin, a radicalized white-supremacist murderer named Brenton Tarrant was parking a silver Subaru loaded with weapons. When Tarrant blasted his way through the doors, shotgun in hand, militaristic music blaring from a belt-mounted speaker, Rashid reacted the same way as everyone else—he froze.

Put yourself in Rashid's shoes. A monster has just entered your place of worship. That monster fires nine times with a shotgun, killing or wounding an untold number of people you care about, before switching to a semi-automatic rifle. The strobe light attached to this weapon further disorients an already stunned crowd. You stand in shock as dozens of people tumble to the floor. The fear has sent your friends and loved ones—people you have worshipped alongside for nearly ten years—into a state of shock. Your son, a bright young civil engineer engaged to be married, is murdered right before your eyes.

How would you react?

After that initial moment frozen in terror, Naeem Rashid did what most people don't, and this is why we remember his name. He dodged his way through the panicking crowd and attempted to tackle the monster. In so doing, he saved many lives by allowing an untold number of his fellow worshippers the time they needed to escape the attack. Unfortunately, overcoming his natural fear response wasn't enough to allow Rashid to stop Tarrant entirely. The supremely heroic attempt to tackle the shooter around the waist came at the cost of Rashid's life.[5]

---

5   In any worthwhile training program about the disarming of firearms, the primary lesson is that it is the perpetrator's hands and weapon that

We know all this not because of eyewitness accounts or the exceptional investigative work that followed. We know all this because the Christchurch mosque shootings, as the event would come to be called, was the first of its kind to be broadcast via Facebook livestream. For decent people, the video is extremely hard to watch, but many of the images are particularly illustrative of the range of human responses to true survival-level fear.

In the video, it is difficult to comprehend, let alone accept, what we see in the foreground: a pile of people lying on top of one another, most of them very much alive, offering no response—not even so much as a flinch of pain—as the shooter fires into them. These people are alive, but they look dead already.[6] Tarrant shoots round

---

will kill you. Though it might seem counterintuitive, it is always a better strategy to go for the gun rather than the body. This is not to take away from the heroism that Naeem Rashid displayed that day; it is merely to point out that while training is no panacea, it does give you critical advantages in situations like these.

6  Their natural response of playing dead so convincingly, in fact, compelled several well-known conspiracy theorists to interpret this as evidence of a false flag operation—the theory being that whatever shadowy entity would have wanted to fake a mass shooting in a pair of mosques in New Zealand had helped enhance the ruse by carting in piles of already dead bodies for Tarrant to fire into. This is of course preposterous. The far simpler, more logical explanation is that the victims of this shooting suffered from a natural, instinctual reaction known as tonic immobility, a subject we will cover in greater detail in chapter 4.

after round into the mass of people at close range before turning and leaving the mosque.

Outside, en route to his Subaru, he shoots more people as they flee. He gathers another weapon from his car, then charges back into the building to fire again on the wounded. The second time he exits the mosque, he murders a woman on the sidewalk as she cries out for help.

Tarrant then flees to his car and drives three miles down the road to the Linwood Islamic Centre, police cruisers screaming past him in the opposite direction, unaware that their suspect has slipped right through their grasp. Just as he arrives at Linwood, the livestream video cuts out, and we receive the remaining details from eyewitness accounts.

Perhaps disoriented by the effects of extreme adrenaline, the killer fails to find the main door to the Linwood Islamic Centre. So he resorts to shooting at congregants through a window. This allows more people to escape and effectively take cover than had happened at Al Noor. It also affords our second hero the time he needs to collect himself and begin a counterassault.

Abdul Aziz Wahabzada, armed only with a credit card reader, escapes through a side door and charges at the unsuspecting shooter. Abdul throws the makeshift improvised weapon at Tarrant, causing him to panic, drop his shotgun, and run.

Just as standing up to a bully often causes him to back down, this reaction is not uncommon among those who perpetrate predatory violence against the innocent, and it is particularly true of mass shooters. A common theme among mass killers is the fantasy to wield godlike power and control over others. But in reality, when someone resists or turns the tables on this kind of killer, the true brittleness of his psychology emerges, the fantasy shatters, and his aggressiveness collapses like a house of cards. As counterintuitive as this may seem, even though someone is bigger, stronger, or faster than you—or even if he has a gun or a knife—that does not mean he is truly in control, or even powerful.

Outside the Linwood Islamic Center, Tarrant runs to his car, where he retrieves another weapon to fire at Abdul, who ducks behind a line of cars outside the mosque. What follows is a cat-and-mouse game, where the killer keeps trying to shoot Abdul, who maneuvers and draws enough attention to keep the killer distracted and away from the mosque. Abdul repeatedly shouts out his own location, drawing fire in his direction. Eventually, he finds the discarded, empty shotgun and tries to use it on Tarrant. Once again, even though he knows it's out of ammunition, Tarrant runs.

This time, however, he runs into the mosque, where the spree continues until a total of seven people lie dead and many more are wounded. As the police sirens draw nearer, the killer heads back to his car, purportedly with the intent to stay one step ahead of the police and hit yet another mosque. However, Abdul is waiting for him. Even though he must know the shotgun Abdul carries is empty of ammunition, Tarrant nonetheless panics and attempts to flee. Seeing this, Abdul throws the otherwise useless gun at the car, shattering the windshield.

It is this final act of bravery that leads to the killer's swift capture. That silver Subaru might have blended back into the traffic of the city—and indeed, Tarrant might have been able to carry out his plan to attack at least a third mosque during the spree—had Abdul not fought back and smashed that windshield.

There are many questions we might ask about the horrific events of March 15, 2019, but the one we will focus on in these pages is this: what was it about Naeem Rashid and Abdul Aziz Wahabzada that compelled them to act? Neither of the heroes that day had any training. Neither wore armor, carried weapons, or possessed any special combat skills. They were just family men able to keep their wits about them, and through good thinking and courageous action, they saved many lives. So, was there something special about them, or can any one of us learn how to act with the lifesaving decisiveness they displayed that day?

## Staying SAFE

Imagine someone getting the drop on you and sticking a gun three inches from your face. How do you respond?

Ninety-nine percent of those reading this book have never encountered something like this in real life, but if you are among that other one percent, I would wager that it wasn't a pleasant experience. For most people, this scenario represents the epitome of the myth of helplessness: "He's so close he can't miss, and everyone knows you can't beat a gun." Most people would admit that they would simply freeze, or panic, or submit to doing whatever the Bad Guy tells them.

But what if I told you that you—yes, even if you aren't trained in martial arts and aren't the most physically fit or fast person in the room—could redirect that gun before the Bad Guy could pull the trigger and then disarm him before he could do anything about it?

In my training classes, I've performed the following demo thousands of times before audiences ranging from schoolteachers to chiefs of police, to soldiers, to federal agents, and to members of Congress. I've even done it live on the TV news. No matter what the crowd or setting, the results are the same every time.

The demo goes like this: I hand the gun to a volunteer and ask him or her to hold it on me. "As soon as you see me move," I tell the volunteer, "yell the word 'BANG!'"

Every time, when I make my first move, there is a short but noticeable delay before the volunteer says "BANG!" In that short window, I grab and redirect the gun away from me before the would-be shot can go off.

The outcome of this demo is predictable because we're seeing a demonstration of something that we all understand intuitively: that there is an inherent delay between action and reaction. Even in an experiment such as this, where the opponent is ready and waiting for the first impulse of movement to execute a simple response, we know this delay will be present. We have all seen and know that this delay exists—from driving a car to playing sports, or even just throwing a ball to a child—but few people understand the science behind what causes the delay or how long it lasts.

What causes the delay is the time it takes to recognize the stimulus, mentally process it, and electrically begin a response. This sequence exists as a definable, physiologically hardwired, four-phase process that our minds go through every time we are reacting to anything—whether it's a gun, a punch, or a deer jumping in front of our car. I call this process SAFE (Stimulus, Analysis, Formulation, Execution). As the acronym suggests, SAFE begins when you receive a stimulus. You hear something, feel something, see something that requires a response. As soon as you recognize the stimulus, your mind immediately enters the second phase, analyzing the stimulus against your previous experience. If you have experience with this stimulus, you then progress to the next phase, where you begin to formulate a plan or plans. If you have the ability to form plans, you can then decide whether or not you want to execute on that plan.

At its fastest, all of this happens in about a half second.

To be more clinically precise, it happens between 0.3 and 0.6 seconds. Dr. Bill Lewinsky of the Force Science Institute, the world's leading research group studying reaction time, performance, and behavior under extreme stress, has studied the phenomena of human reaction time since 2004. The conclusions of his research limit visual reaction time to 0.3 to 0.6 seconds, regardless of whether you are an Olympic athlete or a dedicated couch potato. And this is under ideal circumstances, when you are ready and waiting for the first impulse of stimulus to respond without thought (or what is called a "primed" reaction). When the situation is "unprimed," requiring decision making or involving the elements of stress, confusion, fear, and consequence that come with any real situation involving a gun, the reaction time gap is extended significantly.

If you have spent any time in or around the military, you may be saying to yourself that SAFE sounds somewhat similar to OODA, which stands for Observe, Orient, Decide, Act. The OODA system was pioneered in the 1950s by Colonel John Boyd, a "fighter pilot who changed the art of war."[7] The notion is that when you're flying, you must make split-second decisions that require you to Observe the problem, Orient to it, Decide on a course of action, and then Act.

I do not intend to convince the military and tactical communities to abandon OODA (it has merit and value), but at the same time, I believe that the model is missing a rather large piece. OODA doesn't answer the question of how your brain processes information. Instead, it assumes that all you really need is to Decide what to do in any given moment. It assumes you are fundamentally able to think, process, and make decisions in any circumstance.

SAFE does not make this assumption. SAFE recognizes that the ability to think and make decisions is fundamentally predicated on our experience with similar stimuli, and that absent the right experience—especially in life-threatening situations—the decision-making process that OODA is based upon is compromised from the outset.

---

7    Robert Coram, *Boyd: The Fighter Pilot Who Changed the Art of War.* New York: Back Bay Books/Little, Brown, 2004.

Fundamentally, your ability to have a choice and to make decisions (particularly good decisions) is entirely predicated on your personal experience when you hit the analysis phase. To quote the Greek warrior poet Archilochus, "We don't rise to the occasion; we fall to the level of our training." If you have no experience with the stimulus, or the only experience you have had was negative or even traumatic, then the likely outcome is that you will simply lock up during the analysis phase and enter into one of two extreme states: panic or paralysis, the latter being that freeze reaction, or what I affectionately call "a big fat 'oh shit' moment."

The primary difference between these two states is that panic may be considered a phobic-scale response—a true, irrational, uncontrollable flight reaction that can be every bit as dangerous as the threat itself. Fortunately, only a small percentage of people default into panic.

But wait. What about situations where we see crowds surging and stampeding in panic, trampling and crushing people in the process? What we're seeing here is not an individual-level phobic-scale response, but rather what you might call contagious behavior. Imagine a room full of people where everyone is frozen in paralytic fear. Then one person runs. The part of our brain that controls our survival mechanism says to us, "Well, if they're doing it then that must be the right solution," and we follow as a herd.

We could theorize that this all made perfect sense as a preprogrammed response at an earlier stage of our evolution as a species. Picture a tribe of our distant ancestors milling around on the savannah. The panicked reaction to scatter as a crowd is incredibly effective when, say, a lion suddenly springs from the underbrush. One of our friends or family will almost certainly be caught, but at least the rest of will escape. Unfortunately, in these modern times, where the lion has been replaced by the human predator, our instinctual behaviors have become problematic. Panicking crowds are more likely to complicate the situation than resolve it.

In any case, whether we find ourselves in the same camp as the majority who freeze during life-threatening situations or the minority who fly into panic mode, we have lost control—and a loss of control is exactly the opposite of where any of us ever wants to be. Fortunately, as Archilochus's quote suggests, training can change this dynamic completely. Human beings are capable of incredible feats. We can fly through the air, swim like dolphins, ski down mountains at 60 mph, and yes, disarm a Bad Guy during that half-second window before he can shoot. But only if our mindset accepts that it is possible and we've trained the right skillsets. Learned helplessness can be unlearned.

## *Primed and Unprimed*

Of course, not all decisions are created equal, and as a result, neither are the reaction times we can expect.

Let's start all the way back in the 1860s with Francis Donders, the father of something called "Mental Chronometry."[8] He and his student Johan Jacob De Jaager

---

8    Jensen, Arthur R. *Clocking the Mind: Mental Chronometry and Individual Differences.* Elsevier Science Ltd., 2006.

set up a comprehensive series of tests designed to analyze and measure the reaction time of subjects attempting to perform a simple task. There were three different kinds of tasks assessed in this study, the first being a simple response-time task like responding to a light bulb turning on by pressing a button; the second being a choice response-time task that introduced a second light bulb and required the subject to press the correct button based on which light turned on; and a "go/no-go" discrimination response-time task where the two light bulbs come with only a single button and the subject must press the button only when the correct bulb turns on.

The theory was that the first task would require the quickest response time while the third task would require the longest. The theory turned out to be correct, and it led Donders to formulate something of an equation that could predict response time based on perception plus motor time required to complete the simple task. Choice time adds another layer of reaction time to the equation, while discrimination time adds another layer still. It all boils down to the response time being equal to the number and types of mental stages involved in completing the task.

Flash forward to much more recently, and we arrive at further complicating factors, dubbed "primed" and "unprimed" decision making, mentioned earlier in the chapter. A primed decision is one you've prepared for. For example, picture me preparing demonstration participants to say "Bang!" at the first moment of stimulus. This is a primed decision. Unprimed decisions tend to bring slower responses, as they are not expected or trained for, and that element of surprise, coupled with the universal startle response and hesitation caused during the analysis phase, adds to the delay Donders identifies in go/no-go decisions.

The typical human response to traffic conditions is the perfect example of reaction time for an unprimed decision. As referenced by Marc Green in *Roadway Human Factors: From Science to Application*, when a driver on a highway spots the brake lights on a car ahead, the reaction time depends not just on attention and perception, but also on the movement of the two vehicles in question. Though the results vary wildly, the average unprimed reaction time is 1.4 to 1.6 seconds.[9]

According to *Motor Control and Learning: A Behavioral Emphasis (6th Edition)*, a book focused primarily on sports performance, the normal primed reaction time for a healthy, college-age individual is 0.12 seconds for touch stimulus, 0.16 seconds for audio, and 0.19 seconds for visual. These measures start from the time that the stimulus occurs and end in the instant that the subject activates muscle movement in response under an electromyography (EMG) scan, which can measure the moment of muscle activation.[10]

When you add actual movement to the equation, things tend to slow down slightly. Tack on another 0.06 seconds for pulling a trigger, for instance. If the movement is related

9    Green, Marc. *Roadway Human Factors: From Science to Application*. Lawyers & Judges Publishing Company, Incorporated. 2020.

10    Schmidt, Richard A., et al. *Motor Control and Learning: A Behavioral Analysis*. A Human Kinetics. Sixth Edition. 2018.

to a go/no-go decision, then it slows by another 0.5635 seconds.[11]

What about the speed of assault? How long does it take you to react with a physical response? A punch or kick requires 0.20-0.25 seconds, while a weapon strike with a stick or a knife takes 0.14-0.20 seconds. The first shot from a handgun is 0.25-0.50 seconds.[12]

The conclusion we can draw from all of this is that primed reaction time is somewhere around a third of a second at the absolute fastest, to realistically about a half second most of the time. If it's a go/no-go decision, your reaction slows by another half second. And with the element of surprise mixed in, the reaction time jumps to an average of 1.5 seconds.

What can we take from this? First, the speed of assault is considerably faster than any of the reaction times above— and this is without factoring in how adrenaline tends to adversely impact response time. Depending on your distance from the Bad Guy, and your willingness to react, it is well within your ability to disrupt an attack.

---

11  https://www.forcescience.com/2014/08/police-officer-reaction-time-to-start-and-stop-shooting-the-influence-of-decision-making-and-pattern-recognition/

12  https://www.forcescience.com/2006/07/new-study-launched-on-hit-probability/

## PRIMED REACTION TIME

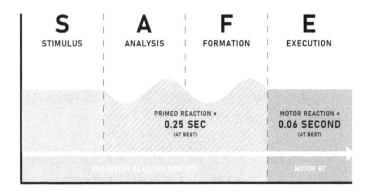

## UNPRIMED REACTION TIME

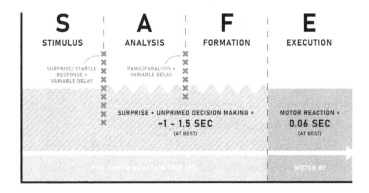

Now, if we're talking about a primed decision—for instance, you're in a boxing match that you've been training the past year for—then it is possible to jump from stimulus directly to response. If your opponent throws a punch, the primed response is to block, and you can do so basically without thinking. This same primed response can be trained for in a violent encounter that happens in the real world, but there are rules. The key rule is to have a one-for-one stimulus-to-response motor program. For instance, if someone throws a straight right-hand punch at you, your primed response may be to parry or block it with your left hand. When you're driving and you see an accident ahead, your reflexive primed response might be to hit the brakes.

While this is all well and good, the problem with primed response time is that you have to be highly focused in the moment and really paying attention to those visual cues, and this is simply not generally possible all the time. You would burn out. More on this subject (along with some strategies on how to overcome it) in chapter 6.

The second problem is that primed response leaves no room for adaptation. If your reaction to every situation on the road is to slam on the brakes, you're not helping yourself much if your car starts to slip on ice, or if the better solution is to swerve to avoid a collision.

What we need to achieve is balance between the speed of decision making and a flexibility of options to allow for adaptation, with stimulus-response programming being very carefully applied to critical reactions like punch defense or a sudden assault with a knife. When we work for this balance, we will find certain factors that emerge as critical—such as distance control and management or exploitation of the universal startle response, along with simple "vertical" decision making (see chapter 11 for much more on this concept). But whether through training for primed responses or through streamlined vertical decision making, reaction-time gaps can be minimized or exploited.

## *The Situational Factors*

Most people think about that half second and make the mistake of assuming that it's not nearly enough time. In the personal protection field, we quickly learn the reality that this half second is contextual. We can never remove the stimulus (what is happening in that moment) from the situational factors surrounding it (how that stimulus is being played out).

For example, if you entered a room and saw a guy pointing a gun to someone's head, who would you immediately assume is in control?

The guy with the gun. 99.9% of people say the same thing.

But what my gun-disarming demo proves is that not everything is as it seems. Situationally, we are seeing the myth of helplessness hard at work: the assumption that because someone has a gun they are therefore in control. However, if the victim moves first, he/she will have that critical, physiologically hardwired half-second reaction-time advantage—which, believe it or not, is plenty of time to redirect a gun. Of course, doing so requires that you have the follow-up skills necessary to manage the situation beyond the initial moment. But thanks to the reaction-time gap, even someone with relatively little training can pull this off.

On top of this, if we add the situational factors into the equation, and if everyone assumes that the Bad Guy with the gun is in control, what do you think the Bad Guy with the gun thinks? He also thinks he's in control. So if the victim moves first, and moves decisively, we can count on the element of surprise.

How this element of surprise impacts the Bad Guy cannot be quantified the same way as the physiologically hardwired reaction-time gap, but we do know that surprise is one of the most decisive factors in any physical engagement, whether we're talking about war (which is violence on a macro level) or two people fist fighting in the street (the micro level of violence).

Not only do we have a half-second, hardwired reaction-time gap working to our advantage; we also have the element of surprise, which will extend our advantage, at the minimum, into the range of unprimed decision making. But here's the most important aspect of this whole equation: if you turn the tables on a Bad Guy and respond competently, odds are good that you have just put him into a situation that he has never experienced before. What do you think will happen when the Bad Guy's brain goes from stimulus to analysis in this moment? Panic or paralysis. Why? Because that's all that *can* happen. After all, he's human, just like you and me.

I use this demo in my sessions because it is the most efficient (and, in my opinion, elegant) way to demonstrate the difference between the realities of managing violence compared to the fictions we've all been led to believe in. We have all been led to believe that we are fundamentally helpless, especially if the Bad Guy has a gun. This quick demonstration, and the science behind mental chronometry, prove how untrue this is.

Still, people have a tendency to cling to previous biases, particularly as they relate to the myth of helplessness. So the natural follow-up question is, "Okay, so that works, but what if the Bad Guy is ten feet away?"

Obviously, distance, obstructions, and physical position will all impact your tactical response to the Bad Guy. Fortunately, there are methods to avoid, deter, and manage the violence no matter the circumstances. We will be covering the specifics of these methods in the chapters to come. For now, the takeaway message is that distance equals time. You're not helpless in this (or any) situation, and that is entirely because the brain controls the body. Improving how you manage the SAFE continuum and use it to stop any Bad Guy in any situation therefore starts with an exploration of the human brain and the factors that impact our performance under stress.

# CHAPTER 4

# The Physiology of Fear

KARINA IS ONE of the strongest, most capable women I've trained. As a career executive and also a competitive athlete, Karina had the uncanny ability to command any room, from conference room to boardroom to ballroom. She was accustomed to issuing commands and feeling in charge—not just of her workplace but of everything about her life. Her self-assurance carried over to a belief that she could protect herself if she ever needed to.

That all changed when, weeks prior to beginning her training with me, she was attacked in the lobby of her condo complex.

"I didn't see him coming," she explained. "Which is weird, because I noticed that the lock on the lobby door wasn't working right. I remember thinking how odd that was, but I just figured it was nothing. I should have looked around to make sure I was alone...

"I'd just opened my mailbox when he grabbed me from behind. He told me not to scream or he'd kill me. I could smell his horrible breath and remember trying to figure out if he had a weapon or not, but I couldn't be sure. I wanted to fight back, but my body wouldn't move. I couldn't even scream… I've never felt so helpless."

Like so many others who suffer through a similar immobilizing response during an attack, Karina made the mistake of believing that there must be something wrong with her—that she was somehow to blame for her reaction: that she must be a coward, or that she must be fundamentally incapable of defending herself. But the truth is that freezing of this nature is instinctual, and that any one of us can succumb to it without proper preparation or training on how to react to such a violent, terrifying stimulus.

Regrettably, Karina's story is frighteningly similar to so many others that survivors have shared with me. The circumstances differ wildly. Some are attacked by people they know, others by strangers. Some perpetrators have weapons, while most—at least in cases of sexual assault—do not. But what is resoundingly similar is the physical response the victim experiences: that ever-present and extremely terrifying inability to move. When we engage with a particularly horrific or frightening stimulus, one with which we have no prior experience, our freeze response may go beyond the inability to think and process. It may run much deeper and can be far more damaging to the victim, both physically and mentally.

Clinically known as tonic immobility, this physiological response is characterized by an inhibition of movement that results from encountering a seemingly inescapable threat. It is a reaction born of the evolutionary process, an instinct designed to keep us safe from deadly harm by flooding the body with enough adrenaline to effectively shut it down. This forced, instinctual version of "playing dead" can manifest itself in many sobering forms. Recall the livestream from the Christchurch mosque shootings; that pile of living people showing no reaction to being shot were experiencing tonic immobility.

A recent study led by Dr. Anna Moller of Stockholm South General Hospital and the Karolinska Institute revealed that seventy percent of women who had been raped reported a similar inability to move or fight back during the assault.[13] It isn't that some victims of rape didn't want to fight back; it's that they simply couldn't.

Research published by John Leach for the Aerospace Medical Association concluded that when faced with a life-threatening situation, seventy-five percent of people will freeze, despite having clear opportunities to escape or evacuate.[14] Freezing behavior can range from acting bewildered, confused, and slow to comprehend and function, to complete tonic immobility. The same research found that ten to fifteen percent of people panic and engage in irrational, counterproductive behavior that decreases their chance of survival. This leaves only ten to fifteen percent of people capable of engaging in productive behaviors that contribute to survival.

---

13  Carolyn Crist. "Many rape victims experience 'paralysis' during assault." Reuters Health. June 15, 2017.

14  https://pubmed.ncbi.nlm.nih.gov/15198281/ Aviat Space Environ Med. 2004

This instinctual freeze reaction can also trigger psychological damage that often lasts far beyond the event. Dr. Moller's study concluded that those who experienced tonic immobility were more likely to develop PTSD and depression. The role of tonic immobility in symptoms of PTSD is so direct, in fact, that a new and separate distinction has emerged. Known as Complex Post-Traumatic Stress Disorder (CPTSD), this classification differs from PTSD in that it results from the offending behavior being specifically of human origin. For both PTSD and CPTSD to manifest, there must be some exposure to a traumatic event, where conditions of extreme fear, helplessness, and horror are present. But CPTSD results from violent trauma, often over time, caused by another human being. It results from violence like rape, physical abuse, or torture.

Why does this distinction matter? Because it speaks to the natural human aversion to violence perpetrated by another person. The aversion is so powerful, so damaging, and so long lasting that it accompanies only the most extreme experiences a person can endure. Those who are victimized, whether through domestic violence, sexual assault, mass homicide, torture, kidnapping, or becoming a prisoner of war, often develop CPTSD.

Ultimately, what the research shows is that most people, when exposed to violence perpetrated by another human being, will experience an almost phobic-level fear reaction. If a person has not been trained or conditioned in how to manage that reaction, it can overwhelm them. This is the bad news. The good news is that while physical training is important, this natural reaction can be overcome with the right mental training—training that anyone can master, no matter their size, background, or skillset. It all starts with a deeper understanding of the physiological processes that lead to your physical response in the face of danger.

## *The Red Zone*

Tap the back of your neck. Go ahead and put the book down if you have to and just tap lightly on the area right at the base of your skull. Feel that? If you're like most people, depending on how hard you just hit yourself, you might feel a little woozy or wobbly. At the very least, your vision might have blurred there for a moment. This is because you just struck one of the most sensitive parts of your anatomy, the area that houses your brain stem. This is the hub of your central nervous system, what amounts to the fuse box of your brain.

If you travel the world studying competitive fighting, you will see many brutal things. Some competitions allow bare knuckles. In others, you can throw elbows or send knees to the face. Some even allow you to strike your opponent's groin. But you will be hard pressed to find a competitive fight that allows a combatant to strike the back of his or her opponent's head or neck. Why? Because if you effectively impact the brain stem, then you trigger a disruption to the central nervous system, causing a sudden loss of equilibrium and/or a knockout. It's like a power surge that blows the fuse box. One carefully placed blow, and the fight is no longer competitive.[15] If you're ever in a life-threatening situation that involves hand-to-hand combat, remember that lesson, as it will help you incapacitate anyone, even if they are considerably larger than you.

The brain stem connects to the cerebral cortex, where the SAFE process takes place. Between these two regions is a key part of the brain known as the limbic system, sometimes referred to as the midbrain. The limbic system's primary function is to ensure your survival. It doesn't care about your hopes and dreams for the future, or your dignity, or your concern for what others think of you. All it cares about is keeping you alive. To do so, it focuses on two primary functions: 1) your radar, defined here as your ability to perceive danger and potential danger in your surroundings on an unconscious level (this is what sparks those intuitive feelings of unease or fear you sometimes experience); and 2) your ability to mobilize your physiological resources to either fight to survive or flee to escape.

We will dig deeper into your radar and how to further tune your situational awareness and the intuitive side of the limbic system in a later chapter. For now, let's drill down into the fight-or-flight process. First off, "fight or flight" is a bit of a misnomer. Most people are familiar with the concept of fight/flight, but the term was never meant to

---

15   The brain stem is so sensitive, in fact, that you don't necessarily have to hit that spot directly. Even a well-placed punch to the jaw can lead to knockout, as the jaw will slide just enough to impact the mastoid process, a part of the brain stem located just behind the ear.

THE PHYSIOLOGY OF FEAR

denote a behavioral response. Our behaviors are far more complex. We may fight, flee, freeze, submit, or pretend to submit to create an opportunity to fight back; we may negotiate, bargain, or use deception; the list goes on. The term "fight or flight," rather, was meant to denote a physiological response to danger, wherein your body activates adrenaline, cortisol, and other stress hormones to maximize your physical ability to survive danger.

This response is largely controlled by something called your autonomic nervous system (ANS), which can itself be broken down into two separate, unconscious systems called the sympathetic nervous system (SNS) and the parasympathetic nervous system (PNS). Think of the SNS as your combat troops—all those men and women with guns, tanks, fighter planes, etc. designed to fight to keep you safe. The PNS, meanwhile, is like the support troops—the doctors, nurses, and supply/maintenance crew dedicated to keeping the whole system going. Put simply, SNS handles fight or flight, while PNS handles resting and digesting.

For most of the day, provided you are not under threat, your autonomic nervous system exists in a state of balance between alertness/awareness of your environment (SNS) and the resting/digesting process that happens constantly (PNS). A study led by Lt. Col. Dave Grossman and Bruce Siddle identifies this state as occurring while your heart functions between sixty to eighty beats per minute.[16]

---

16  Dave Grossman and Bruce Siddle, *Psychological Effect of Combat.* Academic Press, 2000.

This is when you feel normal, when you're in homeostasis, when the PNS and SNS are in balance (or at least close to balance).

When you go to bed at night, you end up in a near-total stand-down mode, and the SNS becomes repressed to the point where you can sleep, your PNS can take over, and your body can dedicate more resources to resting and digesting. The SNS never fully shuts off, however. This is why you wake up when your kid's bedroom door opens at 3 am, why you don't sleep as well on your first night or two in a hotel room or a new house, or why it takes some time to get fully comfortable in a new city. Your limbic brain is still assessing stimuli like air pressure, sound, and space, and searching to create a baseline of normalcy that will allow it to fully reach homeostasis. Once you acclimate, the scales rebalance, and you can relax.

Whenever you are faced with a life-threatening situation, the SNS controls your adrenaline response. Grossman and Siddle reference these effects with a model that looks like stairs, or even a thermostat. I personally view it more like the RPM gauge on a car. While there are levels of RPMs where your car performs best, there are certain levels that can place stress on the engine or even shut it down. The effect of adrenaline on your heart, and on your body's resulting functions, is similar.

While normal homeostatic heart rate is typically between 60 bpm and 80 bpm, adrenaline increases heart-rate almost instantly. The first phase of adrenaline jumps your heartrate to somewhere between 115 and 145 beats per minute. We classically refer to this as the Performance Zone—or in sports, simply "the Zone." Here, adrenaline is optimizing your performance. You're faster, stronger, more aggressive, and more decisive. If you're playing sports, flying an airplane, driving a race car, or trying to win a fight, this is exactly where you want to be.

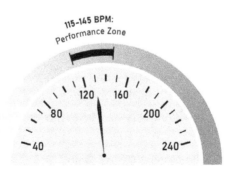

When we climb above this level, adrenaline begins to have a negative effect on our performance. The higher our adrenaline-induced heart rate rises above 145 bpm, the more profound the impact on performance.

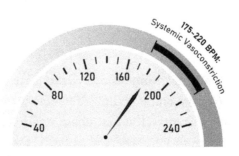

For most people, when the adrenalized heart rate reaches 175 bpm and above, we've officially entered what I refer to as the Red Zone, where the RPM meter is redlining. At this point, adrenaline leads to a cascade of negative effects.

Note: the zones we are discussing are not related to exercise-induced heart rate. Anyone can jump on a treadmill and elevate their heart rate to 145 bpm or more, but you manifest very few of the physiological effects we're discussing here. The effects on performance we are discussing relate exclusively to the effects of stress hormones on the body and mind.

One of the most universal, and noticeable, physical effects of adrenaline on performance is vasoconstriction.

Vasoconstriction is when the blood is pulled from the extremities into the core of the body and the major muscle groups. Most people experience vasoconstriction as extremely cold hands, and the fingers become clumsy. In the Red Zone of adrenaline, this effect is systemic and can be quite extreme. Vasoconstriction purportedly occurs as a mechanism to keep you alive, should you suffer penetrating trauma. Whether you are shot, stabbed, or mauled by a bear, every physiological system in the body is working to keep the blood in your body and maintain hydraulic pressure to the brain to keep you alive, conscious, and capable of fighting or fleeing until the danger passes.

The problem is that vasoconstriction manifests a number of physiological effects on the body that impact performance. Some of the best research on the effects of life-threatening stress on performance comes from Dr. Alexis Artwhol and Lauren Christensen, both internationally recognized behavioral science researchers, authors, and educators. In their most recent study involving law enforcement officers who survive deadly force encounters, the effects of Red Zone adrenaline are quantified.

At the top of the list is auditory exclusion—meaning that everything gets really quiet. Eighty-four percent of survivors reported this phenomenon, even during loud and dynamic gun fights.

Tunnel vision is the second most common, at seventy-nine percent.[17] This is where we lose our visual perspective field, focusing all attention typically on the perceived threat, to the exclusion of almost all other visual stimuli.

Both of these experiences are forms of "sensory gating," or "selective attention" driven by the limbic system. On the positive side, selective attention demonstrates our brain's incredible ability to focus on just the most important stimuli in a crisis—such as by sharpening our vision to the exclusion of virtually everything else. On the negative side, the loss or distortion to our perceptive faculties (termed "inattentional blindness"), can pose a significant problem to our overall situational awareness. We dive deeper into the issues of selective attention and inattentional blindness in chapter 6. For now, it's just important to understand the effects of tunnel vision and auditory exclusion on our ability to perform under stress.

Another common and significant perceptual distortion is that of experiencing tachypsychia—or "slow motion time"—reported in sixty-two percent of cases. You may recall my story about facing a gun as a bouncer in the first chapter. I personally experienced all three of the above phenomena firsthand.

Mechanically, one of the most significant effects of adrenaline and vasoconstriction is a drastic loss of fine and

---

17    Alexis Artwohl. "Perceptual and Memory Distortions During Officer Involved Shootings (2008 Update)." https://www.aele.org/law/2008F-PJUN/wb-19.pdf

complex motor control. All the cool martial arts and spy thriller movies you have seen that depict fist fights as forms of high art? That kind of thing is virtually impossible at this level of adrenaline, due primarily to the vasoconstriction effect. Here, if you engage in a fight, you can expect to be quite a bit less graceful than you see on TV. This is why your average street fight between amateur, inexperienced fighters doesn't look like a calculated boxing match; it looks like a couple of grunting cave people flailing at each other.

Experienced martial artists, soldiers, police, and professional fighters may still be able to access complex motor patterns and techniques in the Red Zone of stress, but only those skills that have been trained to the point of automaticity—or unconscious competence.

Unconscious competence is the top level of the "four levels of learning" model first introduced by Martin Broadwell in 1969.[18] The lowest level is "unconscious incompetence," meaning that you don't know what you don't know; the second is conscious incompetence, meaning you know what you don't know; the third is conscious competence, where you can execute skills while your mind is focused on the skill itself; and finally there is unconscious competence, where the skills are automatic based on the situation and adaptation of the response.

When the skill is unconsciously competent, adrenaline stress becomes less inhibitive and more like fuel for

---

18    Broadwell, Martin M. "Teaching for Learning (XVI)". *The Gospel Guardian*, wordsfitlyspoken.org

performance, action, and determination. Achieving this level of performance ability is a matter of knowing your objective, understanding what to look for and when to look for it, knowing what action is required, and then training on all of the above.

Yet, even when such training exists, stress at this level degrades performance. A principle called the Yerkes-Dodson Law[19] shows how this works.

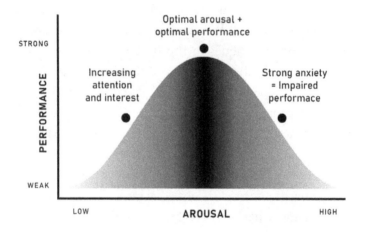

Note the inverted "U" shape of a person's performance relative to the adrenaline response. What we see is that performance improves at first before degrading as more and more stress enters the equation.

---

19   Yerkes, R.M. and Dodson, J. D. "The Relation of Strength of Stimulus to Rapidity of Habit Formation." *Journal of Comparative Neurology and Psychology* 18(5): 459-482.

Most people have never experienced the Red Zone of adrenaline that typically only accompanies life-or-death stress, but if you've ever had a near-miss car accident, where you felt your heart instantly start to pound, your hands shake, and your voice quiver, you have experienced a tiny dose of this effect. If you've ever been in a stressful situation that later on you wish you'd handled better, you've experienced the Yerkes-Dodson Law. It should be noted that some extreme emotional reactions, such as anger, can cause similar adrenaline reactions, with varying degrees of Red Zone effects on performance, but nothing affects us as significantly as fear, as evidenced by the most extreme physical Red Zone response to fear: losing control of our bowels and bladder, something that doesn't happen with other states of extreme emotional arousal. As I mentioned, the limbic system doesn't care about your pride or dignity; its sole goal is to maximize your ability to survive, and it will do whatever it takes to ensure that this happens when you are faced with survival-level fear. It is for these reasons that the Red Zone can be so debilitating during experiences with violence. Too much adrenaline and we essentially lose our ability to function. Beyond the physical dynamics, the greatest issue that comes with Red Zone stress is the loss of higher cognitive function. Access to long-term memory disappears, along with your ability to competently think and process in the moment in order to make decisions or solve problems, OODA be damned.

Panic and tonic immobility are almost universal behavioral responses at Red Zone levels of adrenaline, with the default being tonic immobility. It is for this reason that many have taken to renaming the "fight-or-flight" process the "fight-flight-freeze" process. Freezing at the level of tonic immobility is a survival mechanism that may keep you alive if you're being attacked by a bear, but that can get you seriously injured or killed if you're being attacked by a human predator. As such, it is something we need to learn how to manage.

## *Controls and Expectations*

An old friend of mine is a former UFC fighter and Strike Force Champion with a twenty-plus-year career as a world-class Mixed Martial Arts competitor. Once considered one of the greatest standup strikers on the planet, here was a man whose training made him uniquely capable of winning unarmed hand-to-hand fights with single opponents. Shortly after his retirement from the sport, while on set for a film he was acting in, he learned the hard way that this training was too narrow to keep him safe in every situation.

During the filming of a fight scene, one of his opponents—a former Spetsnaz soldier (an elite member of the Russian Special Forces) serving as a stunt double to my friend's costar—took a cheap shot. My friend's response was reflexive: he hit him back, knocking him down. Before he knew it, he saw three big, serious, former Russian Spetsnaz converging on him, one of them wielding an improvised club.

As he later explained to me, it was the first time he had experienced a level of adrenaline that made everything seem to go in slow motion. Weird details were burned into his brain, like the veins bulging in the neck of one of his opponents and the look of rage on another's face. The fight devolved into a melee. As you might imagine, as an experienced and highly skilled fighter, my friend handled himself much better than most would have, but he quickly realized that his MMA, one-on-one fighting tactics weren't entirely adaptable to some of the dynamics of a street fight. He had never been trained to fight multiple opponents or to disarm a weapon. He was one of the toughest fighters in the world, and he found himself in real trouble.

Fortunately, this was a movie set, so the fight was broken up before my friend could take any real damage. But the situation left him shaken and motivated to train solutions to these problems.

UFC light heavyweight fighter Anthony Smith engaged with a similar situation back in 2019. A man named Luke Haberman broke into Smith's home early one morning while his wife, three daughters, and mother-in-law slept. Despite Smith's far superior training in hand-to-hand combat, Haberman managed to put up a fight for more than five minutes. Smith had been trained as one of the most devastating strikers in the world, and Haberman took every punch, elbow, and kick he threw.

In an interview after the event, Smith admitted that this was the toughest fight of his life, all because combat of this nature in real life—outside the controls and expectations of an MMA fight—causes a much more debilitating adrenaline response. The fear of death in this case served as the great equalizer. Fortunately, police arrived and arrested Haberman, but Smith was left shaken and with a new perspective on the nature of self-defense.

As Smith learned the hard way, the limbic system simply does not evaluate a competitive fight in the same way it does a fight for your life. If you and I enter a Mixed Martial Arts cage fight with each other, we both know that this will be a stressful event, but we also know that we will benefit from a series of controls and expectations geared to our relative safety.

I know, for instance, before I step into the ring, that my opponent is not bringing a knife or a gun to the fight. So my chances of dying are considerably lower than they might be in a no-rules street fight against an unknown opponent. Further, if things get too bad, I can always tap out and end the fight, and if I can't tap out, the referee is there to save me.

All of these controls and expectations mean that, functionally, the limbic part of my brain does not see this event as survival stress. It interprets it primarily as performance anxiety, meaning that my stress and adrenaline will be related more to a concern about what people will think of me and less to whether I will walk out of this ring alive. I'm not worried about losing my life; I'm worried about the potential impact on my dignity, income, and profession.

But in the real world, when danger presents itself—particularly if it comes as a surprise and happens in an instant—you have no controls or expectations about how this is going to play out. It is that lack of knowledge that threatens to send your adrenaline and heart rate into the Red Zone.

This is part of why martial arts and competitive fighting training do not guarantee that you will react to violent situations in the real world much better than an untrained person. For one thing, martial arts can fail you, at least in part, if the moves are too complex. If we are in a competitive setting, there is a degree of predictability which allows the opportunity for more complex athletic moves. The timing and gamesmanship of the environment almost require them. But in the real world, most of this goes out the window.

Now, this is not to say that martial arts are not useful. My Strikeforce champion friend's experience, and Anthony Smith's experience as a UFC fighter, made all the difference in warding off their attackers, allowing for the execution of unconscious-competent skillsets. But when they encounter Red-Zone-level adrenaline, even the world's best martial artists can find themselves struggling. If you never train beyond the controls and expectations, you're in some ways preparing yourself to be *less* adaptable than you might be if training yourself to the reality of a life-or-death situation.

If you have ever served in the military, you have likely experienced an exercise designed to force you past controls and expectations and trigger a stress reaction. The exercise is called the False Finish Line, and it is profound in its simplicity. It starts with your drill instructor telling you that you will be going on a five-mile run. Because your brain has just been assured that it must control your body for the expectation of running five miles, as soon as you see the finish line, a wave of relief washes through you, and your body begins to enter a parasympathetic response in anticipation of slowing down and beginning to recover from your exertion. Then, the drill instructor reaches the finish line and veers off to start another loop.

Upon learning that they are not finished with the run, many of the runners find themselves physically and psychologically ready to collapse—especially if this is the first time they've experienced this. Even if their bodies are fully capable of running another five miles or more, having the expectation of reaching the finish line torn away from them causes a Red-Zone stress backlash that demoralizes and challenges performance.

Of course, as training progresses, false finishes don't affect recruits nearly as much. They may still hate them, but because they come to expect the unexpected, they're able to simply roll with the punches. They've learned not to get overly attached to expectations, and never to let their guard down. It becomes harder and harder to shake them, or to elicit an adverse adrenaline response.

The more closely training resembles reality (one that mirrors the appropriate levels of stress and unexpected challenges), the more inoculated our mind and our limbic system become to adversity, including the adversity of violence and life-or-death stress. In many ways, this is the key to unlocking our greatest potential.

### Controlling the RPMs?

David recently turned fifty, and for his birthday, his wife Angela surprised him with tickets to a huge three-day music festival, where he would get to see some of his favorite country stars in concert. David was blown away by the first two days of the festival—not just by the music, but by the incredible displays of patriotism and military might.

On the second afternoon, for instance, military helicopters performed a flyover of the festival; their sound and power was visceral.

But out of everything, David was most excited to see Jason Aldean perform as the headliner on the third and final night of the festival. "It was a cooker that night," David said, "so we went up to the mezzanine level at the House of Blues to get some air and a better view of the show."

Not long after Aldean took the stage, David recalls the confusion of this loud *whoop-whoop* sound coming from above. His first thought was that the helicopters were making a return appearance. "Why would they be flying these at night when you can't even see them?" he wondered. It wasn't until the second burst of sound, when Aldean dropped the microphone and ran offstage, that David, Angela, and his friends realized that what they thought was helicopters was in fact gunfire.

In the close protection field, we refer to this as *attack recognition*, that moment when you realize that a critical incident is occurring. Attack recognition is always accompanied by a surge of adrenaline, and in a situation like this, few people have experience to draw from and inform their physiological response.

David, Angela, and their friends discovered this the hard way at the Route 91 Harvest Music Festival that began on September 29, 2017. On the final night of the festival, from his 32nd-floor suite, mass murderer Stephen Paddock fired more than a thousand rounds into the crowd gathered below, killing 58 people and wounding 413, with the resulting panic injuring an additional 456.

Once he overcame that initial moment of shock, David immediately took stock of the environment. He realized that most of the people around him—perhaps two thirds of the enormous crowd—were frozen in fear.[20] Everywhere he looked, people were engaged in that paralytic moment so many of us experience when we encounter an immediate threat to our lives, some simply freezing, others exhibiting tonic immobility.

Then it happened: people started panicking, shoving, trying to get away. David couldn't find Angela or their friends, as they had been swept up in the stampede. The crowd's surge came toward the mezzanine, making his position a death trap. People were piling up against the wall below them, trying to hide. Finally, David found his wife and friends, and they made the decision to jump off the mezzanine level into the pile.

Below, they realized just how pinned down everyone was. One heroic man was standing beside the exit, trying to direct the panicked crowd down the steps.

"We had to take turns," David explained. "Had to wait for the shooter to blow through his magazine and reload. Every time there was a pause, one of us would jump up and start running toward the stairs."

David was wearing sandals that day, and he lost one of them at some point, so his run toward the stairs was hobbled. Once out in the open, they caught a break: the

---

20    If you're wondering, the other third of the people were completely oblivious to the danger. This is typical, no matter what the environment.

cyclone fence surrounding the festival had been trampled—not quite to where it was completely flat, but low enough that they could scramble over it and run northeastward toward a nearby industrial park. It wasn't until they reached a distance where they felt safe that David realized he'd been shot. The moment he saw the wound, his leg began to lock up. A strange thing happened to him then.

"I went from afraid to furious," he said. "I wanted to go back in and take the bad guys out."

A military veteran who'd escaped the massacre happened to notice David's wound. He created a pressure dressing out of a jean jacket to staunch the blood flow. David and his wife and friends hobbled through the terrified crowd looking for ways to help, as the rest of the eleven full minutes of shooting passed. They came upon a young lady who'd been shot through the chest, her husband out of control with desperation and fear. A brown dually pickup full of veterans pulled up and put the dying woman, David, and his wife along with five or so others into the truck bed, racing for the hospital. One of the uninjured passengers, a young man, irrationally stood up in the back of the fast-moving truck, screaming at the top of his lungs. David grabbed him and pulled him down to keep him from flying out of the truck as another casualty.

"After that, I just remember the noise," David said. "The roar of the truck. Screaming. Sirens everywhere. The triage area at the hospital was like a war room, so many wounded and dying, so many young kids who'd gotten separated from their parents or groups and couldn't remember any phone numbers to call."

Since he didn't seem to be critically injured, and was fully alert and decisive, the nurses asked David to help them triage and prioritize people with the worst injuries. Eventually, he took his turn in the ER, where the one thing he remembers is asking that the doctors and nurses not cut his shorts off him, as he wanted to save them as a souvenir. They only saw the hole in his quadriceps and believed there was no exit wound in David's leg, so they stitched up the wound and sent him home.[21]

Though David and his loved ones were still rattled from the experience, that night they ended up at the UNLV Convocation Center, where they joined other volunteers in helping the wounded and lost.

When I asked him what lessons he could share from this experience, David said one thing that didn't surprise me and another that did.

"Always know your exits," he suggested, which is absolutely a key lesson to take into situations like these. David explained that he had never given a thought to how he and his wife might get out of there if they needed to, but now, the first thing he does in any public setting is to check his exit routes.

When I asked him if he might have done anything differently—worn shoes that made it easier to run, for instance—he told me no.

---

21    Later, David found out that he had actually been shot through his gluteus, and the hole in his quad was actually the exit wound. He still recovered just fine.

"I don't want to change anything about how I would normally go to a show," he explained. "To allow the Bad Guys to stop you from going to concerts and enjoying your life is to let them win."

David's is an extraordinary psychology. Not all of us can be so calm and take such decisive action under pressure of this magnitude. So the question becomes, if we can't all be exactly like David, are there ways to at least manage our natural fear response and achieve a similar result? The answer is yes, but it requires an ability to pull yourself from the Red Zone of stress back into the performance zone, where you can think effectively, make decisions, and communicate.

But how do you do this? Unfortunately, the parasympathetic and sympathetic components of the autonomic nervous system exist in a black box that we simply can't control in this way. Your thoughts alone can't manifest 175 bpm of adrenalized heart rate accompanied by some tunnel vision and stress diarrhea. Nor can you bring such a reaction under control through your thoughts alone. To exert this level of control over your physical response, your physiology has to play a role as well.

Conventional wisdom is that this requires you to slow down and take a deep breath. While conventional wisdom is true to a degree, the most effective strategy is more complex.

Would it surprise you to know that combat soldiers, Navy Seals, and SWAT teams are learning yogic breathing exercises? It's true, except that they call the exercises "tactical breathing," mostly to ensure that their members will want to participate.

Marc Divine, author of *Unbeatable Mind*,[22] introduced a proven tactical breathing technique called Box Breathing to the Navy Seals, and subsequently to much of the tactical community. It involves modulating your breathing through your nose and bracketing your inhales and exhales with a hold. Begin by inhaling for a count of five. Then hold for a count of five. Now exhale for a count of five. Finally, hold for a count of five before restarting the process.

Most people feel more relaxed after just a few cycles of this. And this isn't the only version of controlled breathing that can help in tactical situations. For another excellent strategy, I recommend looking into the Wim Hof Method.

---

22    Divine, Mark. *Unbeatable Mind: Forge Resiliency and Mental Toughness to Succeed at an Elite Level.* CreateSpace Independent Publishing Platform, 2014.

Whichever controlled breathing strategy you prefer, here is the real trick: you need to practice this in non-stressful situations for it to be truly effective in situations like taking cover and planning your response while a gunman attacks a concert. When you're not in the Red Zone—when you're just dealing with the everyday anxieties that we all manage—functionally speaking, it is easier to practice a breathing exercise like this, and it is therefore easier to train your physiological response. The more you perform this exercise under controlled conditions, the more effective it will be in training your nervous system to respond under extreme stress and bring your heart rate back to the performance zone in times of mortal threat, the more capable you will be of managing your fear.

Now, while this is indeed an effective strategy, there are obvious limits. Under certain circumstances, breathing alone isn't enough. You're trapped at that concert, or in your home or your office, and you hear an intruder getting closer. Tactical breathing has helped to bring you back from the Red Zone to the performance zone, so you can think and make decisions. But when the door opens, and you come face to face with that attacker, breath control will be irrelevant. You won't be breathing consciously, and your adrenaline likely will be spiking through the roof again. At a time such as this, there's only one way to ensure that you have the ability to perform.

That way is training.

We simply don't rise to the occasion; we fall to the level of our training. The best time to figure out how to manage crisis is not during the crisis; it is now, beforehand, when you aren't under pressure, when you can strategically evaluate all your options and seek professional guidance, train, and then develop tactics you can be confident in. This is part of what you're doing by reading this book.

The hard reality is, no matter what the crisis, you're going to be on your own. There won't be any lifeguards to save you. And the greater the crisis, the longer you're likely to be on your own. So now is the time to learn and rehearse what to do and how to do it.

Bear in mind, when I speak of training, I'm not exclusively talking about physical training. In fact, I would go so far as to say that the *real* goal of any decent personal security training program shouldn't be to make you a ninja; it should be to ensure that you can think and make decisions under pressure—that you can override your limbic system's default into tonic immobility or panic, so that you can keep your wits about you, even when everyone else is losing theirs.

"Train the body and the mind will follow" is a core tenet of my philosophy, which is why in chapter 11, I will detail the five steps you need in order to systematically take total responsibility for your personal security, and if needed, find the right physical training. But before those action steps can be viable, we must first recognize that violence is fundamentally never random, and that trouble can find anyone.

Part 2:

# THE MYTH OF
# RANDOMNESS

## CHAPTER 5

# Think Like a Bad Guy

As a successful wealth manager, Ben could afford a very nice home with a high-end security system in a trendy Manhattan neighborhood. But he never considered himself high profile enough that he or his family could become the target of professional criminals. Neither he nor the people he loved noticed the surveillance operation that the Bad Guys undertook in the days prior to the attack.

The operation catalogued Ben's typical arrival and departure times, along with the patterns of his wife Lauren, their children, and the housekeepers and landscaping crews that had access to the home and yard. This allowed the Bad Guys to time their attack for when Ben would be out, the plan being to kidnap Lauren and the kids.

Ben may not have considered himself wealthy enough to ever have to face a nightmare like this, but he had overlooked a key component of Bad Guy psychology: they will leverage any advantage to get what they want. They weren't after Ben's money; they were after his access to the money belonging to his extremely wealthy clients. The thinking was that those clients, some of whom were billionaires, would be significantly harder targets, but Ben would never see it coming. As it turned out, the thinking was correct.

On an otherwise typical Monday morning, Ben left for work, and that was when the Bad Guys struck. They entered the house through the front door. They knew that Ben and Lauren weren't in the habit of setting their alarm during the day. How? Because their surveillance location allowed them to see the security panel through a window, including its easy-to-spot indicator light—green for disarmed, red for armed. Their plan was reasonably well crafted, timed, and executed, except that they failed to account for a babysitter who had stayed over the night before.

The babysitter was the first to spot the intruders. She screamed and ran out the back door, retreating to a neighboring house to call the police. This unexpected trouble made one of the two Bad Guys panic and flee the scene immediately. The other continued with the plan. The scream, however, alerted Lauren, who otherwise might have been taken totally unaware. Now, when the remaining Bad Guy found her in the first-floor laundry room, she was prepared to act.

Ben had attended a training session with me a year prior. One of the lessons—about striking an attacker's nervous system in a way that can cause an immediate equilibrium disruption—stuck with him to such a degree that he went home and taught it to Lauren. In the heat of the moment, Lauren recalled these lessons. She grabbed a nearby clothes iron and smashed it into the side and back of her attacker's neck. This stunned him sufficiently to give Lauren just enough time to get out of the area. When the Bad Guy recovered, he fled the scene.

If this incident had been discussed on the eleven o'clock news, you can bet that at some point we would have heard catchphrases like "In another act of random violence..." or "No one saw it coming." Had this incident included the undertones of workplace violence, we would have heard the old saw, "The perpetrator simply snapped..."These phrases have a way of suggesting to the viewer that there is an epidemic of violence in this country and it is unpredictable. Random. Not something that any of us is equipped to foresee or prevent.

This same line of thinking contributed to the events that led to Lauren having to defend herself. When the police finally arrived nearly thirty minutes after the incident (no, you didn't read that wrong), they gathered the details and began an investigation to track down the Bad Guys. The evidence led to a successful arrest, but the forensic analysis afterward caused Ben a number of sleepless nights.

"The police told me the kidnappers had been watching the house from an unmarked van across the street," he explained. "And you know, I remember seeing that van and thinking, *Why has that van been here all week?*"

At the time, Ben brushed it off as coincidence. He figured it was probably nothing. There was no way this unmarked van had anything to do with him and his family. There had to be a logical, perfectly normal reason for it to have been there for such a long time.

In making this assumption, Ben, like Karina entering her apartment complex, fell into the trap that ensnares so many victims. He minimized and dismissed the critical warning signs that could have alerted him to danger.

After all, why should Ben need to be on the lookout for violence? Violence is random, isn't it? It just happens, and there's nothing you can do about it, right? It always seems like bad things happen to others, usually after they put themselves in bad situations. "This is a safe neighborhood," Ben had told himself. "Nothing like that ever happens around here…"

The myth of randomness is pervasive and compelling. If we label violence random, it is therefore unpredictable. And if it is unpredictable, then what possible responsibility could we have to prevent it or respond to it? The myth is powerfully seductive primarily because, in our core, we want to believe it. It's a scary concept to accept that there are people out there who actively and methodically choose to prey on their fellow human beings; that there are people who perceive kindness as weakness; that there are people who don't victimize others as often as they would like, only because the opportunity wasn't quite right; that there are those who would enter your home, or your life, and take from you and all you hold dear for nothing more than a little profit, pleasure, or feeling of power.

When you couple the fear of these realities with the myth of helplessness—that pervasive belief that you are helpless to do anything about violence, should the worst occur—the true and genuine danger to our safety emerges: denial. Just as we tell a restless child that there is nothing to worry about so they can sleep at night, we tell ourselves a similar story. But this story is as effective in warding off danger as pulling the covers over your head when you hear a bump in the night.

Ignoring these realities—embracing the "save now, pay later" mentality that so many people and organizations fall into—does not make you safer. It makes you more vulnerable.

Even the most unspeakable acts of violence make sense on some level to the perpetrator. This is the bad news. It is also the good news, because accepting this truth allows us to learn the techniques for spotting and then avoiding or mitigating violence before it can start.

The reality is that violence is never random. As security specialist and bestselling author Gavin De Becker once wrote, violence "is a process as observable, and often as predictable, as water coming to a boil."23 I would add to this quote, "provided you know what to look for and are in a position to see the signs."

## *The Three Ps*

The first thing to know about the non-random nature of violence is that all Bad Guys, no matter what their crime of choice, fall into one of three categories: Professional, Potential, and Predatory.

---

23    Gavin de Becker. *The Gift of Fear: Survival Signals That Protect Us from Violence.* Bloomsbury Publishing PLC., 2000.

*Professional Bad Guys*

The Professional Bad Guys category includes, first and foremost, all mass killers—school shooters, workplace shooters, and domestic or international terrorists. To me, all of the above are fundamentally terrorists, as the only differentiating factor is ideology. Some are personally motivated while others are politically motivated, but what they hope to achieve, how they plan and execute their attacks, and ultimately what they are most afraid of are all foundationally the same.

This category also includes members of organized crime, serial killers (who are relatively rare), serial rapists, and child molesters (who are unfortunately not rare).

The Bad Guys that Ben and Lauren met with on that terrible day are ones that we would describe as Professional, despite their relative incompetence. This is because I do not define these Bad Guys as "professional" by virtue of them being necessarily any good at what they do; rather, I define them as professional by virtue of their "mission" orientation. Mission-oriented Bad Guys choose very specific targets for very specific reasons and often engage in a meticulous level of planning or grooming of the target prior to taking action.

*Potential Bad Guys*

At the opposite end of the spectrum, we have what I call Potential Bad Guys. I half-jokingly say that this category represents anyone on a bad day. Unlike the high-level predisposition to violence evident in Bad Guys in the Professional category, Potential Bad Guys are rather more affected by prevailing situational factors. He's drunk, or high, or just got dumped by his girlfriend, or just lost his job.

You may be fully unaware of these situational factors, but if you look at this kind of Bad Guy sideways, or you cut them off in traffic (for example), you have the potential for violence to erupt. This is the closest we come to describing someone who seems to "just snap," although the truth is that no one "just snaps." Potential Bad Guys still follow a predictable and observable process in their escalation of behavior, and they are still careful in the selection of their targets. Given the nature of situationally driven violence, most interactions with Potential Bad Guys can be defused, mitigated, or disengaged from, as long as you recognize them for what they are and manage them correctly.

*Predatory Bad Guys*

This final category encompasses the criminal element that comes to mind for most people when they think of a Bad Guy—namely, those looking to commit rape, robbery, murder, assault, or some combination thereof. Some attack their targets using brute force, while others use charm and persuasion to create the right circumstances for an attack.

Some Predators may actively hunt for their victims, while others might be going about their everyday life when a suitable target strolls across their path and they choose to jump into predatory mode. Whatever their crime of choice, Predatory Bad Guys absolutely have a mission in mind, but they fundamentally need the right situational factors in play to pull it off. The combination of these two dynamics we define with the word "opportunity."

## *Threat Assessment*

In the highest echelons of the personal security industry lies the process of "threat assessment." The purpose of threat assessment is to determine if someone who is making threats, or acting threateningly, in fact poses a threat. There is a significant difference between the two. Lots of people make threats; very few actually pose a threat.

Posing a threat goes far beyond simple access to weapons or a history of violence. It is fair, after all, to assume that everyone who has a motive can access a weapon of some sort, and as you will see, just because someone has no history of violence, that does not mean they cannot become violent.

True threat assessment resides in the interplay between a perpetrator's predisposition (or mission orientation) as we can evaluate it, and the situational factors surrounding the case.

*Pop Quiz:*

If your goal was to predict the potential for violence in a given situation, which of these two elements—*predisposition* or *situation*—would you guess carries more weight on the scale of whether violence may actually occur? Both are important, but which do you think is more predictive?

Some jump to predisposition, because we like to believe that only bad people do bad things, but most intuitively recognize that situational factors carry far more importance. There are three key reasons why this is the case:

1. Some violence is situationally driven alone.

   Picture a twenty-five-year-old woman pushing a stroller in New York. She has no history of violence. No criminal record. She doesn't own firearms and has never practiced martial arts. She doesn't even like to watch violent movies or TV shows. There are no indicators that she possesses even a small degree of predisposition toward violence.

   But in the stroller sleeps her newborn baby.

   If someone were to come along and try to take or harm her baby, could you predict a violent outcome? You better believe it! Not only could we predict that violence is likely to occur; we could even go a step further and suggest that someone who previously had no violent predisposition, considering the situational factors, might in fact *want* to do violence.

   This alone tells us that situational factors trump everything else.

2. Just because someone wants to hurt you doesn't mean they can.

   Consider the would-be terrorist. The world suffers no shortage of people who have become radicalized by religious, political, or social fundamentalism, but relatively few take the leap to committing acts of terror. Mission-oriented Bad Guys like terrorists are almost always deterred by situational factors that cause them to question their ability to successfully complete the mission.

In most cases, the desire to commit violence does not by itself lead to violence. Bad Guys still need to have the ability to pull it off.

3. YOU can control the situational factors.

No matter what the dynamics, and no matter who you are or what your training is, as long as you understand the situational factors that you can control—and you never relinquish control of them—you can control, or at the very minimum significantly influence, the potential for violence and the outcome.

### *The Situational Factors of Control, or "Defense in 3-D"*

In nature, predators naturally and instinctively target the weakest, most vulnerable prey. This behavior is as predictable as it is logical. It's like a law of nature. The only time predators deviate from this law is in times of extreme desperation.

Humans who choose to prey on other humans—be they Professionals, Potentials, or Predators—behave in much the same way. Whether the Bad Guy is a terrorist, con artist, schoolyard bully, or a hardened street criminal looking to commit rape, robbery, murder, assault, or some combination thereof, he is fundamentally looking for the same qualities in his targets: vulnerability. Weakness. A target who cannot or will not fight back. They are looking for what we in the security industry call a "soft" target.

I would argue, based on over two decades studying and defeating Bad Guys, that they not only *want* a soft target; they fundamentally *need* a soft target.

But why? What are they afraid of?

Most people immediately think of the three most common fears that we might ascribe to Bad Guys: getting hurt, getting caught, or getting killed. Perfectly logical. But unfortunately it's not quite that simple…

Take a look at a "top of the food chain" Bad Guy, an international terrorist. Is he afraid of dying? The answer of course, must be *no*. Being willing to die for the cause is almost a prerequisite of terrorism. If they aren't afraid of dying, then they aren't likely to be afraid of getting hurt or killed in the process.

So, if a terrorist isn't afraid of getting hurt, killed, or caught, how do we deter him? Can he even *be* deterred?

I argue that he can. In fact, I would suggest that terrorists can be deterred fairly easily. The key is in understanding that while they may not be afraid of dying, they are deathly afraid of being stopped before they complete their mission.

They fear failure.

Obviously, we can't read people's minds. Certainly, different Bad Guys fear different things. A Potential Bad Guy might be afraid of going to jail, while a Predator might not fear jail, but the idea of getting hurt or killed stops him in him tracks. Ultimately, though these fears may seem disparate, they all equate to that same fear in the mind of the Bad Guy: failure. To each of them, failure means succumbing to whatever they fear most, whether that is getting caught, hurt, or killed.

This is why even the most desperate Bad Guy is careful about selecting his prey; why he is so tuned in to finding a soft target. It is also why deterrence and defense are far less complicated than most people think. You don't need to have a PhD in criminal psychology or even a black belt to defend yourself from them. You simply need to represent enough potential for failure that they decide to move on to easier, softer targets. Bad Guys are remarkably detached from ego in this manner. They're not looking for a challenge. They don't feel a need to prove themselves. They simply keep hunting.

In many ways, this makes deterrence much like the joke about the bear: how fast do you need to be to outrun a bear? Faster than the next guy...

This means you don't need to be bigger, stronger, and faster than every Bad Guy you might encounter. And it means you don't have to put your workplace on lockdown or live in a house with Fort-Knox-level security. You simply have to understand what threats you are trying to mitigate and stack the deck enough in your favor to project a high potential for failure to the Bad Guys who may try to target you.

Understanding who our adversaries are, what qualities they are looking for in a target, and ultimately, what they are afraid of, allows us to articulate a defense—one that's centered around the situational factors you can and must control.

Whether we are protecting a person, place, or thing, my close protection teams (and those we train) follow the same 3-D process: Deny, Deter, Defend.

1. Deny

> Rule #1 of all security, regardless of what kind of security we are talking about—physical, financial, digital, etc.—is to deny opportunity. If you remember only one thing from this book, let it be this: you have the ability to deny opportunity. Based on the choices you make related to the situational factors, you can successfully avoid most attacks.
>
> Denying opportunity means more than just avoiding trouble. Embedded in the principle is the ability to recognize danger—specifically, to recognize when you might be being set up or targeted.
>
> Many pay this principle lip service by saying things like "I don't go out at night," or "I don't go to bars," or "I don't go downtown," as if violence only occurs to certain people, under certain circumstances, at certain times, or in certain locations. This is the myth of randomness hard at work! The reality is that anyone can be targeted anywhere, and at any time. The critical facet of avoidance is in knowing what the warning signs

are that a Bad Guy may be targeting you and then actively responding to avoid further trouble.

If you know the warning signs, you can recognize danger before it reaches critical levels and can actively avoid the trouble before it escalates. Of course, some Bad Guys are better at masking their intent than others, and sometimes even the best-trained people can miss the signs. When this happens, we must progress to the second step.

## 2. Deter

Deterrence can be defined simply as creating, in the mind of the adversary, fear. But to do this effectively, we have to remember what Bad Guys are afraid of and use that fear to become a hard target. This means you MUST be willing and able to participate in your own security. But while willingness is a state of mind, ability is a statement of fact.

If you are not willing and able to respond, the Bad Guys will spot you as easily as a lion spots the softest gazelle on the savannah.

## 3. Defend

Sometimes, in the realm of personal security—as in life—even though you do everything right, you still find yourself in the wrong place at the wrong time. Sometimes you're outnumbered, or the Bad Guy has a force multiplier like a weapon, and the balance tips in his favor. Sometimes, despite your best efforts to deny or deter, the only way out is through, and you're going to have to physically respond and defend yourself.

As first quoted in chapter 3, "We don't rise to the occasion, we fall to the level of our training." I'm not going to sugarcoat it: without proper training and possibly the right tools, most people simply will not be equipped to defend themselves or their loved ones. This is a hard reality of nature. As humans, we simply aren't born with the innate capacity to defend ourselves. We don't have claws or fangs, or even combative instincts to guide us.

In fact, absent the right training, what we are left with is a limbic system hardwired to reflexively panic, or more likely, freeze under extreme stress.

The good thing is that this same human mind that sometimes betrays us also allows us to learn. We are equally well programmed to study, store, and recall lifesaving information—such as how to commit violence, should it become necessary. Equally fortunate is that, contrary to popular belief, learning the right skillsets for personal defense does not require years of dedicated martial arts practice, great athletic ability, or constant sparring.

## *The TIME-Line of Violence*

Imagine the moment when the perpetrators of the September 11th attacks arrived at the idea to hijack a series of planes and crash them into the World Trade Center, the Pentagon, and the Capitol. Intrigued by the idea, Osama bin Laden and his followers collectively committed to gathering the information they needed to formulate a plan to make that happen.

The intelligence they gathered suggested that the best way to ensure the desired outcome would be to hijack planes routed on long flights, thereby maximizing the explosive payload delivered to the target. And the best way to avoid detection would be to rely on hijackers permitted to fly within the United States, arming them with boxcutters—weapons that, if discovered during security screening, would not raise so much suspicion as to thwart the entire plot.[24] Finally, they would need to coordinate flight departures so that the four separate attacks could occur almost simultaneously.

Next came the effort to vet, or stress test, every component of the plan, searching for ways that it might go wrong and then course-correcting accordingly. They spent years on preoperational planning, recruiting, training, testing, selecting the weapons, probing and surveilling the targets,

---

24  Believe it or not, pre-9/11, it was legal and acceptable to fly with pocket knives below a certain blade length.

and rehearsing the steps of the attack. They tracked airline routes to identify the flights that best met their criteria and timing. They took flying lessons. They tested whether their passports would raise red flags at the locations where they intended to board. They tested and rehearsed whether it was possible to get boxcutters onto an aircraft undetected.

The process looks similar for most mass shooters as well. Prior to killing twelve people and injuring seventy more in the Century 16 theater shooting in Aurora, Colorado, James Eagan Holmes gathered intelligence, meticulously planned the attack, and even fabricated a device that would allow him to open the theater's emergency exit door from the outside. At a film showing several days prior to his attack on July 20, 2012, he installed this device and tested it to ensure that he would have access to this entry point on the day he intended to carry out his plot.

These Bad Guys followed a specific, predictable, and identifiable process for selecting a target, planning the attack, and then executing that attack in a way that achieved the desired outcome. I refer to this process as TIME, or Target selection, Intelligence gathering (aka the Interview process), Moment of attack, and Escape/Exploitation.

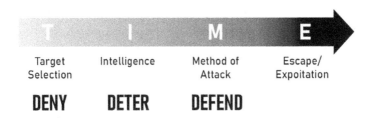

| T | I | M | E |
|---|---|---|---|
| Target Selection | Intelligence | Method of Attack | Escape/ Expoitation |
| **DENY** | **DETER** | **DEFEND** | |

In the stories about the 9/11 terrorists and Holmes, we have seen what Target selection and Intelligence gathering look like. This moves us along to the M, where the first thing you might notice in the graphic above is the flame. This image represents the Moment or Method of attack: the instant when the planes hit the building, when the shooter enters the theater and opens fire, when the Bad Guy makes his intentions known.

In their book *Left of Bang: How the Marine Corps' Combat Hunter Program Can Save Your Life*, Patrick Van Horne and Jason A. Riley, both Marine Corps veterans and security experts, define this as the "moment of bang."[25] As the title of the book suggests, the authors advocate for strategies to disrupt or deter an attack "left of bang," meaning before those attacks occur.

On the TIME-Line of Violence, the moment of bang is exactly where you don't want to be, because if you have sacrificed preparation and insight during the left of bang period, then the Bad Guys bring to bear the considerable advantages of timing, surprise, resources, and weapons. This leaves you in a totally reactive state, which heightens the chances that the Bad Guy will succeed and you will be victimized.

Finally, the E on the TIME-Line carries a dual meaning, as some Bad Guys leap into an Escape plan while others enter into what I call the Exploitation phase. The

---

25    *Left of Bang: How the Marine Corps' Combat Hunter Program Can Save Your Life.* Patrick Van Horne and Jason A. Riley, Black Irish Entertainment LLC, 2014.

escape side of the coin is more obvious. Nikolas Cruz, who carried out the mass shooting at Marjory Stoneman Douglas High School in Parkland, FL, planned to escape by ditching his weapons and blending in with the terrified student population fleeing the scene. This plan initially proved successful, though he was caught and arrested an hour later in Coral Springs.

The 9/11 terrorists, and to a lesser degree, James Holmes, did not enter the M on the timeline with an escape in mind. For them, the desired aftermath was exploitation. For the former, the exploitation involved Al-Qaeda claiming credit for the attack, demonstrating that a single, well-funded terrorist cell could do considerable and lasting damage to the world's greatest superpower, thereby destabilizing the global power dynamic forever. For the latter, the exploitation involved the bombs rigged to go off when investigators searched his apartment for clues as to his motive. This portion of Holmes's plan thankfully failed, but he was certainly not alone among the ranks of mass shooters who wished to leave a message after the attack.

For many, the exploitation takes the form of the manifesto—or the "legacy token," as the FBI describes it—discovered in a locker or on social media and released to the public by the media. For any terrorist, whether a suicide bomber or a mass shooter, the exploitation is what defines his success. It is what delivers that desired notoriety, media attention, and perceived lasting impact on society. For them, killing people is not the end of the mission; it is the means. The end mission is for everyone to know *why* they chose to kill.

LIVE READY

## *Is TIME Universal?*

It's easy to see how mission-oriented Bad Guys dedicate themselves to a meticulous and discernable planning process, but what about street criminals—the kinds of Bad Guys who pick pockets, mug passersby, and commit assault? Do they follow the same TIME-Line?

The answer is yes; it just happens faster. No matter what kind of Bad Guy we're talking about—Professional, Potential, or Predatory—they still follow the TIME-Line of Violence. Just like any terrorist, they engage in target selection, observing their potential prey, assessing strengths and weaknesses, and where applicable, getting to know routines. All of them gather, test, and probe their intended targets to validate their selection prior to committing the act.

With street criminals, we often refer to the I of TIME as an "interview" process. Interviews often take the form of the Bad Guy approaching the target and engaging them in conversation. Sometimes, it takes the form of a pursuit, such as following or observing the target to see if they are even aware of the Bad Guy's presence. They certainly have a mission or method of attack in mind, but they want to evaluate the potential for success or failure. The purpose of the interview is the same, therefore, for a Predator as it is for a Professional: ultimately, to validate if the target is indeed soft, and to confirm that their method of attack is sound prior to execution.

Keep in mind that attacks don't always immediately follow an interview. Sometimes, how you conduct the interview will determine whether you are targeted hours, days, or even weeks later.

Once they're confident they've selected the right target, the Bad Guy may commit to the moment of attack, whether it has been rehearsed through repetition, imagined and meticulously plotted, or sprung simply because opportunity presents itself. And they all have either an escape or an exploitation goal to meet; otherwise, they would not be contemplating and committing a crime in the first place.

Knowing that this TIME-Line exists for all Bad Guys, the next logical question is how do we disrupt it? As Van Horne and Riley point out, we have far less control over the outcome during the moment of bang.

So can we avoid being targeted?

When I ask this question of the attendees to my training sessions, it's about a fifty/fifty split between people who say you can and those who say you can't. The answer is unfortunately that you can't.

The Bad Guy is ultimately in control of whether or not to target you. You can be the kindest person in the world who goes out of her way to treat everyone with respect and dignity and still be targeted for violence. You could be the most emotionally intelligent, sensitive business leader and still be faced with mission-oriented targeting when a ter-minated employee shows up six months after termination saying, "When you fired me, you destroyed my life…" You could do everything right in an intimate relationship and still have to deal with "If I can't have you, no one can…" just like one in six women in the US experience at some point in their lives.[26]

However, you can *influence* the targeting. In following the progression of the 3 Ds, you can avoid targeting by denying opportunity; by actively avoiding the potential for trouble and not putting yourself in harm's way; by listening to your radar and recognizing the early warning indicators, and thus reducing the likelihood of being seen as a viable, soft target.

But in the end, never forget that it can and does happen, and if you get targeted, it's not necessarily because you did anything wrong! You can do everything right, denying opportunity at every turn, and still find yourself targeted. If you do, don't blame yourself. Ultimately, target selection is the only part of the TIME-Line that the Bad Guy controls.

### *The Exploitation Cycle*

Recently, I hosted a training session on spotting the indicators of intelligence gathering and the interview process for a group of college students. One of the key messages in this course is that the TIME-Line of Violence may be

---

26  CDC. National Intimate Partner and Sexual Violence Survey. 2010. "One in 6 women (16.2%) and 1 in 19 men (5.2%) in the United States have experienced stalking victimization at some point during their lifetime in which they felt very fearful or believed that they or someone close to them would be harmed or killed."

predictable, but some Bad Guys are sophisticated enough that you may not spot their intent until it's too late. Some are so charming and persuasive that we don't even realize we've been targeted, even as we're trapped in the middle of the interview. They have honed their craft to the point where they can commit horrifying, ongoing, long-term crimes with impunity.

Imagine a fifteen-year-old girl at the mall with her friends. The group is approached by an attractive Predatory Bad Guy in his early twenties.

"You're so beautiful," the predator says to his target. "You should be an Instagram model."

The young woman might roll her eyes at this, refusing to believe the predator's sincerity.

"No, I'm serious," he says. "How old are you?"

"Fifteen."

"Fifteen?! I would have definitely thought you were at least eighteen." He hands her a business card. "I'm a talent scout. Text me if you're ever interested in doing some modeling."

Most young women are educated enough on the dangers of the modern world to recognize that all of this was probably a line, and most will refuse to share any personal information with someone they have only just met by (supposed) chance. Few recognize, however, that this is potentially just the first phase of the Predatory Bad Guy's interview process.

A day or two later, having followed his target and learned her routines, the predator will bump into the young woman at a convenience store or Starbucks.

"Hey," he will say, feigning surprise. "Aren't you that girl I ran into at the mall the other day? What a crazy coincidence. Have you given any more thought to modeling?"

Now we have a fifteen-year-old girl who was already flattered by the idea that someone thinks she is beautiful enough to be an Instagram model, and here she has bumped into that same someone in a second location. It must be fate! All those movies she has seen where the main characters meet by happenstance and fall in love, maybe it's all really happening in her own life.

In the intelligence community, this is a technique called a *bump*. Essentially, it is nothing more than an extremely powerful icebreaker or rapport-building tool—a means to deliver the sense that this second meeting is serendipitous; why wouldn't his target let her guard down, if only a little?

I'm enough of a romantic to want to believe in serendipity, but I also want you to remember that there really is no such thing as a coincidence, at least not in the popular sense. Most people use the word "coincidence" to describe remarkable events that happen by chance. But from now on, I want you to think of coincidence through the lens of its original mathematical definition, meaning to "coincide perfectly." Bumps don't typically take place through happenstance. Assume that they are contrived. When they occur, rather than lowering your guard, raise it and look for other warning indicators that you may be being interviewed.

For a persuasion-oriented predator, the interview process is often very sophisticated and sometimes longer term than most potential targets might realize. Their process gets into very similar dynamics as child molesters use to *groom* their victims, systematically breaking down natural inhibitions and defenses in a way that shapes their victims' belief that this abnormal behavior is normal. Perhaps it starts with slightly improper physical contact, like a socially inappropriate or too-intimate hug or touch of the hand on a leg. It progresses to using a position of authority to get the victim alone (privacy always works to the advantage of the would-be predator). Maybe he introduces the victim to pornography, alcohol, or drugs, or he engages in subtly increasing inappropriate touching or "accidental" intimate contact designed to continuously desensitize and normalize the abnormal behavior. If you know what to look for and are watching closely, these interviewing or grooming behaviors are easy to see for what they are.

As the Predatory Bad Guy cycles through this interview process, he is always gathering intelligence on what his target needs, whether socially or psychologically. Does she need affection? Attention? Does she need to feel attractive? Or is it something more physical like food, drugs, or money?

Once the Bad Guy has identified this need, his method of attack takes the form of providing for that need. In this way, he creates an environmental or psychological dependency that suggests he is the only person in a position to continue providing that need. This is when the victim is primed for exploitation and the real victimization begins. Most commonly, this takes the form of sexual victimization. The sense in the victim is that while he/she knows that what's going on is wrong, he/she has been positioned and systematically maneuvered to feel trapped, lost, unable to seek help, and ultimately totally dependent on the predator for his/her needs.

When that dependency actualizes, the I-M-E phases of TIME become a recurring exploitation cycle. This is how abusers, pimps, loan sharks, bookies, drug dealers, and every manner of persuasion-oriented predators victimize people: by identifying unfulfilled needs and then exploiting them. A similar dynamic occurs in relationships that involve ongoing domestic abuse. From the outside looking in, it might be difficult to imagine why someone would stay with an abusive partner. It's not because the abusers are master psychologists; it's because they recognize their partner's insecurities and how to provide just enough for them to feel secure. In this way, the victim believes themselves so dependent on the abuser—for childcare, for money, for food and shelter—that they believe they have no choice but to stay. "He's going to get drunk and hit me from time to time, but he doesn't really mean to. He'll always apologize. And anyway, it's not like I can do any better."

The fifteen-year-old girl flattered about the prospect of becoming an Instagram model might be coerced into doing something that introduces crippling shame. The predator invites her to a party for all prospective models, but the only catch is that it's in Vegas. He's happy to buy her plane ticket and put her up in a hotel room, but her parents will never approve of such a trip, so she will have to lie to them and say she is staying with a friend for the weekend.

Because the predator is so skilled at his craft, he proceeds to break down any obvious objections the young woman might have to this idea. Eventually, he talks her into joining him, and they travel to Vegas, where he puts her up in a hotel room and spends whatever time it takes to break down her remaining resistance. He coerces her into having sex with him, or his friends, or a stranger. The act fills her with shame, which makes her even more vulnerable. Now is when he springs the trap that enters her into the exploitation cycle. He leverages that shame to convince her that she can't tell her parents about any of this now or they will disown her. And if she doesn't do what he asks of her—if she doesn't repay the favor of that free ticket and hotel room in Vegas—then he will just have to leave her here to fend for herself.

Or perhaps he takes a different tack. "I owe money to these three guys," he says. "They're going to kill me if I don't pay, but they said they'll forgive the debt if you have sex with them."

Of course the young woman resists at first.

"But don't you love me?"

Of course she loves him. Or thinks she does. She's fifteen.

"Well this is just how people who love each other are supposed to behave," he tells her. "You're supposed to do things for each other. Help each other out."

This logic makes sense to the young woman. She does what is asked of her. This brings more shame, which only leads to more control for the predator as he reinforces her fear about what her parents or others might think of her if she ever tells the truth about what happened. The cycle continues again and again, the Predatory Bad Guy always returning at the right moment to give his victim what she thinks she needs, locking her further into the exploitation cycle and under his control.

## *The I of TIME*

We cannot fully control whether we will be targeted. If the Bad Guy reaches the moment of attack, he already holds the advantage. And if we find ourselves at the point of escape or exploitation, our victimization has already occurred.

Fortunately, this does not mean that we are all simply waiting to become victims. There is still that one spot on the TIME-Line, the phase where we can exert the most control: the I of TIME. This is where we spot the warning signs that we're being interviewed or watched/followed as part of intelligence gathering, where we deter the Bad Guys before they can commit to the moment of attack.

Knowing how to leverage your advantages during the I of TIME is your first and best line of defense. This defense involves a series of strategies you can follow regardless of your physical size, training, or experience with Bad Guys. The foundation of this process is to hone and listen to your sense of intuition, to enhance your natural radar's ability to pick up on the warning signs or "indicators" that you may be being targeted. To do this, you have to first understand that you don't see with your eyes… You see with your mind.

## CHAPTER 6

# You See with Your Mind, Not Your Eyes

ON THE MORNING of September 11, 2001, US Airways ticketing agent Mike Tuohey was working the check-in desk at Portland International Jetport, just as he had done nearly every workday for the past thirty-seven years. Right before he was scheduled to go on a break, he noticed two nicely dressed gentlemen approaching the ticketing counter with first class tickets. Those men were Mohamad Atta and Abdulaziz Al-Omari.

Tuohey went through his normal procedures. He asked the well-dressed men if they had any bags to check. He rattled off all the usual security questions. He checked their IDs.

"Then I looked at them," he explained later on NBC News, "and it made the hair on the back of my neck stand up. You could feel it. It was palpable. You could feel the anger coming out of this man, for some reason. Then a thought registered in my head. It had never, ever done that before… It said, 'If this guy doesn't look like an Arab terrorist, nobody does.' That's the exact words that ran through my head. Then I gave myself kind of a mental slap and I said, 'That's not right.'"[27]

Despite his misgivings, Mike Tuohey wasn't about to "profile" or prejudge these strangers based on their race. That would have been rude—and culturally speaking, it would have been rude in one of the most socially unforgivable ways. So, without consciously realizing what he was doing, he dismissed the warning signal in his mind and let the men proceed to security without further screening. Atta and Al-Omari boarded the US Airways flight to Boston, where they caught their connection with American Airlines Flight 11, the plane they would hijack and crash into the north tower of the World Trade Center.

"I felt terrible," Tuohey said. "I put two guys on that plane… I put two guys in first class on that plane, and here I am thinking they're terrorists, and now the poor buggers are dead. Then I found out about the next plane hitting the other building, and I thought, 'I was right…they were terrorists. These guys caused that American Airlines flight to crash into that building.'"

In the many years since that attack, Mike Tuohey has suffered as a person of conscience. He has gone on the record as feeling partly responsible for the events of that day.

---

27 Associated Press. "Ticket agent recalls anger in Atta's eyes: Tuohey was suspicious of 9/11 plot boss but let him board plane." NBC News. March 7, 2005.

So as we examine his story, I want to accentuate the point that what happened that day was in no way his fault. Between the restrictions placed upon him by his job as a ticketing agent and our natural tendency as human beings to ignore the warning signals we receive when danger is near, any one of us could have and likely would have done exactly what he did. He was simply trapped in a no-win situation.

The reason I share Tuohey's story is because it represents a remarkable example of how fast and accurate our radar can be. I also marvel at how he, without realizing it, so accurately and succinctly describes how our radar works. But the truly haunting message is that his story illustrates the key factors that inhibit our ability to listen to our radar, factors that actively prevent our best defense against danger from keeping us safe.

## *How Does Our Radar Work?*

As first described in chapter 4, what I refer to as your radar is the collective process of your limbic system's unconscious ability to perceive danger or potential danger in your environment, along with your conscious processes of interpretation.

It is important to keep in mind that your limbic system does not care one bit about your social contracts, political correctness, or what anyone else might think. All it cares about is your safety, and it will do what it needs to do to alert you to perceived danger.

Whether physical or mental in nature—or more often, a combination of both—these warning indicators are what

I refer to as "Alarms." Physiological alarms are often unsettling. The hair standing up on the back of your neck. That skin-crawling sensation. That sinking feeling in your gut. Your hands shaking. Your heart palpitating. That cold sweat erupting on your brow.

The mental side of alarms is often just as unsettling. The thoughts triggered by alarms will startle you with their unusual nature, and often with their insensitivity. This is by design, as their purpose is to get your attention by any means necessary. In Tuohey's case, the mental alarm was, "If this guy doesn't look like an Arab terrorist, nobody does." To him, that was a startling thought because it sounded so unlike the way he usually thinks. In his own words, he had never experienced a similar thought in his thirty-seven years on the job.

Now, to avoid giving the wrong impression, I want to be very clear that in encouraging us all to pay closer attention to our alarms, I am in no way espousing racial profiling. In fact, I intend to do the exact opposite.

Understand that if you do stereotype or profile, you will greatly interfere with your ability to recognize true alarms from the noise of inappropriate perceptions or biases. This will ultimately blind you from seeing what may actually be there. As Henry David Thoreau once said, "In the largest sense, we find only the world we look for."[28] If we enter a neighborhood we are not familiar with and we experience an alarm that someone nearby intends to do us harm, and

---

28    Henry David Thoreau. *Journal.* July 2, 1857.

the local news has led us to believe that most crimes are committed by young black men in hoodies, then we might wind up focusing too intently on young black men in hoodies. We become fixated, lose our objectivity, and run the risk of being victimized by someone who doesn't fit that image.

Listening to our radar and engaging in prejudiced thinking are two very different things. You might have the out-of-nowhere thought that someone looks like a rapist, for instance. Or a pickpocket. Or a scammer. Or a child molester. These thoughts can occur no matter what the race or religion of the Bad Guy in question. The critical difference between an alarm thought and one generated by implicit bias is rarity. Biased thoughts occur with varying levels of regularity, whereas an alarm, by definition, does not happen often, if ever.

Again, while the specific words that entered Mike Tuohey's head were certainly insensitive, what mattered more was that he had never experienced a similar thought in his thirty-seven years on the job serving people of every race, color, and creed. When you couple an alarm like this with a physiological reaction, like the hair standing up on the back of your neck, it is clear that you are experiencing an alarm worth listening to.

## Knowing Without Knowing Why

But if it isn't a matter of profiling or prejudice, then what triggers these alarms? There are three components, all of them delivering more from our unconscious rather than conscious observations of our surroundings.

"Situational awareness" is a term commonly used in the self-defense and tactical communities to describe alertness to your surroundings and the goings-on within them. However, it is also commonly used to describe a type of levelheadedness often demonstrated by experienced operators—specifically their ability to think three-dimensionally and make good decisions in high-stakes situations. Both are valid uses of the term, but for the most part, when I refer to situational awareness, I am referring to the first definition, and our ability to pay attention to our surroundings sufficiently to feed our radar information.

Your radar is dependent on your senses. It can't function in the absence of input and stimuli. So, the most critical thing you can do as someone who wants to stay safe is to not shunt your radar by intentionally ignoring your environment or blocking your sensory inputs. Put another way, if you find yourself in an environment you are unfamiliar with, don't bury your nose in your phone, wear ear buds, or simply tune out.

While you are reading this book, if I asked you to bring your awareness to the feeling of your feet, toes, and shoes, or the way your belt or waistband feel around your waist, your mind will become aware of those sensations. Unless something was causing you pain, you were likely unaware of the specific sensations until I asked your mind to focus there. This is called Sensory Gating.

Sensory gating is the process by which your mind selectively chooses what sensations you need to pay attention to and shunts awareness away from those that are unimportant at the moment. This happens because we all have a very limited capacity for attention, and the miraculous design of our mind gives us the capacity to switch focus to only those senses we absolutely need in the moment.

This effect is massively exaggerated when high levels of performance are required, such as in sports, in war, or in matters of survival. This sensory gating is what causes the tunnel vision and auditory exclusion so often experienced in the Red Zone of adrenaline. It is the mind-enhancing focus—for example, on the visual—and the reduction of focus and awareness to other senses, such as hearing, taste, or smell. The modern term for this phenomenon is Selective Attention, which means that we become so dialed in to a specific stimulus that we fail to notice others that could impact our decision making.

That's the bad news. The good news is that this means that under most circumstances you do not need to remain on high alert. If you're in a known safe place, you can relax. But if you're in a public place, or are uneasy about your surroundings or the people around you, pay closer attention, put the phone down, and turn up your level of situational awareness. If you allow your senses to feed your radar input, you can remain calm, knowing that your radar will alert you if there is trouble.

Obviously, this does not mean that you shouldn't seek to consciously enhance, tune, and expand your awareness skills and your radar's capabilities; it just means that even if you don't, you can trust your radar to work for you. Just don't block it.

How your radar processes and assesses input is based on the simple concept of the *baseline*.

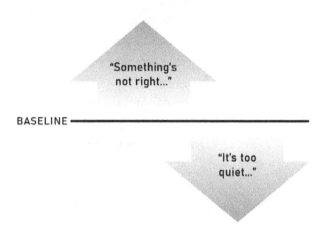

Everyone has a baseline, and all baselines are environmental. My hometown is Pittsburgh, Pennsylvania. My baseline in Pittsburgh will be different from my baseline in Islamabad, or Paris, or Mexico City. While some human dynamics like interview behavior are universal, oftentimes social and cultural norms will vary from place to place, meaning that your radar will need to adjust and establish a new baseline whenever you enter a new environment with which you are unfamiliar.

This is typically why we are uncomfortable while traveling. That discomfort is our radar adjusting to a new baseline. In my experience, it typically takes about forty-eight hours to develop this new baseline, and then your mind starts to relax.

Baseline also serves as the foundation for the next component of your radar, your intuition. The word "intuition" stems from the Latin *intueri*, which means "to watch over." Once you have developed a baseline sense of what is normal, you are immediately able to recognize when something is abnormal, doesn't fit the situation, or just doesn't seem right. Like the tumbleweed rolling across the empty town square in a cowboy movie, or like that sense that everyone else knows something you don't, our intuition tells us exactly when we need to go on alert. It helps us know that something is wrong without necessarily knowing why. It is at these moments that our radar triggers an alarm.

Usually, after an alarm is triggered, the third component of our radar kicks in: rapid cognition. Rapid cognition is our ability to make rapid, highly accurate assessments based on limited evidence.

Rapid cognition is a process that uses what we call the adaptive unconscious, meaning that 1) it is adaptive to our state of knowledge and experience, and 2) it can be trained to arrive at more accurate conclusions. If you can do this, then you improve your ability to observe and absorb information about the potential for violence or criminal behavior, thereby bringing you one giant step closer to accurately assessing the intentions of the people around you.

To understand the adaptive unconscious, it is often useful to consider a concept known as thin-slicing, a term used by psychologists to describe a person's ability to identify patterns based on brief encounters or experiences. This innate ability allows us to reach conclusions about people and places with incredible accuracy even when we are exposed to them only in so-called thin slices of time. Put simply, given only a few seconds of interaction, we're all pretty exceptional at judging a person's character.

The concept has received considerable public attention thanks to Malcolm Gladwell's massive bestseller *Blink: The Power of Thinking Without Thinking*,[29] although it originated in a 1992 meta-analysis titled "Half a minute: predicting teacher evaluations from thin slices of nonverbal behavior and physical attractiveness" by social psychologists Nalini Ambady and Robert Rosenthal.[30]

As the title of their study suggests, Ambady and Rosenthal focused on the question of whether a person is capable of accurately assessing a total stranger's qualities based on small nonverbal samples of that total stranger's behavior. Participants in the study were shown a series of five-second, ten-second, and thirty-second clips of college professors and schoolteachers giving lectures to a class. These clips were completely silent, a control that limited participants to making snap judgments about each educator based solely on visual assessment of their body language and presentation.

Based on these thin slices of silent video, the researchers asked participants to grade each teacher on categories like how accepting they thought the professor might be, along with how active, attentive, competent, confident, dominant, and so on—qualities that one might typically assume would

29   Gladwell, Malcom. *Blink: The Power of Thinking without Thinking*. Penguin, 2006.

30   Nalini Ambady and Robert Rosenthal. "Half a minute: Predicting teacher evaluations from thin slices of nonverbal behavior and physical attractiveness." *Journal of Personality and Social Psychology. 1993.*

require a significant amount of time to assess accurately. What Ambady and Rosenthal found was that not only were the thin-slice assessments incredibly accurate, but in many cases the thinner slices did not lead to significantly less accurate assessments than the longer exposures. Students exposed to five-second clips of college professors could arrive at judgments almost exactly as accurate as students who were shown the thirty-second clips, and even as students who had sat in on that same professor's class for a full semester.

What this means is that the average person not only possesses an incredible capacity for intuition; we also have a remarkably sophisticated ability to instantly and accurately assess the people we meet. Again, I am not referring to profiling or prejudice either, which, as I mentioned, are in fact hindrances to our radar. What I am referring to here is an ability to make accurate judgments of individuals based on snapshots of information. It is precisely how Mike Tuohey was able to make such an accurate judgment of Atta and Al-Omari on September 11th. Unfortunately, as Tuohey's story also illustrates, taking action based on those judgments is sometimes the most difficult part.

## *The Veils of Denial*

"Denial" is a refusal to accept something that is true. When we find ourselves engaging with Bad Guys or even facing potential violence, our natural tendency is to deny what we are seeing. We strive to find evidence to invalidate the information being presented by our intuition, and to avoid the emotions and consequences that come from accepting that we may in fact be in danger or that someone may want to victimize us.

Denial in this context manifests itself in the form of three very distinct and interwoven veils:

1. **The Veil of Normalcy**
   *"I'm just overreacting."*
   *"It's probably nothing."*

   This first veil is often referred to as "normalcy bias." As strange as this may seem, one of the most pervasive and natural tendencies that people demonstrate in the face of danger is to search for and cling to the belief that what is going on is in fact "normal," even if there is more than enough evidence to the contrary.

   This desire for things to be "normal," and therefore safe, is universal, powerful, and incredibly seductive. It is extremely uncomfortable—and potentially even damaging to our psyche and our worldview—to accept that someone we are interacting with may want to do us harm. We don't want to believe that we could be victimized, or that evil people may exist… We want things to be normal. So we'll say things like "It's all in my head," or "I'm overreacting," or "I'm just being paranoid."

   The veil of normalcy is the very essence of denial, and it is every bit as dangerous as it is common.

## 2. The Social Veil

*"I should say something or do something, but I don't want to be rude or politically incorrect."*
*"I have every right to be here, doing whatever I want, and I'm not going to be pushed around…"*

The second veil has always been powerful, but it is particularly so in today's world. It is difficult to imagine a time when there were more pressures to avoid being socially inappropriate.

In addition, we are living in a time of ever greater equality—a wonderful and long overdue dynamic. But purely from the lens of personal security, a risky byproduct of this movement toward equality is what I have observed as a sense of entitlement to safety. This entitlement manifests in a belief that one should be able to do whatever one wants, even going so far as to engage in risky behavior, with an expectation of guaranteed safety. The problem is that Bad Guys—particularly Predatory Bad Guys, who are motivated primarily by opportunity—are out there, and unfortunately, they are a big part of the safety equation.

Philosophically speaking, people should be free to do whatever they want (so long as they are not hurting others) without fear of being victimized. But such a utopia does not exist in the real world. As with the laws of nature, the deer should be free to frolic in the meadow and drink in the babbling brook without fear of being eaten, but in the real world, there are predators, and they are hungry for their next meal. No amount of outrage or righteous indignation will change this fact.

The responsibility for your safety once again falls to you and your ability to decide how to behave in the given circumstances.

Certainly, all decent people want to see society continue to improve toward greater inclusivity, safety, and freedom. But with freedom comes responsibility, and if your goal is to keep yourself alive in the face of a deadly threat, the social veil can be extremely dangerous.

Now, I am not for a moment suggesting that we all need to walk around being mean to each other, shunning political correctness, or avoiding having fun… I mean simply that, as responsible people, we need to understand that there are times when prioritizing our safety has to take precedence.

### 3. The Veil of Reciprocity

*"Maybe if I'm nice to him, he'll be nice to me."*
*"If I just give him what he wants, he won't hurt me."*

As a close cousin of the veil of normalcy, this final veil refers to the erroneous belief that if we behave kindly toward someone we will receive kindness in return.

The concept of reciprocity is part of the glue that holds a society together. It helps to define social expectations and appropriateness of behavior for everyone. The problem is, once again, that Bad Guys simply do not think the way we think, nor do they conform to societal rules. To those who prey on their fellow humans, kindness is most often interpreted as weakness… or opportunity.

The challenge is, much as with the veil of normalcy, that we want to treat people kindly and be treated similarly. We don't want to accept the possibility that someone may want to hurt us, and we believe, based upon societal conditioning, that if we are kind to them, they will want to be kind in return.

Now, I'm not suggesting that belligerence is the best solution when dealing with those who set off alarms—far from it. Life and confrontational management require a far more nuanced approach than simply going around yelling at people. Rather, I want to shine a light on the simple reality that just because you are kind to someone does not guarantee that they will be kind to you in return. When we act kindly out of a sense of fear, we're unconsciously broadcasting submissive behavior, which can itself trigger a greater predatory response and possibly an escalation to violence on the part of the Bad Guy.

In this context, kindness, delivered from a position of perceived weakness, is viewed as a type of submission. It is just one more step down the slippery slope that can lead to tonic immobility, as discussed in chapter 4.

In the animal world, when one animal submits to another of the same species, it almost never results in violence. In fact, it is a predictably safe conclusion to conflict. Through the submission the pecking order has been reestablished and society's order maintained. Obviously, this same behavioral logic does not extend to predator-prey relationships, as with an interaction between a wolf and a deer. These interactions follow an equally predictable but very different dynamic.

The problem is that humans are one of few species that routinely preys upon each other, for no reason other than power, pleasure, or profit. But for most people, the veil of reciprocity is hard to overcome for the same reason that it is so difficult to cast off the veil of normalcy: it's uncomfortable for decent people to accept the notion that some people will view them as nothing more than prey.

So, the issue of reciprocity is not that we can never be kind; it is that we must do so from a position of strength, and from a position of control over critical situational factors that change the perceived power or opportunity dynamic between us and the Bad Guy.

We will discuss how to do this in depth in
Part 3: Navigating Violence. For now, it is vital
to shine a light on this final veil so you can avoid
falling into its deceptive trap.

Each of these veils on its own has the potential to interfere
with our ability to listen to our radar, recognize danger,
and do what is necessary to escape or protect ourselves.
When the three veils work in combination, our radar is
easily negated.

In Tuohey's case, the social veil prevented him from
listening to his alarm about Atta and Al-Omari looking
like "Arab terrorists." In response, he took comfort in the
veil of normalcy, telling himself that there wasn't enough
evidence to believe his alarm. The veil of normalcy was so
strong that even after hearing about the first plane hitting
the World Trade Center, his immediate reaction was not
to assume that the men he had encountered were among
the hijackers, as he initially suspected. Rather, it was to feel
grief that he had put two men on a plane that had crashed.

Fortunately, there are ways to pull back the veils of
denial. It starts with improving our observational skills,
enhancing our knowledge of what to look for in a Bad Guy,
and assessing situations more accurately through objectivity.

### *Selective Radar*

When I train groups on how to tune and trust their radar,
I often refer to a clip from the 2002 movie "The Bourne
Identity." In the clip, the hero, Jason Bourne, an elite covert

operative coming to grips with total amnesia, explains to his companion Maria that his awareness of his surroundings borders on supernatural. Where most people might be able to tell you a few details about the café in which they sit, and maybe a few more about their server or the patrons at the next table, Bourne reveals that he automatically memorized the license plates of the six cars outside, identified every potential exit and entry point in the café, and even sized up every patron who looked as if they could do him harm, and he doesn't know how or why he did so.

After people watch this scene, they often question whether this is just a Hollywood gimmick or if this level of awareness and recall is actually achievable. The answer is a little of both. It is absolutely achievable. With extensive training, and with the help of mnemonic devices first pioneered by the ancient Greeks and now employed by the military and the intelligence and close protection communities, almost anyone can replicate Bourne's seemingly photographic memory. But it is also a Hollywood gimmick because keeping up this high level of alertness at all times would be far too taxing to be practical. Imagine trying to consciously study the face of every person you meet for indicators that they intend to do you harm, sizing up everyone's potential to carry out violence, and memorizing their description along with every license plate you see. The burnout would come quickly. So yes, these are learnable skills, but following them on a constant basis is simply not realistic or practical.

Instead, to keep yourself safe while also maintaining your sanity, you need to understand how to trust your radar, how to overcome the veils of denial that interfere with it, and just as importantly, when you can relax and when the situation calls for you to switch on. If you know what to look for, how to look, and when to look, you don't have to be Jason Bourne all the time, just during the times when it matters.

So when does it matter? In Part 3 of this book, we're going to get in depth with some very specific techniques that will help you recognize if you're being targeted, followed, or interviewed. We will examine how to manage these situations if the Bad Guy in question is Professional, Potential, or Predatory. For now, the question at hand is when you need to switch on and focus on what your radar is telling you.

The answer, thankfully, is that on a daily, moment-by-moment basis, you don't need to be switched on. What you do need is to know that your radar is always on; it's just up to you not to block it. If you find yourself in an environment that you believe (or know) is safe, then you can relax. There is no need to consciously maintain a high level of vigilance. You can relax and trust that your radar will warn you if something arises out of baseline.

However, if you are in an environment that makes you uncomfortable, it is critically important that you allow your senses to pick up on all the possible signals around you. Your radar relies on these senses to create those intuitive alarms. So, once again, if you have your nose buried in your phone or earbuds in your ears, you are actively shunting your natural ability to keep yourself safe. Allow your senses to work fully, keep your eyes on your environment, and pay attention.

But what, specifically, should you look for?

## *Lost in the Details*

In the late 1990s, psychology professors Christopher Chabris and Daniel Simons conducted an experiment designed to measure study participants' ability to spot details in a controlled setting. The experiment gave rise to a video called "The Monkey Business Illusion," and later, to their brilliant book, *The Invisible Gorilla: How Our Intuitions Deceive Us.*[31] In the experiment and subsequent video, three women dressed in white T-shirts and three in black T-shirts line up at random on a stage backed by a red curtain. One of the players in white holds a ball, as does one of the players in black. Viewers are then invited to "count how many times the players wearing white pass the ball."[32] The players then circle around in a crisscrossing pattern, those in white passing the ball only to their teammates and vice versa.

The intricate though seemingly random pattern of movement and passing causes the viewer to focus intently on counting the number of times the players in white pass the ball—so intently that many viewers fail to notice something startlingly obvious that happens halfway through the video. Without warning, straight into the center of the circle steps a person in a gorilla suit. The gorilla beats his chest several times, making a grand show of his presence

---

31    Christopher Chabris and Daniel Simons. *The Invisible Gorilla: How Our Intuitions Deceive Us.* Harmony, 2011.

32    https://youtu.be/vJG698U2Mvo

before exiting the other side of the frame. All told, this hilariously conspicuous interruption to the game stands right in the center of the frame for nearly nine seconds, and yet approximately fifty percent of first-time viewers simply do not notice the giant gorilla.

Because this video became so popular in corporate settings—so popular that, at the time of this writing, it has been viewed nearly eleven million times on YouTube—Chabris and Simons later tweaked it so that they could measure whether people who knew about the gorilla in advance would be more or less likely to notice subtler changes occurring in the background and foreground. Over the course of this new version, the curtain changes color, and later, one of the players in black departs the game entirely.

When surveyed, only seventeen percent of participants who were familiar with the original gorilla video noticed one or both of these new changes. Meanwhile, twenty-nine percent of participants who had never seen the video before correctly identified either the change in curtain color, the departure of the player in black, or both. The study concluded that simply expecting the unexpected does not enhance a person's ability to spot the unexpected. In fact, if one goes in looking for a gorilla, one is far less likely to notice any other strange or unexpected events.

This groundbreaking study demonstrates the natural human tendency to miss the forest for the trees. Our minds have an incredible ability to filter out even the strangest visual or other sensory input when we're focused intently on a certain task or observation.

Knowing how to look for danger is important, but if we allow ourselves to become too focused on a specific type of danger or a specific perceived threat, then we risk missing other salient clues about what is actually happening to or around us. If you're too busy looking for the gorilla, you could miss the wolves watching you from the forest.

From a personal protection standpoint, if you're too worried that someone will open fire on the market where you're shopping, and you're so busy looking around for the person who might be carrying a gun, you might miss any number of other extremely relevant threats or concerns in your immediate vicinity. This also dispels forever the notion that racial profiling is a useful tool. Racial profiling actually makes us more vulnerable, because if we tell ourselves that someone of one race is always more likely to be dangerous, we fail to notice the warning signs that someone of another race is about to victimize us. The same goes for the ill-conceived notion of "Stranger Danger." The huge problem with convincing an entire generation of children never to trust strangers is that the unintended counter-lesson is that the people they know are always safe. This is particularly damaging because children are far more likely to be victimized by people they know than by people they don't.[33]

Learning to be focused without becoming too narrowly focused is a matter of teaching yourself the specifics of

---

33   Lawrence A. Greenfield. "Child Victimizers: Violent Offenders and Their Victims." Bureau of Justice Statistics, US Department of Justice, 1996. https://www.bjs.gov/content/pub/pdf/CVVOATV.PDF

what to look for. This way, your radar will alert you to threats—genuine threats, and not just imagined ones—instantaneously, rather than having to expend too much time and energy on keeping your radar on alert at all times.

Consider the following image:

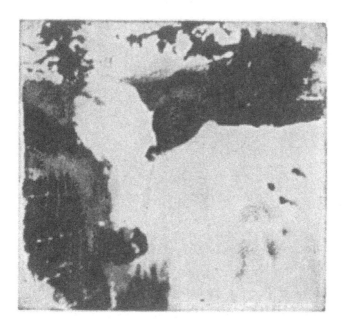

If you have never encountered this image before, what do you see? In my training sessions, I have heard responses ranging from a grainy satellite image of the Middle East to a cat curled up in a ball. But if you have seen this image before, you know exactly what you are looking at:

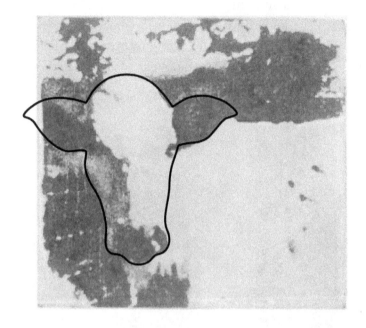

The above image was part of a tachistoscopic training system originally developed by experimental psychologist Dr. Samuel Renshaw as a means to aid the Allied war effort during World War II. The "Renshaw Training System for Aircraft and Ship Recognition" taught Navy sailors to identify enemy planes and warships with shocking speed and accuracy, a measure credited with saving countless lives.[34]

---

34   Nick Joyce. "Spotting the enemy: The Training System for Aircraft and Ship Recognition designed by psychologist Samuel Renshaw saved untold lives during World War II". American Psychological Association. March 2010.

The system is based on a pair of simple premises: 1) if you train your mind to quickly process visual information in a lab setting, it will be more effective at making snap decisions in the real world; and 2) once you see something, you can't unsee it. If you had seen the above photo of the cow prior to reading this book, you immediately saw a cow. If you had never seen it before, chances are, you didn't pick it up right away.

If properly trained, your mind can make similarly rapid, accurate assertions about dangerous or potentially violent situations, even based on limited information. This training helps you recognize danger in your vicinity more quickly, which positions you to make better decisions about how to mitigate that danger. Sometimes the best option is to take the nearest exit; other times, it is to confront the Bad Guy directly. If you can spot danger before it escalates, then you can quickly ascertain the best strategy for avoiding or ending it.

Never forget that your limbic system only cares about your survival, not what others think about you or what society expects of you. Often, it will alert you with a thought that will definitely not feel politically correct. Your radar's job is to get your attention and wake you up to the presence of potential danger. Your job is to avoid shunting your senses, to listen to your radar, and to consciously counter the veils of denial that make us more vulnerable.

It really is that simple. And you can easily tune your mind to recognize danger sooner, and with less obstruction from the veils. I will systematically break down these tactics in chapter 9. The good news is that once you have tuned your mind, even experienced predators who use charm and persuasion to cloak their intentions will be spotted as easily as a mugger jumping out of the bushes wearing a ski mask.

The bad news is that there are other Bad Guys in the world, ones of a more professional nature. These are often the most dangerous and the most challenging to spot. To get to the bottom of how to deny, deter, and defend against them requires a deeper dive.

# CHAPTER 7

# Killer Culture

THE MEDIA LOVES to label violence as "random." At the top of the list of stories that the media—and as a result, society at large—likes to label as "random" are mass killings like school shootings, workplace shootings, and the like.

In reality, when the media labels the indiscriminate targeting of innocent people as "random," it does so erroneously. These events are anything but random. Nor are they "senseless"—at least in the eyes of the perpetrator. As we have examined in previous chapters, violence is never random. It is always an observable and predictable process, provided that you know what to look for, know how to read the signs, and can avoid falling into the veils of denial that inhibit our ability to see what's really in front of us.

The myth of randomness is seductive, particularly when it comes to extreme violence, because it lets you off the hook. If this horrifying occurrence is random, then it is therefore unpredictable. And if it is unpredictable, then how could anyone possibly have anticipated, intervened, or responded better? In the most specific sense, if violence is random, then there is nothing anyone can really do to stop it. This is the final upshot of the veils of denial, and it represents a total abdication of our own responsibility to address and prevent violent behavior.

Part of the reason the myth of randomness is so compelling to decent people is because of the "unthinkableness" of the act itself. "I can't even imagine who would do such a thing or why" is the common refrain. Viscerally, any decent person can relate to this thought process. But by embracing such thinking, you inhibit your ability to discern and understand the motives behind the act. Refusing to understand "why" someone commits an atrocity disables your ability to predict and prevent similar behavior in others. If you can't imagine it, then you can't anticipate it or stop it.

To overcome this mythology, we need to take a clear-eyed look into the mind of those who choose to commit some of the most extreme forms of violence. Never make the mistake of simply labeling them as "crazy." They may very well be. In fact, they may be disturbed in a variety of ways. But crazy or otherwise, their actions are a choice, and as such, we need to understand how someone can arrive at the decision to commit an atrocity in order to understand how to predict, discourage, and altogether prevent similarly motivated offenders in the future.

The mass shooting at Marjory Stoneman Douglas High School in Parkland, Florida, dominated the national conversation for far longer than many similar shootings for two reasons. First, it surpassed Columbine as the deadliest school shooting in American history. Second, in the aftermath, it stirred a widespread, longstanding, and especially passionate debate about gun control in the US.

Lost in this debate were two other important lessons: first, the Parkland shooting was particularly illustrative of the way Bad Guys of this nature think; and second, law enforcement often cannot stop them before they commit violence, even in cases where they have received ample evidence of a threat in the days, weeks, and even years prior to the act. Part of the reason Parkland stirred up so much rage from proponents of gun control is that even though many, many people saw it coming, no one in a position of authority did anything to stop it.

Dozens of Parkland students interviewed after the terrible events of that day pointed out that Nikolas Cruz didn't exactly hide his intent to bring a semi-automatic rifle into his school and shoot his classmates and teachers indiscriminately. Maybe if the sheriff's office had taken the series of tips it received in 2016 and 2017 more seriously; or maybe if the FBI had taken more aggressive action upon being alerted to a video posted to YouTube by a user calling himself "nikolas cruz"—a video making it abundantly clear that its author intended to become a school shooter; or maybe if any law enforcement agency, whether local, state, or federal, had made an arrest in January 2018 after receiving a direct complaint that Cruz had made a death threat, the seventeen deaths and seventeen injuries that occurred on February 14, 2018, could have been prevented.

But none of these law enforcement authorities took proactive measures. And why would they? Proactively protecting the students of Stoneman Douglas High School, proactively protecting the countless victims of gun violence, abuse, and rape across the country, and proactively protecting people like you is not their job. Their job is to step in and stop the violence once it has already started, apprehend the perpetrator, and represent the state or federal government in the resultant criminal case.

If any case shows the limitation of law enforcement, it's the case involving the incomprehensible actions of Scot Peterson, the School Resource Officer charged with protecting Stoneman Douglas High School. All throughout the massacre that day, Peterson remained outside the building, retreating to an area of safety instead of attempting to seek out, engage, and take down the shooter. Peterson was fired, but later won a lawsuit to be reinstated with back pay.[35]

Of course there are many more stark examples like Parkland, and they all add up to one conclusion: that the responsibility of protecting you and your loved ones is yours alone. This is not to say that law enforcement, schools, or society in general, wouldn't want to protect you and your children; merely that this responsibility always ultimately falls back on you. In times when the response is late in arrival, out of position to help, or simply does not take action in your defense, you must be equipped to respond.

In situations involving a mission-oriented Bad Guy, you must first put yourself into the mind of the kind of person

---

35  Associated Press. "Sergeant fired in Fla. school shooting response to get job back." May 14, 2020.

who would try to kill or hurt people indiscriminately. We have already begun this process with our examination of the Three Ps, but this is merely the tip of the iceberg when it comes to the psychology of a Professional Bad Guy like Nikolas Cruz, like Adam Lanza, like Seung-Hui Cho, or like any of the next and inevitable school shooters to dominate the national conversation.

## A Culture of Killers

If you have ever read the book *Mindhunter* or seen the Netflix series of the same name (or for that matter, if you've seen any of the entries in the Hannibal Lecter saga), then you are familiar with the groundbreaking work of John E. Douglas and Robert Ressler.[36] Douglas and Ressler pioneered the science of criminal profiling, established the Criminal Profiling Program at the FBI, and dedicated themselves to decades of data collection and study that helped create a method for profiling serial killers that is still in use today.

In the 1960s and '70s, when serial killers began to spring up in alarming numbers, the prevailing assumption was that this brand of criminal was born evil and that there was nothing law enforcement could do to identify or stop them.

---

36  See, for example, Bonn, Scott A. "The Birth of Modern Day Criminal Profiling." Psychology Today, May 26, 2015. https://www. psychologytoday.com/us/blog/wicked-deeds/201505/the-birth-modern-day-criminal-profiling

They simply had to wait and hope the killer would make a mistake, creating an opportunity to catch him.

Thanks to the tireless work of Douglas, Ressler, and their fellow researchers, investigators could now draw from a wide array of contextual clues that could give them great insight into the killer and his motivations. For instance, from crime scene evidence alone, they could often accurately gauge whether the killer knew the victim and why they likely chose them as a target, and could often infer almost prescient details of their sex, race, sexuality, age, or background.

Eventually, the deductive reasoning based on experience and systematic data collection and interpretation from hundreds if not thousands of murder cases allowed the FBI to pinpoint the profile of individual serial killers with remarkable accuracy. They went from being completely unable to understand what would compel a person to become a serial killer to being able to say, "We believe that the killer is a white male between thirty-five and forty-eight years old, knew the victim, was having financial problems, likely lived in a lower middle-class neighborhood, possessed a below-average IQ," and so on.

During Douglas's career with the FBI, serial killers were unsettlingly common (their numbers peaking at 193 separate active killers in 1989), while incidences of mass homicide were relatively rare.[37] Curiously, right around the

---

37   Taylor, David. "Are American serial killers a dying breed?" The Guardian. September 15, 2018

same time that the total number of operational serial killers began to decline, the total incidences of mass homicides—which the FBI defines as "an individual actively engaged in killing or attempting to kill people in a confined and populated area"[38]—began to rise.

There was a time when decades passed between mass homicides. Between 1970 and 1997, only forty Americans were killed in acts of mass homicide in the workplace.[39] This infrequency led many to view these incidences as Black Swan events, here defined as events that come as a surprise, impact a person or culture in a profound way, and are then rationalized in some way after the fact. Incidentally, the final component of that definition returns us to the myth of randomness:

"No one saw it coming."

"There is no known motive in the case."

"The killer just snapped."

"Thankfully, this could never happen to me."

Viewing mass homicides as Black Swan events helps fuel that comforting normalcy bias that allows us all to return to our everyday lives without having to consider what makes these killers so similar or to engage with the systemic problems that could be contributing to the occurrence of their unthinkable acts.

---

38  "Active Shooter: How to Respond." US Department of Homeland Security. October 2008.

39  Lee, Seungmug; McCrie, Robert. "Mass Homicides by Employees in the American Workplace." 2012.

Normalcy bias and the myth of randomness have caused the prevailing sentiment regarding mass homicides, at least among the public, to sound exactly the same as it did back when Douglas began developing the psychological profile of serial killers: this brand of criminal is simply evil. They are born that way. And there is nothing law enforcement can do to identify or stop them before they commit their crimes.

The problem with that line of thinking is that it is every bit as inaccurate as it was when applied to serial killers. Take workplace violence, for example. According to a recent study conducted by the Department of Justice, during the five-year period between 2015 and 2019, an annual average of 1.3 million people became victims of this brand of violence. It is the fifth-leading cause of worksite deaths in the US, with 454 workplace homicide victims in 2019.[40]

The statistics become even more troubling when we expand our horizons to mass homicides. Right around the time when the number of active serial killers started to decline, the rate at which these mass homicides occurred began a rapid climb to the waking nightmare we're experiencing today.

I refer to this as a waking nightmare in part because these acts are always unspeakably tragic, but also because

---

40    Harrell, Erika; Langton, Lynn; Petosa, Jeremy; Pegula, Stephen M.; Zak, Mark; Derk, Susan; Hartley, Dan; Reichard, Audrey. "Indicators of Workplace Violence, 2019." United States Department of Justice, Bureau of Justice Statistics. July, 2022.

there is a huge psychological leap between a disgruntled worker wanting to kill his boss and a child wanting to bring a gun into his school and kill his classmates and teachers indiscriminately. It's so much more comfortable to see something like this and retreat into normalcy bias, to tell ourselves that this was unpredictable, a Black Swan event, the perpetrator was simply a monster, and that there is nothing wrong with a society where this kind of thing occurs with such frequency. But according to the FBI, from 2000 to 2018, there were 277 of these incidents, with 2,430 casualties, not including the offenders.[41]

It's time to take the blinders off. It's time to engage in a Douglas-like codification of the psychological profile of mass killers. If we do this, then we can begin to see ways to blunt these occurrences, and perhaps even to stop them before they occur.

The FBI agrees with this sentiment, having tasked its Behavioral Analysis Unit (BAU) with managing this growing manifestation of violence. The trouble is that unlike serial killers, whose numbers overwhelmingly fall into specific demographic categories, mass killers—particularly of the workplace homicide or terrorist varieties—seem to come from any number of demographic backgrounds.

Since 1991, when mass shootings first entered the national conversation following two different incidences of postal workers killing their coworkers almost within

41  https://www.fbi.gov/how-we-can-help-you/safety-resources/active-shooter-safety-resources/active-shooter-incidents-graphics

a month of each other (and incidentally, when the term "going postal" entered the lexicon as a descriptor of workplace violence), there have been cases of workplace killings carried out by men and women from any number of age, racial, religious, political, and socioeconomic backgrounds. Fortunately, there is plenty of data to contribute to the development of a psychographic profile, helping to pinpoint the motives of a mass killer, even in the absence of demographic consistency.[42]

For generations, humanity has been plagued by mass killers—from Genghis Khan to Hitler, from Stalin to Mao to Idi Amin—but never before have we seen children deciding to go on a killing spree at school. In the old days (pre-1990), if a disgruntled terminated employee was so disturbed as to want to seek revenge, they might have killed their boss and then themselves—which is of course bad enough—but rarely, if ever, would they have viewed the indiscriminate mass killing of coworkers as the means to showcase their grievance to the world. So what changed? If we can look at that period in the early '90s as the inflection point, then what can we point to as significant

---

42  *Psychographic profile* is a term typically applied to marketing theory. From a marketing perspective, psychographics are the influences that determine why people buy something. In our study, we broaden the term to address the question of why people do what they do. This is not a term that psychologists or the FBI typically use (that I know of), but from my experience in close protection, it is an apt descriptor for a Bad Guy's broader motivations.

changes in our society that could have contributed to this new manifestation of violence?

1. The dawn of reality TV and the notion that "anyone can be a star"

In 1992, MTV ushered in a new era of entertainment with "The Real World," showcasing the lives of supposedly everyday people in a way that generated a new brand of fame. This imprinted on all subsequent generations the notion that it is possible for anyone, no matter who they are, to become famous.

In my career, this effect was never more evident than when a professional baseball player engaged my company's services. His wife at the time had risen to a small level of fame by giving a series of sexually explicit interviews on the radio and appearing on the cover of a few men's magazines. By the time we first met, she and her publicist had begun the process of rather desperately trying to get her on a reality TV show. Noting the seemingly random pattern of her public appearances, I asked her whether she was trying to be a radio personality, a cover model, or a TV star. "I don't care," she told me. "I just want to be famous."

The unfortunate dark side of this cultural phenomenon is that, for people of a certain psychographic profile, it also fosters a sense of *entitlement* to fame and fortune. The problem has only been exacerbated in the years since. In just two short decades, reality TV has come to dominate the programming space of most networks, forever changing the average person's perceptions of fame, for better or worse.

2. A drastic change in the nature of violence depicted on television

Early '90s television also ushered in a massive shift in how our culture engages with violence. For someone like myself, who grew up on "Buck Rogers in the 25th Century" and "The A Team," where the height of onscreen violence might have involved Mr. T throwing a Bad Guy into a pile of mattresses by a dumpster, the depictions of murder, rape, and mass violence on network television represents a dramatic change. This change definitively contributes to a mass desensitization to violence in the general society, especially among children, and distorts the gravity of violent acts. As my dad used to say, it "makes life cheap..."

According to Lieutenant Colonel Dave Grossman and Gloria DeGaetano, authors of *Stop Teaching Our Kids to Kill*, "Since 1982, television violence has increased 780 percent and in that same time period teachers have reported a nearly 800 percent increase of aggressive acts on the playground." Part of the problem at hand is that many of the violent depictions are aired during periods when children are most likely to be watching television, with "Youngsters who watch two hours of cartoons each day …exposed to five hundred high-risk portrayals of violence per year," and "nearly 40 percent of violent incidents on television are initiated by characters who possess qualities that make them attractive role models," where "at least 40 percent of the violent scenes on television include humor."[43]

So if depictions of violence on TV are escalating every year, and those depictions consistently place the good guys as perpetrators of violence in a just, cool, or even humorous way, depict the bad guys as escaping consequences for violent acts, and generally make the whole prospect of violence seem more attractive, funny, and less consequential than it would be in real life, what exactly is the message we're sending to children?

3. The introduction of realistically violent, first-person-shooter video games

In 1993, the first-person-shooter video game "Doom" was released for use on personal computers.

---

43  Grossman, Dave; DeGaetano, Gloria. *Stop Teaching Our Kids to Kill: A Call to Action Against TV, Movie, & Video Game Violence.* Crown Publishers. 1999.

Though its depictions of violence are almost childish by today's standards, this game brought the public face to face with multiplayer interaction as well as intensely realistic depictions of killing for the first time—so intensely realistic that they elicit a physiological SNS reaction (more specifically, an adrenaline reaction) in the limbic system of the player.

There have been countless studies into the subject of whether violent video games contribute to desensitizing our society to violence, so I will not reiterate the numbers or the arguments here. I will say, however, that during my Marine Corps career, the military experimented with encouraging the use of first-person-shooter games as a type of combat simulator to help train and desensitize soldiers.

Because of that SNS reaction, games like these become what psychologists call "pathological play." They help override the body's natural resistance to violence and killing of other human beings; and because of point systems, level ups, and in-game awards, you're actually being rewarded for committing violence—usually with bigger guns and better ways of killing.

4. The 24-hour news cycle

While CNN created the concept of the 24-hour news cycle in 1980, it wasn't until the murder trial of OJ Simpson in 1994 and 1995 that 24-hour cable news became the norm.

In any 24-hour news cycle, particularly disturbing and egregious acts of violence are showcased with regularity because, as mentioned before, "if it bleeds, it leads." This further desensitized our culture through the second half of the 1990s and beyond. Then, in 1999, coverage of the Columbine High School Shooting forever changed our society, inspiring and emboldening generations of brittle, disturbed children to idolize mass killers and seek the same notoriety and attention the media granted to Eric Harris and Dylan Klebold.

5. The growing ubiquity of the Internet

The early '90s saw the meteoric rise of both personal computing and the Internet, with roughly 23% of homes in the US owning a computer by 1993. 1995 was a watershed year, with Microsoft releasing Windows 95 packaged with Internet Explorer, and Amazon, Yahoo, and eBay all launching. By 2000, 51% of American households had a computer, with 50.4% using the Internet.[44]

---

44  Census.gov. "Computer and Internet Use in the United States." May, 2013.

As home computing and Internet use became more and more ubiquitous, so too grew generations of children living in the dual worlds of the physical and the digital. Social skills, play, and personal interaction began to drop. This increased isolation led to a rise in antisocial behavior.[45]

6. Personal communications arrive, slowly evolving from cell phone to social media.

1991 introduced the broader world to consumer handsets, with personal cell phones becoming available and more widespread with each passing year. Later in the '90s, social media began with companies like Friendster laying the foundation for MySpace and eventually Facebook, Twitter, YouTube, and the like in the early 21st century.

These sea changes in daily life led to a psychological shift from collective culture to intense individualism. We now lived in a society where anyone could be reached at any moment, where everyone could have a public voice, where anyone had the potential to be a celebrity, and where we celebrated major news stories (almost always of the negative variety, and often featuring violence)

---

45    ADHD – https://pubmed.ncbi.nlm.nih.gov/29499467/

Reduced ability to discern body language: https://www.winchester-hospital.org/health-library/article?id=907792

like never before. As of the writing of this book, the majority of kids ages eight to twelve in the US and the UK say they want to grow up to be YouTube stars over other paltry professions like teacher, professional athlete, musician, or astronaut.[46]

Do you see a pattern here? The processes outlined above—coupled with an intensely narcissistic, character-disorder-driven society where everybody just wants to be famous, believes their own opinion is just as important as everyone else's, contributes to outrage culture, and so on—is exactly what makes mass killers appear in ever larger numbers.

## Why Isn't Everyone a Killer?

The objection to this claim is a natural one: if reality TV, social media, and violent video games make mass killers, then why doesn't every kid become a mass killer? This question once again comes from normalcy bias. But the answer is actually quite simple. The military might use violent video games to desensitize their soldiers to violence and help entrain the instinct to kill the enemy, but not every soldier leaves the military an unhinged killer. This is because they were taught these lessons in an environment

---

46    Leskin, Paige. "American kids want to be famous on YouTube, and kids in China want to go to space: survey." Business Insider. July 17, 2019.

that imbues high levels of personal responsibility. The military trains morality just as readily as it trains violence. In fact, I don't think you could point to a more moral, responsible, restrained, and professional military in all of human history than what exists today in all branches of the US Armed Forces.

This is not to suggest that you can't have some rotten apples; rather, it is to illuminate that the cases where a seemingly normal kid devolves into a monstrous mass killer always come from a place where that sense of personal responsibility and morality is absent, usually in their early upbringing. Kids who are allowed to play these games and submit to this culture without moral and personal oversight have the potential to develop violent tendencies, and even then, those tendencies are not enough on their own to make them killers. There is a massive difference between being systematically desensitized to violence and being capable of murder. The latter requires intense underdevelopment, character disorder, narcissism, paranoia, and a malignant lack of personal responsibility.

Put this way, the profile of a mass killer starts to sound similar in many ways to the profile of a serial killer. Both are mission oriented. Both take pleasure in violence. Both are ultimately seeking notoriety from a society that they believe has ignored or mistreated them. They are mad, and they want everyone to know why. Just as importantly, they are so narcissistic that they actually believe everyone in the world will care.

All of them, no matter what their demographic background, fit these characteristics—even the ones who publicly claim not to. Consider Ian David Long, the twenty-eight-year-old Marine Corps veteran who killed thirteen people including himself in the Thousand Oaks, CA, nightclub shooting on November 7, 2018. In the aftermath, the media uncovered a series of Instagram posts he published even as he carried out the murders. In one, he wrote:

> *It's too bad I won't get to see all the illogical and pathetic reasons people will put in my mouth as to why I did it. Fact is I had no reason to do it, and I just thought… fuck it, life is boring so why not?*

The media latched onto this message as evidence that this killer just snapped. There was nothing to suggest society had somehow made him crazy. We could all go back to our everyday lives, comforted in the knowledge that this kind of thing is just random and unpredictable. The trouble is that this line of thinking ignores another message Long posted that day:

> *I hope people call me insane* 😊 😊 *would that just be a big ball of irony? Yeah… I'm insane, but the only thing you people do after these shootings is "hopes and prayers"… or "keep you in my thoughts."*

What the killer is saying in this second message boils down to this: all of society will pay attention to me because of this, and I alone have brought their attention to how ineffective their reaction always is to these events. This represents an uncommon level of narcissism, evidence that this kind of killer thinks of himself as so special that everyone in the world will want to know everything about who he is and will care about what he did and why.

So yes, conditions in our society and culture are making it more possible for people to evolve into killers of this nature, but what makes them killers is a (thankfully) rare psychological cocktail dominated by intense paranoia and this specific brand of narcissism.

There is an upside to this predictability. It means that dangerousness is not a fixed condition, that there is no such thing as someone who "just snaps," and that very few violent events can be accurately defined as Black Swan events. Violence isn't random; its perpetrators always fit into specific psychographic profiles. If you know what to look for, you can identify potentially violent people before they commit violence, or at least you can spot the indicators that someone may be moving in that direction.

## CHAPTER 8

# The Descent into Violence

As the **CEO** of a mid-sized manufacturing company in Florida, Frank Thompson just wanted to push through the mountain of work on his desk that Friday afternoon before Memorial Day Weekend. He and his wife Julie planned to spend the evening making last-minute preparations for hosting a large family gathering, so he knew that the sooner he could get home, the sooner they could begin. Busy as he was, he let the call from the unrecognized number go straight to voicemail.

Not until he was back home late that night, exhausted from a long day's work, did Frank finally find a moment to sit down and catch up on the message he had missed. The following is a transcription of the actual voicemail, with a few identifying details changed to protect the identities involved:

> *Hello, Frank. This is Randy Smith calling. I'm sure you remember me, but just to refresh your memory, you fired me four years ago after lying to my face.*

*You are reprehensible, you are immoral, you are unethical, and you are in violation of so many different labor laws I can't even begin to count.*

*[long pause]*

*I hope you are doing wonderfully well. I hope everything is just peaches and cream for you. Because guess what? You fucking destroyed my life.*

*When you fired me, I had depression and chronic pain. I should have been on disability. I should not have been let go as brutally as I was. I am still in intensive psychotherapy and psychiatric treatment. I cannot get a handle on my medical problems. And why can't I do that?*

*Because. I. Can't. Get. Over. Your. Fucking. Betrayal.*

*You fucking stabbed me in the back, Judas, and I hope you have a really, really, great Memorial Day Weekend with you and your precious family. I know you don't give a SHIT about me or my family... [long pause] ...but we think of you all the time. You made us what we are today.*

A voicemail like that has a way of ruining a weekend. One moment, Frank was unwinding before what promised to be a memorable three days with loved ones, and the next, he found himself unable to think about anything but protecting those loved ones from an apparently unhinged former employee.

In response, Frank and his leadership team did what almost every business leader does in this scenario, and in fact, what pretty much everyone would do because it seems so logical: they called the police. Imagine their surprise when the police told them they couldn't do anything about the situation.

Again, in this swimming pool of life, there are no lifeguards—only the appearance of lifeguards. It is your job to know how to swim. While protecting yourself is a fundamental human need, it is also an individual responsibility.

In Frank's case, the police suggested that the company's best recourse would be to file a harassment complaint with the local magistrate. Frank followed this advice by calling his attorney, who did a very wise thing and suggested that they instead get a threat assessment. I call this a wise thing because filing a complaint of this nature with a magistrate is often a swing-and-miss situation. Experience has taught me that Bad Guys of this type will simply take the stand in magistrate court and lie.

"I was in so much pain and on so much medication at the time," Frank's threatener would say. "I don't even remember making that call."

The magistrate likely would decline a restraining order and opt instead for a stern warning. Swing and miss. Worse, the failed attempt would reinforce in the threatener's mind that threatening Frank had led (and would continue to lead) to exactly the level of fear and disruption for Frank, his family, and his company that the threatener had originally intended.

So instead, Frank and his attorney called my company and asked us to determine whether this caller presented an actual and credible threat, and if so, what to do about it.

Given the urgency of the situation, we immediately began engaging in two different kinds of investigation. The first is what we call a vulnerability assessment, where we examine the physical locations involved—which in this case centered primarily on Frank's home and workplace—in search of vulnerabilities that a Bad Guy might exploit. The second is known as a threat assessment, which refers to a deeper dive into the background and psychology of the Bad Guy himself. As shorthand, a vulnerability assessment applies to places, while a threat assessment applies to people.

There are further distinctions for the term "threat assessment" as well. There is an official, professional threat assessment on the level of what my company does, and there are what I call "snap" threat assessments that we all perform nearly every day, even though we might not realize it. Many of the strategies we discussed in chapter 7 are forms of snap threat assessments. If we find our radar pinging us that someone in a crowd may be a problem, our snap threat assessment is to scan the crowd for what may be out of the ordinary. Often, this snap threat assessment turns up nothing consequential. If the situation doesn't progress to any further indicators of an interview, we are able to relax.

On the other side of the spectrum, maybe you find yourself on the subway at two in the morning with a single strange man leering at you. In this circumstance, your snap threat assessment formulates an alert based on more than just peripheral intel. The collective situational factors coupled with the man's body language put you on alert and possibly impel you toward protective action.

## *Assessing Threats*

In most circumstances, my company does not wind up performing or even needing a formal threat assessment, as these are only necessary when we can establish an evidence chain that suggests the Bad Guy is escalating his threatening behavior. In Frank's case, that evidence chain almost immediately presented itself. So we pored through the recording in search of clues as to whether this caller in fact intended to harm Frank and his family, focusing first on the words before gleaning what we could from the inflection in his voice.

When I teach CEOs, executive teams, and HR directors at companies from very different parts of the country both urban and rural, this voicemail almost universally gives people the chills. That is not just because of the nature of the call, but also because virtually everyone at these training sessions can relate. Anyone who has managed people for a long period of time has had to fire someone who sends out warning signals in some form or another. Statistically speaking, companies with more than a hundred employees will experience situations where they have to deal with people with drug or alcohol issues or gambling problems, people who are engaged in domestic violence, people who have threatened another coworker already, and so on.

So when I ask these executives to tell me what they think is important about the voicemail Frank received, the answers usually come from a place of experience and are almost always the same. Interestingly, most of the observations that these experts perceive as important are merely the smoke rather than the fire. These observations include:

1. **The threat to Frank's family**

   This point always elicits the most visceral reaction, because everyone can relate to how unsettling it would be to have a Bad Guy threaten harm to the people they love most.

   But here's the thing: Bad Guys who fixate on individuals—whether they actually intend to do harm or are just trying to stir fear—very frequently threaten the target's family in either a direct or a veiled manner. It's the surest, simplest way to terrorize the recipient of the call. It's almost like they can't help themselves.

   Yes, this is a detail we should note, but it's nowhere near the most important. Like the misdirection of a magician, the content of the threat itself is far less important than the situational factors surrounding it. What is really important? Just about everything else the caller says, and more directly, *how* he says it.

2. **The caller's reference to his psychiatric problems**

   In most settings, this detail would be important, since not everyone goes around admitting to psychiatric problems. But when it accompanies a threat of this nature, this is actually something of a garden variety revelation.

   Many threateners talk about how hard their

life is. The important component isn't that he has sought psychiatric treatment; in fact, if true, this could actually represent a stabilizing and threat-reducing factor. Rather, the important part is that he has woven his perceived psychological problems into an intense tapestry of anger and blame. Put another way, he doesn't blame himself for these issues; he blames *Frank*.

Because he blames Frank for not recognizing his pain and psychological problems prior to firing him, and because he blames Frank for every moment of suffering in his life he has experienced since, we know that these statements speak to the caller's predisposition.

This is how he views the world: "My life is full of problems, and they're all Frank's fault." This worldview could be indicative of the caller's chances of following through on the implied threat of violence.

3. **The fact that the caller referenced Memorial Day Weekend specifically**
While this element might at first seem like a throwaway point, it actually should reside near the top of our hierarchy. Referencing Memorial Day Weekend placed a time stamp on the caller's intent. This time stamp indicated a degree of specificity generally uncommon in threats.

Specificity increases the validity of the threat, much in the same way that specificity in a bomb threat escalates the likelihood that the threat is legitimate. Most people assume that the appropriate security response to a bomb threat is immediate evacuation. This might seem logical. We have to take these kinds of threats seriously, don't we? But the professional response—one based on decades of security experience, data, and evidence—says that the calling in of a bomb threat does not alone indicate that there is a bomb in the building. It indicates only that the caller wants to disrupt your organization.

There are a few reasons this logic holds true. First, from a tactical perspective, if a Bad Guy wants to kill as many people as possible with a bomb, then his best strategy is to get everyone outside first. Any bomb he might manage to smuggle into a building would be roughly the size of a backpack, but a bomb that he could position near a building, where everyone would naturally congregate following an evacuation, could be the size of a van or truck. If his goal is to use a bomb to kill as many people as possible, then getting people outside is in his best interest. Similarly, there is precedent for active shooters using evacuations as a means of driving targets into a more open "kill zone."[47]

47   Mary Hollis Inboden. "20 Years After the Shooting on the Playground." The New York Times. March 23, 2018.

Second, if a Bad Guy genuinely wants to blow up a building and kill lots of people, then he just blows up the building and kills lots of people. He doesn't warn you about it in advance. As a general rule, bombers don't threaten and threateners don't bomb.

In 2012, the University of Pittsburgh received a bomb threat written on a bathroom wall. Authorities responded with the decision to evacuate. A series of 160 threats ensued, taking place between February and April, with building evacuations and bomb sweeps occurring every time a new threat was received. This completely disrupted an entire semester for 29,000 students, not to mention faculty and staff. Only after a catastrophically lost semester did the university decide to "tweak" its response tactics to threats and not automatically evacuate, as these evacuations had clearly served only to embolden threateners to further disrupt the organization.[48]

The automatic evacuation mindset comes from a legacy of the decades-long terror campaign of the Irish Republican Army in Great Britain from the late 1960s to the mid 1990s. The IRA would almost always call in bomb threats with high

---

48   James R. Haggerty. "Campus Tweaks Bomb-Threat Response as Finals Begin." The Wall Street Journal. April 22, 2012.

levels of specificity. For instance, they would tell the police that they had rigged a bomb in a car positioned at a specific intersection.

Bombs would almost always be found or detonated according to the specific threat, thereby reinforcing the value of the threat. But in the end, indiscriminate civilian death was rarely the aim. Why? Because the IRA knew that if their bombing campaigns caused too many civilian casualties, public opinion would turn against them and they would no longer have anywhere to hide. The true aim of these terrorizing campaigns was to cause disruption and attract attention. Following every threat, police would have to reroute traffic, everyone in the immediate vicinity of the bomb would have to stop what they were doing and evacuate, and the media would descend on the situation, calling millions of people's attention back to their cause.

Now, I am not saying that the IRA never bombed with the specific intent of killing innocent people—far from it— only that their typical MO suggests an organization that recognized the terroristic value of disruption.

This is why specificity is such a key detail. There is a huge difference between "There's a bomb in the building and you'd better get everyone out" and "There's a bomb in the lobby, and it will go off at four o'clock today." That high level of specificity is atypical and is therefore an indicator of actual intent. In such specific bomb threat cases, the recommended protocol is to quarantine the local area—say the lobby—and visually screen it for any anomalies. Should a package be found, don't touch it, call the bomb squad, and let them do their job. If they are willing, let the bomb squad do the screening as well.

For threats that contain high levels of specificity, caution is warranted.

4. **Situation over content**

Not all mass killers display their anger, but anger that is held onto and nurtured—such as the anger demonstrated by Frank's caller four full years after termination—is never a good sign.

In this case, the caller demonstrated his anger overtly through strategic pauses, inflections, and tone changes. What stood out most to me during my first few listens to the recording were the several moments where the caller loses control of his emotions to such a degree that he has to pause as if to collect himself. There was no questioning the fury roiling inside this man's mind. But then, after listening to the outbursts and the pauses, it occurred to me that much more important was what came after them. No matter how much the caller lost control, he always managed to bring himself back on message. To me, this indicated that he had scripted the call.

If this assumption was correct, and this man

took the time to write down what he wanted to say to Frank in advance, what does that tell us? At first, you might assume that the caller merely intended to frighten. To cause terror (which is the primary goal of most people who make threats) and ruin the weekend of someone he had spent four years quietly hating. But in fact, in cases like these, a script indicates premeditation. It allows us to rule out the idea that the caller had just gotten drunk and decided to take out his rage on his former boss. He had been brewing on this so-called betrayal for four years, and now he had taken the time to script what he wanted to say.

This made it all the more possible that he had taken the time during this period to script other elements of his terror campaign. If the script indicated premeditation on terrifying his victim, then it was only logical to assume that the caller was capable of premeditating a violent act as well.

5. **Grandiose narcissism**

There was little question from the call that Frank received—both from the words and the inflection—that the caller possessed the particular brand of paranoia we often observe in perpetrators of school and workplace violence. But as we will examine in more detail later in this chapter, there is another component to the volatile cocktail that compels these people to take the crime from fantasy to reality. That component is a very

THE DESCENT INTO VIOLENCE

specific kind of narcissism.

Consider the Judas reference. Most people notice the reference on first listen, but very few realize how important it is. At first, it is easy to assume that the reference means that the caller thinks Frank is a betrayer. But there is more to it than that. By calling his former boss Judas, he places himself in the role of Jesus.

So was this man a psychotic who truly believed he was Jesus? I didn't think so. In the simplest sense, a psychotic doesn't know reality from fantasy, or good from bad. A psychopath or sociopath (functionally the same thing) does know the difference; he just chooses to do the bad thing anyway.

My interpretation in this case was that the caller didn't believe himself to be Jesus; rather, he seemed to be posturing himself as a martyr. He saw himself as a victim of persecution. At the same time, the Judas reference provided a glimpse into a sense of superiority such that he would equate himself to the level of Jesus Christ. If it hadn't been for Frank and the other oppressors in his life mistreating him time and again, then his life would have been idyllic, and everyone would have known just how superior he actually was.

History has unfortunately shown us, through case study after case study, a similar pattern of predisposition built upon a sense of persecution and superiority. Like two chemicals that independently are caustic in and of themselves but together make an explosive cocktail, this specific brand of paranoia and narcissism can lead a Bad Guy to all the justification he needs to commit unspeakable levels of violence.

## *The Teeter Totter of Personal Responsibility*

The decision to commit violence does not happen at random; it begins on what I call the teeter totter of personal responsibility.

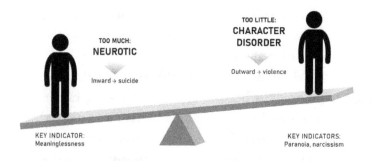

The basis for the above graphic is a book called *The Road Less Travelled: A Psychology of Love, Traditional Values, and Spiritual Growth* by psychiatrist M. Scott Peck.[49] While this work is quite obviously not about human violence, a particularly illuminating passage changed how I think about the subject:

---

49    Touchstone, 2012.

*Most people who come to see a psychiatrist are suffer-
ing from what is called either a neurosis or a character
disorder. Put most simply, these two conditions are
disorders of responsibility, and as such they are opposite
styles of relating to the world and its problems. The neurotic assumes too much responsibility; the person with
a character disorder not enough. When neurotics are in
conflict with the world, they automatically assume that
they are at fault. When those with character disorders
are in conflict with the world, they automatically assume
that the world is at fault. (p. 35)*

Those who commit violence tend to operate on the
extremes of this same spectrum highlighted by Dr. Peck.
On one end of the teeter totter, you have people who take
on too much responsibility for the negative factors in their
lives. On the other, you find people who take on too little.
The former's worldview reads something like "I'm not
happy because I'm not good enough, smart enough, pretty
enough," etc. These beliefs eventually develop into neuro-
ses powerful enough to compel them to commit violence.
Almost always, this violence manifests itself in the form
of suicide or self-harm. The key indicator that drives them
to this self-harm is a profound sense of meaninglessness.
They struggle with questions like "What's the meaning
and purpose of my suffering?" and "Why would I want to
continue living this way?"

On the other end of the spectrum, those who take on

too little responsibility for the negative factors in their lives tend to display character disorder or personality disorder. What I refer to here is the kind of person whose worldview reads like "I'm not happy in life specifically because I'm being persecuted, oppressed, and it's all someone else's fault." This person fundamentally believes they are a victim—that someone, some entity, or some race, religion, or social class is ultimately responsible for all of the problems in their lives. Even in cases where this belief has some basis in reality, the sense of persecution is outsized.

Unlike those who fall into the neurotic category, those who display extreme character disorder are capable of projecting violence outward. Since nothing is their fault, ultimately someone else is always to blame and therefore a justifiable target for violence. I would argue that virtually all manner of criminal violence exists on the character disorder side of the scale. Yes, you can have shoplifting and other typically nonviolent criminality on the neurotic end, but every level of borderline or antisocial personality, all the way out to the psychopath/sociopath extremes, exists on the character disorder side of the scale.

In the most extreme cases, such as perpetrators of mass homicide, we often find a combination of observable paranoia and narcissism. I'm not a psychologist like Peck, who may be focused on diagnoses and treatment. As a threat-assessment and security professional, my only goal is to identify potentially dangerous people and help you do the same. So it is important to note that I use the terms "paranoia" and "narcissism" merely as snapshots of psychological factors that most people can understand and identify. There are of course many more factors and indicators, but for our purpose here, I have found that these two stand at the top of the list.

That said, the paranoia and narcissism particular to those who would commit extreme violence like mass homicide or workplace homicide are not of the garden variety. This is not your average tin-hat-wearing, aliens-are-going-to-abduct-me brand of paranoia. Nor is it the standard "I am worthy of praise and worship" brand of narcissism. The paranoia I'm referring to is the genuine belief that a person or category of people is not only to blame for all of the subject's problems, but as they see it, for all of the world's problems. Extreme examples of this will manifest as malignant racism or misogyny.

This paranoia alone is not usually enough to compel a person to violence. For violence to occur, it must be combined into a volatile cocktail with the level of narcissism that makes a person believe the world at large should worship them or otherwise fails to recognize their obvious superiority.

We find a stirring example of this cocktail in a video recorded by Elliot Rodger, who killed six people and injured fourteen others in the 2014 Isla Vista killings. Before he went on his killing spree, Rodger decided to rant on video about how he had spent his whole life being shunned by women who chose other men for sex. In his view, his decision to carry out this horrific attack was justified because no one in his life recognized his godlike qualities. In his written manifesto, titled *My Twisted World,* he describes a worldview so filled with self-pity, anger, racism, and misogyny that at one point he declares he would "wage a war against all women and the men they are attracted to [and] slaughter them like the animals they are."[50]

That may sound like an unquantifiable level of crazy, but this same pattern appears over and over again in mass killers we see in the United States and around the world. It is what compelled Frank's caller to compare his former employer to Judas and implicitly compare himself to Jesus; it is what compelled him to pick up the phone and leave that chilling voicemail in the first place; but it is not what would ultimately cause him to leap the chasm between the threat and the act of violence.

## *The Descent into Violence*

Most predictive models view the process of behavior leading to violence as an escalation—a process that builds to a crescendo or explosion. One frequently referenced model is known as the "Pathway to Violence," shown below:

---

50    Rodger, Elliot. "My Twisted World: The Story of Elliott Rodger." Contributed by Lauren Johnston (*NY Daily News*) https://www.doc-umentcloud.org/documents/1173808-elliot-rodger-manifesto

While this model is certainly viable, it primarily refer-ences the mechanical or tactical implications of a violent perpetrator's behavior. Put another way, this model primar-ily explains the behavior of perpetrators who have already decided that violence is the answer and then begin to move in a violent direction. In my view, the process actually starts much earlier, and the question must be asked: how does a person arrive at that decision in the first place?

I think of the process more as a descent from some level of "normal" to seeing violence or homicide as the right solution, or maybe even the *only* solution.

---

51   https://www.torchstoneglobal.com/where-the-attack-cycle-intersects-the-pathway-to-violence/ The concept of the "Pathway to Violence" was developed by Frederick Calhoun and Steve Weston in 2003.

*Grievance*

This is the top step on our staircase for good reason: a person does not even begin the process of descending toward violence without believing that he/she is somehow aggrieved. Frank's caller believed he was unlawfully, unnecessarily, and "brutally" fired. This grievance struck him so deeply that he stewed on it for four years. Similarly, in his own mind, Elliot Rodger was aggrieved that he remained a virgin at age twenty-one, that women wouldn't date him, and that "lesser men" were getting all the girls. Again, violence is never random. It always occurs for a reason. Even if the reason might seem trivial or irrational to an outsider, it is never trivial or irrational to the perpetrator.

*Justification*

Once aggrieved, the next step is to create a sense of justification for that grievance. In the caller's mind, the justification is Frank's special brand of injustice—the supposed character flaw that allowed him to overlook the needs of a suffering man and his family and mercilessly kick him to the curb.

Now we're referencing the caller here, but his is an extreme example of how these things manifest. Any one of us can be legitimately aggrieved and justified in that grievance. Many people, particularly those on the character-disordered side of the scale, live in a perpetual state of grievance, victimhood, offense, and outrage. In fact, there may even be real justifications for many of those grievances. While living in this state may not make for a happy or balanced life, the state in itself is not necessarily indicative of someone who could turn violent. It becomes concerning when someone displays the behaviors of what we would call an *injustice collector*—someone who holds onto grievances and focuses on, exaggerates, and amplifies even the slightest perceived offense.

I once took a case in upstate New York where a company immediately terminated someone for threatening to bring his AK-47 into the office to kill everyone. Immediately escorting someone out of the building for making such an overt threat is of course understandable and generally the right thing to do, but typically, by the time a threat like this is made, a multitude of warning signs leading up to it have already been missed. By the time I was brought in to investigate, the horse was already out of the barn from a threat-assessment perspective, and we were principally focused on security, especially as the subject had been seen conducting what we in close protection refer to as "testing and probing" behavior. He had been spotted skulking around the grounds, seemingly looking for weaknesses and opportunities to gain access.

Nonetheless, I conducted a series of interviews with key staff to get more perspective on the situation, and in one case, at the end of an almost hour-long interview with one of the managers, I posed the catch-all question I hold in reserve for the end of any such session: "Is there anything else you can share with me that would help me better understand this situation?"

"Well," he said, "there was this one thing."

My ears pricked up. Whenever someone says this, that one thing almost always turns out to be the most important thing.

"He used to carry around this big three-ring binder. Anytime anyone did something that pissed him off, he would flip to a new page of the binder and start taking notes. Once, when he was away from his desk, I looked in the binder. It was full of all these entries like, 'So and so said this to me on this date. He doesn't know who he's messing with. He's going to get what's coming to him,' and so on."

In addition to these entries, the offender kept dossier-like information on coworkers such as their home addresses and behavioral patterns. I call this an injustice journal. It's not unlike a school shooter's hit-list, where he ranks and re-ranks the top people he hates. There is a huge difference between normal justification of a grievance and injustice collection of this nature. It is a critical warning sign that this person might be moving on to the next step on the descent.

*Fantasy*

In the classic movie "A Christmas Story," the main character, an elementary-school-age boy named Ralphie, lies in bed, upset and crying after his mother responded to his use of profanity by making him wash his mouth out with soap. As he lies there, he drifts into a fantasy where he imagines himself returning to his parents' home after a long absence. His parents are stunned and beside themselves with guilt to learn that the soap punishment has caused Ralphie to go blind. Ralphie delights in the fantasy of his own blindness because he can visualize how terrible it makes his parents feel.

In the real world, similar fantasies sometimes manifest themselves in children wanting to run away from home, or even worse, wanting to commit suicide. "They'll miss me when I'm gone," or "They'll really know bad they treated me…" are common themes with this mindset. Often these fantasies arise because the child feels their parents don't pay enough attention to them or have mistreated them. It is a fantasy rooted in powerlessness, an attempt to assert control over something or someone they cannot otherwise control.

Violent fantasies are different, though they often stem from that same sense of powerlessness and desire to punish those the perpetrator deems to have caused it. This does not mean that you are character disordered just because you feel justified in a grievance and fantasize about getting back at someone. That may not be the healthiest behavior, but there is a difference between a normal psychological coping mechanism and the way a perpetrator becomes fixated on fantasies of revenge. Perpetrators often seek outlets to enact

181

their fantasies, whether through video games or disturbing writings or drawings, or even acting out their fantasies as the Columbine killers did in their haunting home video productions. Fixation on fantasies at this level goes beyond a natural coping mechanism, ending up in what we would classically refer to as ideation (a fixation so intense that the person thinks about it nearly all the time).

Fortunately, during this phase, the would-be perpetrator of violence tends to broadcast their intent. Their fixation on the fantasy is so intense that they often will leak their intent in the form of clues and even admissions to other people. "Leakage" is the term used to describe the sometimes unintentional but often deliberate revealing of clues of the perpetrator's intent. It is a brazen openness about their fantasy to commit violence. In my experience, leakage often behaves in much the same way as those cries for help that a person contemplating suicide unconsciously uses to draw attention and intervention.

Leakage can sometimes look like a casual minimization of an otherwise unthinkable event. Following any story of a school shooting, most people's reaction around the water cooler might be "What kind of monster could do something like that?" But a person experiencing ideation related to a fantasy about mass homicide would react in a way that leaks their intent. "Well, you can only push a person so far," they might say. Or they might make an unsettlingly dark and socially outrageous joke about dead children. This reaction that goes so against the norm is not an indication of a mental disorder; it is the sound of this person trying to justify his own evil fantasy.

## Tethers

If we can assume that many people engage in violent fantasies, then why don't more people commit to making these fantasies reality?

The answer lies in the next step of the descent: tethers. Think of the tethers holding a hot air balloon to the ground. Each positive factor in someone's life is a tether—success, a spouse, work, kids, friends and family, hobbies and personal interests. These tethers serve as inhibitors to violence. They keep a person grounded, even at moments of extreme grievance that lead to the fantasy of violence. If a person is wrongfully terminated, for example, the tethers could include the confidence that they can find a new job. Another tether could be a spouse or parents who care about them. Another could be children or friends who will support them and into whom they can project their self-worth.

In any situation that could lead to workplace homicide, the perpetrator often only has one tether: work. This person will say things like "The only reason I have to get up in the morning is this damn job, and I hate this place." Yes, that is an extremely paradoxical statement. It is also exactly the brand of thinking that allows this person to take the final step into violence. If you hear someone say this, chances are they are putting you on notice that if you sever this tether, their hot air balloon could go off.

Of course, it's virtually impossible to assess exactly how many of these tethers a person will have in their life, but we can eliminate certain categories. For someone who would commit workplace homicide, very often there's considerable self-reported information; enough to form a pattern.

He is experiencing a great deal of financial stress. His wife recently left him, and he's living in his mother's basement. He has no friends—in fact, people tend to find him kind of scary socially. He spends most of his free time shooting guns, talking about violence, killing animals, and posting disturbing things on social media.

If you are in a position of authority at work and you are thinking about terminating someone like this, it is important to exercise caution. The best strategy is to try to install tethers prior to cutting the work tether. Severance, unemployment, EAP programs, extended health benefits, mental healthcare, and so on. A common myth around mental illness is that people who are mentally ill are automatically predisposed to violence, when the reality is that the vast majority of people diagnosed with mental illness are not violent. Put simply, there is great efficacy in identifying people on the descent into violence and getting them treatment.[52]

This is because, in the end, the final tether is always dignity. Someone can feel as if his life has completely fallen

---

52 While it may not be possible to accurately quantify how effective treatment is in ultimately preventing violence—as it's difficult to measure something that does not occur—it makes sense that treatment would be a very effective intervention, as it can address so many of the underlying issues that may be causing someone to see violence as the correct, or only, alternative to their situation. At the very least, treatment may provide a clinician an optic on someone who could be moving in a violent direction and exhibiting signs of leakage. This raises awareness on the part of the clinician that a threat is legitimate and must be defended against.

apart, and as long as he feels heard and respected (by his former employer, for example), it quite often prevents him from taking that next step on the descent.

*Consequences*

The flip side of tethers is the idea of consequences. The fantasy might be incredibly compelling to the would-be perpetrator of violence, but they ultimately decide against acting on it because they don't want to end up in jail, hit with a debilitating lawsuit, dead, or even just socially ostracized.

The danger is when someone crosses the threshold into thinking that the consequence is actually positive or irrelevant. Then it no longer serves as an inhibitor. A potential mass shooter possesses that cocktail of paranoia and narcissism, character disorder, ideation, and has few or even no alternatives tethering him to the ground. When it comes time to assess consequences, he will brush them aside with something like this: "If I do this, everyone will know my name. My cause will live in infamy forever." Again, this is how mass killers, terrorists, and most other mission-oriented Bad Guys justify their behavior. The desire for notoriety outweighs the drawbacks of all traditional consequences.

*Ability*

The final step in the descent is that the perpetrator has to have the ability to pull off the violence. This is the step that you have the greatest chance of controlling in the moment. Just because someone is aggrieved and fantasizing about violence to the point of ideation, has few or no tethers, and believes the consequences of a heinous act are either irrelevant or positive, that does not mean they can succeed in their effort to commit violence. Their belief in whether they can succeed (or fail) in their mission is the final, and often the most effective, deterrent.

This is why I always tell my clients that just because someone wants to hurt you doesn't mean they can. Ultimately, you are the final arbiter in the equation.

- • -

As we sat down with Frank to perform our threat assessments, we engaged with our combined predisposition and descent model one step at a time. From the voicemail itself, it was easy to deduce that the caller felt justified in his grievances. Moreover, he clearly had remained very angry and fixated on those grievances for the full four years since his termination. Couple this with the generally blaming nature of the voicemail and a review of his employee file, which further demonstrated a pattern of blaming rather than acceptance of personal responsibility for failures.

The time-stamp reference to Memorial Day Weekend was critical. Had my firm analyzed this voicemail prior to the weekend, we would have calculated an attack to be likely and would have taken measures to protect Frank and his family. But Frank, not really knowing what to do about the situation, waited until Monday to address it—a very dangerous gamble that luckily did not cost him. The fact that an attack did not occur over the holiday weekend removed the criticality of the timestamp but did not invalidate the specificity of the threat, as there could have been a variety of reasons why an attack wasn't launched. The Judas reference, however, was particularly concerning, with the caller positioning himself as a martyr.

As part two of our investigation, we studied the caller's social media accounts. Social media can be helpful, as it often provides an optic into the perpetrator's state of mind, motivations, and fixations, and it may provide a platform to leak intent. In this particular case, we found long posts outlining his grievances, many of which focused on his previous employer. In one recent rant, we discovered an image of the company headquarters' staff taken after a company outing. The image was defaced, with the CEO, CFO, and HR director circled in red magic marker and labeled Judas, Pilate, and Roman Legionnaire respectively. Leakage.

But as I mentioned, behaviors like this are often more like a cry for help. The would-be perpetrator wants someone to take him seriously. Consciously or unconsciously, they often leave clues that are easily discernable. In Frank's case, the leakage was as obvious as something you would see in a movie. Yet no one saw the signs. Not because they were hard to read, but because no one thought to look.

In one post, the caller referenced how he had begun seeing a new "shrink," as he called him. The psychiatrist had asked him a pretty direct question: "If your life is so terrible, why haven't you killed yourself yet?"

"Well," he wrote in a moment of self-reflection, "the reason why is because of my daughter." In this statement, we found a timely and recognizable tether holding the caller to the ground. Further investigation showed that he remained married—another tether. He seemed to be gainfully re-employed. Even though it seemed likely that he would one day drive his current employer crazy enough to fire him, in the leadup to that Memorial Day Weekend, this detail represented yet another tether.

Yes, many of the posts were quite unsettling, but more evidence of the strength of these tethers could be found scattered throughout. As a result, my team and I concluded that the caller did not actually present an imminent threat to our client's life. *Imminent* being the critical word.

But what could have compelled him to make this call after four long years of leaving Frank in the dark about his grievances? As it turned out, Frank's company had recently been profiled in a local magazine. The company had enjoyed a series of strong quarters that saw its profits hockey-sticking them out of startup status. Seeing his former boss interviewed for a positive story in a local magazine likely stirred up the caller's long-held grievances and triggered the decision to script and make the call. He found evidence of success for the man he hated, and in response, he decided to send a little terror his way.

Given the collective evidence, we considered the situation very serious but not in need of immediate 24/7 close protection. Close protection is something we specialize in, but it is almost always a last resort in our playbook, as deploying it can be so invasive for the family that the cure can feel worse than the disease. In addition, while the voicemail and the social media evidence may have indicated a desire for intervention, my belief based upon the timeline was that any contact would simply encourage more of the same (or worse) behavior.

Instead, based on our vulnerability assessments of the workplace and the key stakeholders' homes, we advised hardening the potential targets. We helped Frank and his key staff enhance the security of their homes, and we trained everyone from the company staff to the targeted executive's families. My company implemented a protective intelligence umbrella, keeping tabs on the caller remotely, following his posts, and checking on his marital and employment status. We asked Frank to report to us if any further spikes in the business led to stories in the media, as we determined that these could lead to further flashpoints and behavior that we would need to monitor and even mitigate, should the need arise.

Some weeks later, Frank and Julie were dining at a restaurant near their home. Based upon his training, Frank positioned himself to allow for maximum situational awareness and close proximity to an emergency exit. Just as their meals arrived, Frank noticed a disturbance near the front of the restaurant. There, near the entrance to the dining room, stood the caller. The man was staring at Frank so intensely that the waiters and waitresses had to go out of their way to walk around him. The moment Frank made eye contact, the caller marched out of the building.

Needless to say, this incident was troubling, but it was not entirely unexpected. As is often the case, since Frank gave no response to the voicemail, we expected some level of escalation. This often takes the form of increased threats (or "proxy" threats), where the threatener attempts to relay veiled threats by way of third parties who know both the threatener and the target.

In these instances, the question often centers on whether to escalate in similar fashion from a legal perspective. "Should we get a restraining order?" the company attorneys wanted to know. I advised against this, as once again, filings of this kind are often swing and miss. Based upon what we believed about this case, we thought such an attempt might either escalate matters further or further reinforce the stalking behavior.

The similarity to an intimate stalking situation is as relevant as it is seemingly counterintuitive. Most people in a situation like this want to tell the threatener in no uncertain terms that they will not be pushed around. The problem is that this behavior, as logical as it may seem, often fuels the pursuer. It gives them feedback. No matter what you say or do, all they hear is that they are getting to you. Much like dealing with a bomb threat, often the last thing you want to do is react.

Just as I would recommend to a victim of intimate stalking, I recommended that Frank and the company not respond outwardly to the threats and intimidations. Rather, they were to maintain or improve their internal state of readiness and continue monitoring and closely analyzing the threatener's behavior without showing any outward reaction. As long as the tethers remained and the behavior did not escalate into more deliberate pre-attack indicators such as surveillance, testing, or probing, we could hold the course until the threatener realized his efforts were futile. This in fact happened shortly thereafter.

To be clear, not all threatening situations can be resolved in this manner. Even though threats and threatening behavior often follow similar patterns, there is no simple playbook of formulaic solutions. Every situation presents different factors that must be carefully assessed based upon the predisposition and situational circumstances at hand.

However, in your own life, if you ever encounter a situation like this, there are a few universal strategies you can use to mitigate danger, even as the would-be perpetrator progresses through the descent into violence. I will cover these strategies in Part 3. But if you ever have to deal with someone who has reached this point in the descent already, the unfortunate reality is that there are few outside forces you can depend on to help. A close protection team can of course keep you safe, but law enforcement is unfortunately too reactionary to offer aid. What, after all, would Frank have had his stalker arrested for? Making a threatening phone call? Showing up to the same restaurant where he was eating? Neither of these actions would remove the threatener from society and thereby make Frank and his family safe.

Think about it. Even if you call the police and tell them that a terminated employee threatened to come into work this Friday at 4 p.m. and kill everyone in the building, what do you think the police will say or do? Likely they will tell you to let them know if he shows up. If your local law-enforcement agency isn't already overwhelmed with other criminal complaints, they might offer to send a patrol car by the building at the time in question, or they might suggest avoidance measures such as closing early that day or hiring security.

The bottom line is that it isn't the police's job to provide proactive security. Generally speaking, they don't typically have the resources to do so, even if they wanted to. Proactive security is your job. There are lifeguards in this world, but you still must know how to swim.

Ultimately, just as Frank learned, you are the final arbiter in the equation. You don't even have to be the cause of the Bad Guy's failure. Often, whether we are talking about a mass shooter or a back-alley mugger, if you can simply become a hard enough target that they see failure as a likely outcome, they can be deterred.

Knowing how a Bad Guy behaves—and more importantly, knowing what he fears—makes you more powerful than any fantasy, any physicality, or even any weapon they might bring to bear against you.

If you are to forge the confidence that you can protect yourself and others, no matter the situation, then there is one final question we must answer: what do you do if, in spite of all your efforts to deny opportunity and avoid trouble, you find yourself targeted, or simply in the wrong place at the wrong time? What do you do when you come face to face with that Bad Guy?

Part 3:

# NAVIGATING A VIOLENT WORLD

## CHAPTER 9

# Deny (Opportunity)

"WHY SHOULD YOU be nice to the police?"

I ask this question when working with teenagers—who, being teenagers, often have some issues with authority. It's an important lesson that needs to be learned, hopefully before it's learned the hard way.

So why should you be nice to the police? Is it because the police have a difficult and often thankless job? Or because you're "supposed" to respect authority? Or because we shouldn't judge all police because of the actions of a few rotten apples that we might have heard about or seen on the news? Or because they are people too, and you should treat them the way you'd like to be treated? All of that, certainly. But there's another, more tactical reason why you should be nice to the police:

Because you simply don't want to give someone an opportunity to negatively—and potentially severely—impact your life. Which the police can do.

Now this last reason isn't as enlightened and altruistic as the others, but I would argue that it's the most important.

From my experience, the overwhelming majority of law enforcement officers are decent people who don't make a practice out of abusing their authority, or others'. But some, unfortunately, are not as decent and do.

To complicate matters, most people I've met over the age of thirty have had some type of negative run-in with the police, whether they were physically abused, made to feel demeaned, or simply not treated fairly or with the level of courtesy they felt they deserved. I know I've had experiences like this, and while these moments always leave a lasting impression, I've found that negative encounters with police are the exception, not the rule. And for the same reasons I preach never to profile Bad Guys, I simply don't believe in judging all cops on the behavior of a few. As with everything we've discussed in this book so far, you have to address the facts and context of each situation as they unfold.

In my opinion, one reason police encounters often make people uncomfortable is that there is danger present. And while being polite and courteous is not a guarantee that someone with authority can't try to harm you if they want to, it does go a long way toward defusing and mitigating such encounters. Even in situations where you feel the police are unjustly harassing you or being less than professional or courteous themselves, it doesn't change your responsibility to manage the situation—and in any high-stakes situation, often the first person you need to de-escalate is yourself.

You may feel outraged at what you perceive to be a violation of your rights, and you may very well be justified in that feeling. Even then, you need to be nice. Don't give someone the opportunity to make you look like a Bad Guy or escalate the situation into an arrest or worse.

"But that's not fair!"

Well, maybe not. Certainly, if you're being targeted by a dirty cop, it's no more fair than having to prevent yourself being victimized by any other type of Bad Guy. But this is all the more reason why Rule #1: Deny Opportunity must be obeyed, and in an emotionally detached way. Get your ego in check and respond appropriately to the situation. Deny opportunity. And in this context, that means—*be nice*.

The same basic logic applies to avoiding car accidents. From my perspective, regardless of who's at fault, the goal is to avoid an accident. Even if this means checking your ego. This again is Rule #1 in action.

Rule #1 is fundamental to your safety, regardless of whether we are discussing financial security, digital security, information security, or the physical security of people, places, and things.

I can tell you from learning some lessons the hard way that you are well advised to make Rule #1 an ever-present concept in your life. Most of the situations that have cost me in my life, whether times I've fallen into the veils of denial, blindly trusting those I thought were friends or business partners, or physical conflicts—all of them, upon reflection, were set in place by clear violations of Rule #1. In the words of Anthony Robbins, whom I had the privilege of serving on a protective detail once, "Discipline weighs ounces, but regret weighs tons." This is never truer than in the application of Rule #1.

At the core of deny opportunity is the ability to recognize danger and adjust our attitude and behavior accordingly to avoid further escalation, exposure, or risk. In the context of dealing with police, if you cannot avoid the interaction, your default tactic should be to be nice. In the context of managing Predators, Professionals, and Potential Bad Guys, as defined in chapter 5, your tactics will vary. But the process always begins with recognizing and accepting the reality that you are in danger; that you may be being targeted; and that you will need to respond appropriately to manage the situation.

## *Enhancing Our Radar*

As our focus now shifts from *why* we need to understand human aggression and violence to *how* we navigate safely in a dangerous world, our goals become very focused.

In this chapter, we will enhance your ability to recognize danger, particularly when someone might be looking to victimize you. To do so, we're going to work together to reinforce your ability to trust your radar and avoid the veils of denial. Next, I'm going to outline some simple habits that you can develop, ones that will allow you to always know your options and avoid trouble, even when you find yourself in the wrong place at the wrong time.

In chapter 10, we will address what to do when avoidance is no longer possible, and you need to deter threats from manifesting into violence. And in chapter 11, I'll explain everything I've learned both performing and teaching physical tactics, so that you can develop the skills you need, beyond this book, to manage violence should a situation progress from talking to touching.

## *The Five Habits of Situational Awareness*

As you learned in chapter 5: Think Like a Bad Guy, there are three distinct types of Bad Guys, and each of them is motivated and operates in different ways. With that in mind, there are of course complexities to this first step in the Deny, Deter, Defend continuum. We will get into these complexities later in the chapter. In the meantime, there are five vital habits that will help you recognize danger in the first place.

From a 30,000-foot view, denying opportunity is a matter of avoidance. It's all about not putting yourself in harm's way. But from a personal security perspective, it's not enough to just say, "Well, that's easy. I don't go out at night. I don't go downtown or go to bars," as if bad things only happen to certain people at certain times and in certain places.

We've already learned that bad things can happen anywhere and to anyone. But living in fear and blindly avoiding certain places or times of day is simply no way to live. Keeping safe shouldn't be a matter of fear and restriction. The better way to balance enjoyment in life and personal security is to know how to recognize the early warning signs of danger by understanding what to look for in Bad Guy behavior. Specifically, the first step to keeping yourself safe in a dangerous world is to know if you are in fact being Targeted. With this knowledge, you will recognize when you're in trouble and will immediately know what your options are to deny an opportunity to be victimized.

Some Bad Guys are better than others at masking their intent, but even those who are well versed in deception can't fool your radar for the most part. As with every skill, you can enhance and tune your radar with the right techniques. Practice these consciously for a while, and in short order they will become automatic.

## Habit #1: Scan from left to right

Good observation skills are arguably the most important tools in your situational awareness toolbox. And the first step is to learn how to visually scan your environment and the people around you. The best way to scan is the way our mind has been programmed for comprehension since childhood: from left to right, just as you're reading this book.

We teach protection specialists to scan from left to right while on duty, anytime they enter a new environment, or while standing watch, and I recommend you do the same. When performing your scans, it is important to keep your mind open so that your radar can alert you to anomalies, or suspicious behavior, or anything that might warrant a second look.

If your radar is alarming you that something's not right, you may choose to do a deep scan on the person of concern. Ask yourself, "Why is this person setting off my radar?" Is he using the environment for the dedicated purpose (see Habit #2)? Is he a watcher (see Habit #3)? Are you in an area of mandatory travel (see Habit #4)? And so on.

If the alarm you are sensing cannot be localized to a single person, you can evaluate the entire environment more consciously. Deep scan the entire visual field from left to right, starting low, then at the mid-range, and then high. This is much the same manner in which you would visually scan a room for a bomb. Your first pass would search for anything out of place or of interest on the ground. Your next would scan at mid- or eye-level for anything that might be of concern. Finally, you would scan left to right above the normal line of sight. Mechanically working from bottom to top, always scanning left to right, allows you to take in all key elements of your surroundings, picking up any warning signs without subjecting yourself to any of the veils of denial that impede your radar.

In this way, the first habit of situational awareness accomplishes two important goals: 1) If you're always following a specific process for scanning, your observations become more objective, meaning that you avoid getting distracted or listening to the veils of denial and talking yourself out of what you're seeing, and 2) you're less likely to overlook key details that could indicate trouble in your environment or the people around you.

The added benefit of scanning is that the behavior can be an incredibly effective deterrent to crime all on its own. Always remember that Bad Guys are looking for a soft target. They want to catch someone unawares. If you're scanning the room or environment, you demonstrate your awareness in a way that would convince most Bad Guys to simply leave you alone.

Once you practice scanning left to right consciously for

a few days, you'll be amazed at how automatic the behavior will become. Just like any other skill, your brain needs direction and training, and this simple technique will enhance your awareness and improve your observational accuracy. Of course, if you sense trouble, then by all means revert to a deep scan and try to consciously identify what is causing your radar to alarm.

*Habit #2: Know that every environment has a purpose*
Every physical environment you encounter serves a specific purpose. Your home is for shelter and relaxation. A public park is for leisure activities. A mall is for shopping. A road is for driving, and so on. This second habit of situational awareness calls our attention to the idea that if you encounter anyone who is behaving in a way that doesn't fit a location's purpose, it may be cause for further observation.

For example, what is a parking lot's purpose? It's for parking your car so you can enter the adjacent building, complete whatever business you have come for, and then return to your car and drive away. When people use parking lots, they park, they move into the building, and then they move out. There's not a lot of wandering or loitering going on.

So if you see someone wandering or loitering, they may be there for a reason other than parking, and if they're there for a reason other than parking, that should raise a red flag. Sure, maybe they're waiting for a cab or a rideshare or for someone to come pick them up because their car won't start. But even without training, it's fairly easy to tell the difference between the body language someone displays when waiting for a ride versus someone who is watching who's coming and going. The former will look either impatient or as if they are just trying to pass the time. They might keep checking their watch or shifting impatiently, or they'll sit or stand calmly somewhere and look at their phone.

A Bad Guy, on the other hand, will wander, look around for people coming and going, or maybe position himself near what we call an area of mandatory travel (See Habit #4) so he can observe and intercept potential targets on their way into or out of the building. Often you'll see these people trying to engage with passersby, conducting interviews. The same is true in any setting. Most people use the environment for its intended purpose; Bad Guys treat it like a hunting ground. In many cases, spotting the difference between the two is a simple matter of noticing who's watching the people around them.

*Habit #3: Watch for the watchers*
One of my clients who lives in New York City once told me that he summarizes some of my situational awareness teachings for out-of-town visitors like this:

"In this city, there are three types of people. There's the people looking down. They're the New Yorkers. There's the people looking up. They're the tourists. Then there's the people who're looking for who's looking up and who's looking down. They're the ones you have to watch out for..."

In many ways this simplified perspective is spot on, as the third habit of situational awareness, watching for the watchers, is an incredibly effective strategy. What's interesting is that when you actively practice habit #1, you too become a watcher. And often that's all you need to keep other watchers from bothering you. Much like two predators spotting each other at the watering hole, the Bad Guy simply recognizes that there's easier prey available elsewhere.

Most people are so thoroughly tuned out of their environments that spotting a watcher is as easy as spotting a cloud in an otherwise blue sky. Of course, when you spot a watcher, it doesn't necessarily mean they are a Bad Guy. It could mean they're like you. If you deep scan them and see that they are using the environment appropriately, they don't approach you or try to engage you and are simply not causing your radar to alarm beyond a general interest, chances are they're not a problem. But if they are in fact a Predatory Bad Guy looking for a target, just visually acknowledging each other is often enough to take you off the menu.

Obviously, I'm not suggesting that you make prolonged eye contact or stare someone down—these behaviors could trigger an escalation, especially if a Predatory or Potential Bad Guy thinks you are challenging or disrespecting them. The best way to avoid inadvertently triggering a challenge reaction is to look more at people's chests than at their eyes and maintain a detached, neutral expression when scanning.

When you combine watching for the watchers with Habit #2: Know that every environment has a purpose, it becomes easy to spot and avoid the people who don't fit.

*Habit #4: Be on alert in areas of mandatory travel*
Areas of mandatory travel are defined as natural choke-points or spaces in which you must predictably travel if

you are to move through an area. To better understand this concept, it helps to consider one of the principal dangers we address in the close protection industry: kidnapping. In many parts of the world, kidnapping for ransom is an everyday concern, not just for the rich and famous, but for practically anyone.

But when we look historically at kidnapping for ransom attacks, where do you suppose you would be most vulnerable as an intended target? Would it be while you are inside your home? Or perhaps inside your hotel room while traveling? What about while you're at work, or while you are driving to and from?

While attacks can certainly occur in any of those locations, the reality is that the vast majority of attacks occur during what we call "arrival and departure" moments, when you are getting into or out of your car, or your house, or your place of work. And an inordinate number of these more sophisticated attacks occur at or around the victim's home.

What makes arrivals and departures appealing for a Bad Guy is that these moments and locations are more predictable. In addition, most people tend to relax when they get home or enter into otherwise familiar territory. These are the places where they feel secure. People who don't believe they could possibly be targeted at all, let alone in a "safe" place, tend to let their guard down.

A good practice is to make a habit out of paying attention when you are arriving or departing from these areas. At the minimum, it is critical to raise your level of awareness during arrivals and departures, specifically in areas of mandatory travel, if you are being targeted or have a specific reason for concern—such as a stalker, or a threat in the workplace.

Areas of mandatory travel are, as you can surmise, mandatory. Let's use a typical suburban cul-de-sac as an example. There might be three different ways for you to get into or out of the neighborhood as a whole, but the street entering that cul-de-sac is an area of mandatory travel. The driveway to the home is another. If this is where you live, then you have no choice but to drive through this location.

When you think like a Bad Guy, the predatory logic becomes quite simple. If your purpose is to execute a mission-oriented attack on a specific target—as is the case with kidnapping or assassination—you typically wouldn't try to hit them while they are on the move even if you have conducted extensive surveillance and learned their patterns. There are simply too many variables, complications, and possible failure points. This is more the realm of Hollywood depictions of a kidnapping situation, because of the dramatic nature of such attacks. In reality, if you were that Bad Guy, you would simply set up a stationary surveillance point and wait for the target to leave or return along an area of mandatory travel. To reduce elements of uncertainty even further, a Bad Guy's plan is often to launch the attack on departure—say from the house in the morning, like what happened to Ben and his family in chapter 5 —or during a time when the victim is likely to be at her least alert, like what happened to Karina in the lobby of her apartment building in chapter 4.

Areas of mandatory travel are everywhere, so you want to get good at spotting them, anticipating them, and if need be, raising your alertness level while arriving to or departing from them.

Another way of thinking about areas of mandatory travel is to think in terms of hard versus soft areas. Just like people, places can be viewed through the lens of hard versus soft targets. For example, where do you think are the most vulnerable, or soft, areas of a hotel? When I ask this question in seminars, people often say the public restrooms or the stairwells. Some even say their hotel room. The reality is that, unless you are being specifically targeted by a sophisticated criminal enterprise or government-level intelligence agency, when you are behind the locked door of your hotel room, you are generally safe (unless you open the door or invite someone in).

The lobby and hotel bar are another story. The lobby is almost always an area of mandatory travel, one that may afford a Bad Guy opportunities to watch and covertly observe and conduct target selection and maybe even interviews. If you think like a Bad Guy, the predatory logic is once again obvious: which is more likely to ensure your success, lurking in a stairwell and just hoping that a soft target strolls by at some point, or selectively targeting a person and then waiting for them in an area of mandatory travel when their guard will be down?

It's easy to see why they usually choose the latter. Years ago, when I would be called to another city for close protection work, if I had some downtime, I would often sit in the lobby or bar of my hotel. You might be surprised how easy it is, if you just pay attention, to determine which people are there on business, which are there for pleasure, who is traveling alone, and who is with a group of family or friends. You can also quickly pick up on status and wealth indicators: clothing, quality of luggage, the person's mannerisms, how they treat the staff, and any number of predictable cues. You don't have to be a trained criminal to pick up an enormous amount of information about everyone you see; you just have to be observant—to be a watcher yourself.

So if you are an experienced predator, or a Professional Bad Guy, where would you go to select or locate your target? Would you sit on the steps in the stairwell? Lurk in the bathroom? Find a dark hallway somewhere? Or would you park yourself in the lobby and watch for a soft target?

The case is similar at the airport. If you were a criminal, what would make more sense, purchasing a ticket for a flight you have no intention of taking so you can get through the security line and target people in their gate area, or otherwise go through the risk and challenge of getting weapons or explosives through security? Or would it just make more sense to observe and intercept a victim, or conduct a terror attack, in the uncontrolled areas of the airport (like baggage claim, ticketing, the lobby, or any of the soft spaces between the parking lot and post-security terminal)?

Of course, this isn't to say that you shouldn't be aware of potential pickpockets or having your laptop stolen near your gate, or that you won't encounter bad people in the terminal or on the plane; it's just that the opportunity for violent crime in these areas is so greatly reduced that it does not need to be a high priority of concern. Obviously, attacks in stairwells or dark alleys do occur—and as such we still need to be alert in any environment that presents opportunity—it is just that areas of mandatory travel, from the Bad Guy's perspective, are usually the most opportune environments to select a target and the first place where you can deny that opportunity.

The world we live in is full of areas of mandatory travel, and every place inherently can be rapidly assessed as either soft or hard relative to the threats you are concerned with. The key is not to fall into the trap of thinking that danger lurks everywhere and living in fear! If everything is important, then nothing is important. Learn when to switch on and when to relax.

Pay attention going to and from the parking lot. Through the lobby of your apartment building. Near the entrance to any ticketed event. Anywhere that crowds of people either congregate or funnel from one place to another.

Scanning left to right and watching for the watchers is not essential every second of the day, but these are the kinds of environments where it becomes particularly important when you need to switch on and pay attention.

*Habit #5: Know your options*
One December, my family and I attended a performance of *The Nutcracker* in downtown Pittsburgh. I'm not sure how my wife managed to score such great tickets, but we wound up in the front row center, right in front of the orchestra pit and stage. This was a great place to take in the show, but from a security standpoint it wasn't ideal.

Think about any concert venue or event that attracts a crowd. Where are the soft areas? Short answer... everywhere.

Generally, the whole thing is a soft target.

Even if the venue has metal detectors, or security at the gate, do not confuse that illusion of security with being safe. I can say with confidence that if I wanted to smuggle a weapon through these checkpoints, I could do so with little trouble, and so could Professional Bad Guys. At best, these security elements serve to deter bad behavior. But make no mistake, if someone wanted to target that venue for an attack, it can be and has been done.

Now, again, this is by no means a recommendation not to go to concerts or events or to avoid participating in anything that draws a crowd. That's no way to live your life. It literally lets the terrorists win. Instead, let's explore how you can still enjoy such venues throughout your life but do so while still taking a healthy responsibility for your own safety.

So let's think about this. If someone were to enter the event with a weapon, where would be the best place for you to be? The simplest answer is almost always "somewhere along the perimeter." You want to be near either an emergency exit or the front entry—locations that will allow you to either quickly escape or quickly take action against the Bad Guy. You never want to be in the center of the crowd or otherwise penned in by people who may begin panicking or freezing in tonic immobility. Put simply, you want the freedom to respond, whether that response takes you away from or toward the threat.

So there we were at *The Nutcracker*, in the best possible place to see the show, but in a less-than-ideal place if something awful were to occur. Even in a less-than-ideal place, however, you can remain safe, as long as you know your options. In public settings, those options do not usually spring to mind for most people. For instance, in a theater, where are the exits? Usually, there's the lobby and the emergency exits on the right and left wings. The exits are positioned this way due to the fire code to ensure that, in the event of smoke or a fire, people can quickly escape in more than one direction.

But there is almost always another direction of escape that most people don't consider: behind the stage. Most venues need backstage entrances to allow the acts to come and go, accept deliveries of equipment, and facilitate any back-of-house needs for the staff and performers. In the event of violence, these exits are just as effective, if not more so, than the ones to which the rest of the crowd is rushing. So why do most people not think of these exits? Mostly it's because we think of the stage and backstage areas as places we're not allowed to go. That location is off limits to the spectator. But in a violent situation, those rules are no longer relevant. Remember the attack on Mandalay Bay that David survived? Want to guess how many of the tens of thousands of attendees decided to escape over the stage? It's an easy answer… zero—at least that I'm aware of.

So, right after we sat down in our best-seats-in-the-house at *The Nutcracker*, I turned to my family and said, "Listen, if anything bad happens and there's an emergency, we're all going to climb the stage and exit the building out the back. Okay?"

Everyone agreed. Between sizing up our location, considering an escape route, and communicating the plan to my family, the entire process took maybe ten seconds. Then, once we had our plan, we could all relax and enjoy the show.

So here is Habit #5: Know your options in a nutshell: if you find yourself in an area of mandatory travel—or any other environment you deem to be a soft area—it is always best practice to identify your exits or other options as soon as possible. This achieves two important goals: 1) it helps ensure that, if something bad happens, you immediately have a plan for how you will escape or respond, and 2) having this plan allows you to relax, lower that Jason-Bourne-level of situational awareness, and not spend your entire experience in some level of hypervigilant adrenaline.

Keep in mind, I'm highly aware of the righteous indignation you might be feeling—that we even need to think about such things when going to a concert with our family—or the similar feelings you may have anytime you send your kids to school. Your outrage is justified. We should all be outraged. But this book is not about trying to solve the riddle of mass homicide or international terrorism. It's about helping you to live your life more confidently by teaching you tactics to take personal responsibility for your own security, and to teach you how to respond if, God forbid, you find yourself needing to. This is—for good or for bad—the world we live in, and blindly trusting in illusions of security is simply a recipe for disaster.

In any case, if you're still reading this book, I know I'm preaching to the choir; so let's move on.

## *Reading People*

You spot an unfamiliar dog up the block. As you approach, the dog begins a low growl. He flattens his ears and lowers his chin, looking up at you through the tops of his eyes. If you move closer, he bares his fangs and the hair on his back stands up. Closer still, and he backs up and enters a crouch.

If you were to put your hand in that dog's face, what do you think is likely to happen? Yep, you're going to get bitten. And if you do, then does it really matter whether the dog was motivated by fear, territoriality, or aggressiveness? Not really. What's important is that you failed to recognize or heed the obvious warning indicators that if you tried to touch him, he would bite you.

Humans, even those trying to actively hide their intentions, give off similar clues—although, because of the complexity of human interactions, particularly the context under which interactions are occurring, the clues are often more nuanced than they are with other species. Part of where our thin-slicing and rapid cognition abilities come from is our ability to read facial expressions and body language, a skill that is meticulously developed and refined from infancy onward.[53] But, as with any skill, a little professional training goes a long way.

---

53 With the exception being those who reside at certain levels of the autism spectrum, where one of the defining elements is an inability to accurately gauge other people's reactions and body language.

When it comes to reading people's body language, I rely on the work of Joe Navarro. As a former FBI agent and a leading authority on body language and nonverbal communication, Navarro dedicated much of his government career to catching spies. His systematic codification of people's body language, particularly under stress, led to an incredibly high rate of confessions and resulting convictions.[54]

Navarro's work focuses primarily on the larger, more easily read nonverbal indicators telegraphed by the human body. To paraphrase Navarro, people may lie, but their bodies cannot. Central to his methodology, Navarro points out that babies only have two operating emotional states: comfort and discomfort. When a baby is comfortable, you'll know it; and when a baby is uncomfortable, you'll definitely know it. The same holds true for adults. People, simply put, are always displaying indicators of either comfort or discomfort, and while the displays are often more subtle in adults than in babies, if you know the signs, they are just as easy to read.

Bad Guys sometimes telegraph their intent in obvious ways that we might call "threat displays," and other times, in much more subtle ways. Yet, all indicators appear as clusters of behaviors that, when added up and evaluated objectively, will tell you a story about what's going on inside his or her head—particularly if they intend some level of harm.

Why is this the case? Because no matter who this person

---

54   See for example Navarro, Joe. *The Dictionary of Body Language: A Field Guide to Human Behavior.* William Morrow Paperbacks, 2018.

is or how they are wired, they are still subject to their limbic system. Since our limbic system is largely unconscious, even a seasoned criminal will display indicators of adrenaline—discomfort or stress—leading up to an attack.

Remember when we discussed the effects of fear and adrenaline on the human body in chapter 4? Well, Bad Guys are human too, even if they sometimes do things that seem inhuman to us. Because of this, most will at the minimum experience and display tangible signs of what we might call "slow-burn" adrenaline. Much like the stress a prizefighter experiences gearing up for a match, or a soldier feels when preparing to execute a mission, slow-burn adrenaline makes you uncomfortable. It causes your hands to shake, your voice to quiver, and your eyes to dart or to go into a "thousand-mile stare." What causes this limbic reaction is fear. For the Bad Guy, it is the ever-present fear of failure—whatever that might mean to them: getting hurt, getting caught, getting killed, failing in their mission. For both good guys and bad guys alike, this type of slow-burn adrenaline-based fear is stressful enough to cause hesitation or even to stop someone from moving forward into greater danger altogether.

These "limbic indicators" are almost always noticeable but are often misinterpreted if the observer doesn't see the signs of stress as being incongruent with, or out of context for, the situation at hand. For example, if everyone at a place of worship is happy, dancing, and engaged, but someone else is sitting, disengaged, profusely sweating, with a thousand-mile stare, some may read these indicators as perhaps the person simply not feeling well. But now that you are thinking differently, you might read such behavior as decidedly disturbing, given the context. The key is to be able to recognize the signs of discomfort, or stress, particularly when those signs are incongruent with the prevailing situational factors.

Unlike limbic indicators, threat displays are more overt movements that are less stress related in nature and more representative of behavioral patterns a Bad Guy might use to try to conceal intent, close with or intimidate a target, or ready an attack. Much like seeing the unmistakable body language of a leopard stalking into position for a fatal charge on a Discovery Channel special, a trained observer can read the threat displays of a Bad Guy that presage an attack.

When you see limbic indicators and/or threat displays, your radar will always alarm. And the more you can consciously and accurately recognize the patterns of behavior for what they are, the less likely you will be to fall victim to the veils of denial. Both limbic indicators and threat displays typically happen concurrently; as such it's easier to explore them together rather than parse them into two categories.

Let's examine some of the most common:

1. The predatory gaze—often described as "he was looking right through me," or "he looked at me like a piece of meat," or referred to as the "thousand-mile stare;" the predatory gaze is a function of the blink reflex slowing due to the adrenaline process.

2. A loss of color in the face—sometimes described as looking "white with fear." This is a critical indicator of vasoconstriction caused by high levels of adrenaline which is almost universal in the Red Zone of stress. The "blood draining" from someone's face is always a sign of extreme stress—possibly fear, as in he turned "white as a ghost," or in the context of an interview that precedes an attack, it is often a critical indicator that violence is intended or imminent.

3. Shaking hands or limbs—no matter who the Bad Guy is or how many times he has engaged in violence, shaking is a very common adrenaline indicator.

4. A quivering voice—the same is true here; a shaky voice is extremely difficult to control and is often the first noticeable indicator of stress or fear in the body.

5. Clenching fists, crossing arms, stiffening of the joints, or "frozen" behavior—all of these are indicative of a person who is trying hard (and often failing) to hide their shaking limbs and quivering voice. When people communicate, they are normally animated. When someone's movements are unnaturally stilted, restrained, or outright frozen—pay attention.

6. Profuse sweating that is inappropriate for the occasion—as we discussed earlier, sweating can happen in times of heat, pain, or illness, so if you know what to look for, you know that sudden,

extreme sweating independent of these circumstances is another limbic indicator representative of extreme discomfort.

7. Approach Behavior—someone walking toward you with purpose or on a deliberate intercept path, particularly if they are walking in an odd manner, such as keeping a hand hidden from view while moving, may presage an attack, or at the minimum an interview.

8. Encircling—A critical threat display is when someone tries to maneuver to your side or rear, or when more than one person attempts to engage you in an interview, while others attempt to encircle you

9. Batoning and wild arm gestures—angrily waving, pointing, or chopping gestures with the arms, typically accompanied by some level of verbal assault, are key threat displays that may lead to violence, particularly if mismanaged.

10. Puffing up—thrusting of the chest toward you, typically while holding the hands back behind the body, or batoning the arms, are critical threat displays.

11. Disrobing—taking off glasses, hats, shirts, and the like are threat displays designed to intimidate and often immediately precede a violent attack.[55]

---

55  http://marcmacyoung.com/immediatethreat.htm

Ideally, we want to identify a Bad Guy's intent and deny opportunity before these limbic indicators or threat displays progress to where we now need to manage the interview in the "I" of TIME, but to do so, we must be aware of the indicators and be able to trust that we know what they mean.

## *Who you are speaks so loudly, I can't hear what you are saying...*

Paul Ekman, another leading expert on human nonverbal communication, pioneered the concept of micro-expressions. The central notion is that humans are incredibly expressive animals, and as such, there are seven universal facial expressions, tied to very specific emotions, that people can't fully conceal no matter how they try. Moreover, these expressions are universal regardless of age, gender, language, or societal conditioning across the global landscape of human cultures. If we know what signs to look for in the unconscious muscle movements of a person's face, and if we are observant enough, we can determine whether someone is experiencing disgust, sadness, happiness, fear, anger, surprise, or contempt.[56]

As Ekman teaches, these seven expressions are involuntary, and therefore unable to be masked. Unfortunately, the

---

56   See, for example, Ekman, Paul. *Emotions Revealed, Second Edition: Recognizing Faces and Feelings to Improve Communication and Emotional Life.* Holt Paperbacks, 2007.

expression is rarely visible for longer than a flash—often for no more than a few tenths of a second (hence the "micro" in the term "micro-expression"). This means that unless you are actively looking at someone's face for that one flash of a moment, you may miss the indicator entirely. On top of this, I have found that you can often misinterpret the expressions you see—mistaking surprise for fear, for example—especially if the expression only appears for a flash.

Even if you read the expression correctly, your ability to interpret its value is based, again, on the situational factors. An expression of surprise has a very different meaning when someone opens an unexpected gift compared to when someone realizes that you have entered the room and quickly tries to hide their behavior. Requiring you to simultaneously spot the micro-expression, do so accurately, and evaluate the expression's congruency or incongruency as predicated on the situational factors is asking a lot in a stressful moment...

This is why I find these techniques incredibly valuable—particularly for detectives and interrogators—but perhaps a bit too subtle for the vast majority of people to use consciously in the context of personal protection. There is one key exception, however: the expression of contempt.

Contempt is defined as the feeling that a person or thing is beneath consideration, worthless, or deserving of scorn. Practically speaking, it means that the person showing you this expression believes himself superior to you. It means that he has effectively dismissed your humanity. This opens the door to victimization. And it is a sure sign that the person you are dealing with is on some level a Bad Guy.

So how can you read contempt in the face of another person? Ekman points out that contempt is the only asymmetrical facial expression. Since it is alone in its asymmetry, this means that it is easier to spot. The contempt expression involves one corner of the mouth tightening and raising slightly, like so:

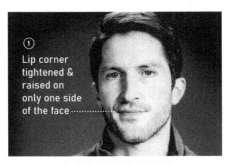

**CONTEMPT**

However, in the context of dealing with Predatory Bad Guys—or even in more everyday questions such as "Is this someone I want to hire, date, go into business with, or be friends with?"—when contempt rears its ugly head, I would urge caution. You can be sure you are dealing with someone who at a minimum feels superior to you and fundamentally disrespects you. No matter what the context, that is not a good foundation from which to build a healthy relationship.

Diane Downs murdered her daughter and attempted to murder her other two children in 1983 and then concocted a story about a carjacking to garner public sympathy. The story was so grandly crafted, and she was such a good storyteller, that the manipulation worked—for a time. In the weeks immediately following the incident, Downs received an outpouring of public sympathy, and she was interviewed repeatedly by the news media.

But if you research her story and see her interviews with your own eyes—and they are readily available—you will see someone whose body language and facial expressions are completely incongruent with the context of her story. Just four days after the incident, while one daughter was being buried and the other two still in intensive care, fighting for survival, Diane is seen laughing and joking during a video re-enactment of the purported attack. In media interviews, you see an emotionally flat affect coupled with deadpan facial expressions that are odd and off-putting, even to an untrained observer. But in one particular interview, you can clearly see her flash what looks like a crooked smile directly after she describes how horrible the events of that night were.

What you are actually seeing is contempt.

In his book *Telling Lies: Clues to Deceit in the Marketplace, Politics and Marriage*[57], Paul Ekman refers to this particular manifestation of contempt as Duping Delight. Duping delight describes the thrill or satisfaction that liars often feel at getting one over on people.

Investigating officers picked up on these anomalies immediately and never believed her story from the start. Doug Welch, the lead investigator on the case, said in an Inside Edition interview, "from the beginning it was wrong..." Too much simply didn't fit—about the case, her

---

57    W. W. Norton and Company. Revised edition, 2009.

story, the forensic evidence, and her subsequent demeanor. Eventually she was charged, and her surviving daughter Christy testified that it was her mom who shot her and her siblings. It is believed she committed the attack because her boyfriend at the time didn't want kids and she needed to get rid of them.

Liars and manipulators don't have to be on national television to display duping delight. It can happen in any setting, and it could be a vital warning sign that you're dealing with someone who doesn't have your best interests at heart. As with Diane Downes, most liars and manipulators will give off multiple indicators of their true nature, but often they are such skilled liars that you might doubt your own impressions. When you see duping delight, particularly when coupled with other body language indicators, pay attention, because you may just be dealing with one of the most dangerous predators out there.

## *The Most Dangerous Animal*

Unlike in the animal kingdom, where predators (even those who use camouflage) are easily identified by their teeth and claws, some human predators become masters at camouflage, manipulation, misdirection, and hiding in plain sight. They are the proverbial wolves in sheep's clothing. These wolves are more dangerous than any animal found in the wild. And as much as you train to be able to identify potential danger, they are equally working to conceal themselves and avoid your detection.

One of the reasons these particular Bad Guys are so dangerous is that they typically use charm and persuasion to lower your defenses and create opportunities, rather than brute force. Whether they are conmen, sexual predators, child molesters or serial killers, those who use charm and persuasion to identify, groom, seduce, and ultimately victimize their targets are all mission oriented and thereby classified as Professional Bad Guys by our definition, as we discussed in chapter 5. This means that they will also fall somewhere on the character-disordered side of the Scale of Personal Responsibility that we discussed in chapter 8. Fundamentally, all violent criminality falls on this side of the scale, but these most extreme dangerous personalities (that are also the hardest to spot) exist at the far end of this scale.

These are people who take no responsibility for their actions, and who have no sense of remorse, guilt, empathy, or conscience as a result. The psychological terms used for these individuals vary—Antisocial Personality Disorder, Sociopath, and Psychopath being three of the most common. Antisocial Personality Disorder refers to a wide range of behavior, and for our purposes more aptly describes the whole character-disordered side of the scale, whereas the terms *sociopath* and *psychopath* refer to the most extreme cases. There's some debate on what, if any, are the differences between a sociopath and a psychopath, but for our purposes of identification and protection, we will consider them functionally the same. For simplicity, we will refer to anyone who meets these extreme behaviors as sociopaths.

A sociopath is different from a "psychotic." Simplistically speaking, a psychotic is someone who doesn't understand right from wrong. A sociopath does but chooses to do it anyway. Often, their moral barometer is not based upon "is this behavior right or wrong?" but rather "can I get away with it or not?" Morality, as decent people view it, simply doesn't factor for a sociopath, except to be seen as a weakness in those they choose to prey upon. These are people whom their victims often describe as evil, inhuman, or diabolical.[58]

Diane Downs is a perfect example of what we are talking about. Conscienceless, deceitful, manipulative, evil. As investigator Doug Welch said, "Diane's the type of woman who, I think, could cut your throat and sit down and have lunch next to your body."

I've met plenty of kind, decent people who refuse to accept that "evil" actually exists. They believe that Bad Guys are simply good people who have just had the wrong upbringing, or life experiences, or have simply made the wrong decisions. I get it, and as I stated in the beginning of this book, when I use the term "Bad Guy," I'm not suggesting that everyone who does bad things is inherently evil. However, I am convinced that there are

---

58  As I've said before; I am not a psychologist, and my objective is not to "diagnose" anyone, as doing so in this context would be functionally meaningless. What I'm interested in is ensuring that you can identify people who may exhibit dangerous qualities or character traits so that you can make educated decisions to protect yourself and those you love.

indeed some fundamentally diabolical, evil people in this world. They live among us; they may be schoolteachers, CEOs, doctors, parents, clergymen, neighbors, or even children; and they are often such masters of deception and manipulators of your veils of denial that you will question your radar even when it screams at you to run as far and as fast as you can.

My goal in examining this subset of dangerous people in this chapter is not to do a deep dive into sociopathy. There are some excellent books that do that already. Rather, I want you to know how to spot them—and just as importantly, how to deny opportunity for them to victimize you or keep you in an exploitative cycle of abuse, as described in chapter 5.

So a key point to remember is that when we use the term *sociopath*, we're talking about someone who fundamentally does not have the same wiring as the rest of us. They lack conscience and empathy. Their disregard for right and wrong is always the same; they just have different modes of victimization.

Why are we focusing on this? I mean, aren't sociopaths rare? Shockingly, some studies estimate that four percent of the US population would meet the clinical definition of sociopath. That's one out of every twenty-five people.[59]

Some will read this statistic and worry that this means there are serial killers and rapists around every corner. This

59   Stout, Martha. *The Sociopath Next Door: The Ruthless versus the Rest of Us.* John Murray Learning, 2021.

isn't true, of course. The vast majority of sociopaths aren't violent—and if they do physically victimize, it's not on the level we observe in a serial killer. This is part of why it's so easy for them to blend in with the rest of us. But while they may not be homicidal or even physically dangerous, they are incredibly destructive to virtually anything and anyone they come in contact with—especially those they choose to target.

Sociopaths are masters of deception. Lying and manipulating are some of their most defining characteristics. They start deceiving early in life and become so gifted at these behaviors that it is difficult even for professional psychiatrists, psychologists, law enforcement, or security professionals to spot them. They're just so good at playing off your emotions and using the veils of denial against you that it's easy for a decent person to get sucked into their narratives and ignore the alarms ringing in their head. Sociopaths build such intricate webs of deception that when you do spot an incongruency and call them out on it, they will often talk their way around it in ways that make you feel foolish for ever doubting them. In other words, they "gaslight."[60]

---

60 "Gaslighting" is defined as a psychological manipulation that causes the recipient to question his/her understanding of reality. In other words, someone who gaslights you is causing you to question your memory or understanding of what has happened or is happening to you. Against all evidence, you question your own sanity.

Psychologist Robert Hare is famous in the field for creating the Hare Psychopathy Checklist,[61] which is a screening test for potential sociopaths. It scores a person based on twenty specific criteria that can be applied to sociopathic behavior. Answers to these criteria are weighted, and anyone who scores above a thirty on a scale from zero to forty can be identified as a sociopath. Since the criteria include more run-of-the-mill impulsive behaviors like sexual promiscuity or a tendency toward short-term marriages or a history of behavioral problems in childhood, the weighting of the score is particularly important.

To complicate matters, it's important to understand that just because someone is impulsive or manipulative or even demonstrates a lack of emotion in situations where an emotion might be expected, it does not make them a sociopath. We all have friends who are impulsive spenders. We've all dated or have friends or family that dated someone manipulative. Many veterans or law enforcement professionals are significantly more desensitized to seeing or even doing violence than the average person—myself included. That does not make them (or me, thank you very much) a sociopath. It is the behaviors taken on a weighted scale that allow us to see to the heart of that definitional lack of conscience.

Since you're functionally never going to have the opportunity to run people who concern you through the

---

61    Hare, Robert D. *Hare Psychopathy Checklist: Screening Version Manual PCLS2J*. Elsevier Health Sciences, 2000.

psychopathy checklist, I will try to categorize and identify sociopaths based on observable patterns of behavior and indicators. There are many ways in which psychologists attempt to categorize sociopathic behavior, but for our purposes here, I rely on the brilliant work of Dr. Martha Stout, author of *The Sociopath Next Door*, and *Outsmarting the Sociopath Next Door.*[62]

With that in mind, we will categorize true sociopaths into three fundamental types:

1. **Parasitic**

   A parasitic sociopath is someone whose primary aim in life is to essentially do nothing. To have others take care of them and to live a life of ease and pleasure. They just don't want to have to work (other than by targeting a host) to achieve any of what they desire. If they can land the trappings of success and status—say through marriage—even better! Parasitic sociopaths want to enjoy life, not work, and find ways to take advantage of others' generosity, care, money, status, etc.

   The classic case is the man or woman who seduces and/or marries someone stable or wealthy. Often, the parasitic sociopath will seem to intuitively fulfill their target's most unfulfilled

---

62   See footnote 58, and Stout, Martha. *Outsmarting the Sociopath Next Door: How to Protect Yourself against a Ruthless Manipulator.* John Murray Learning, 2022.

or important desires—be that sex, attention, adventure, caretaking, friendship, whatever (think about the "I" of Time). But once they feel they have sufficient control over their target, through marriage, pregnancy, addiction, etc., the façade drops, and things start to change. Someone who was once an attentive or giving partner suddenly has little interest other than their own gratification.

Aside from psychological manipulations and efforts generally designed to isolate their host from their friends, family, and anyone on the outside who could see what is really going on, they generally exist without having to put forth any other real effort. "He really is working hard to find a job; he's just overqualified…" or "He's writing an amazing book…" or "She's just having a hard time with XYZ ailment…" or "She's an artist or musician…" These are all representative of cover stories for the sociopath's behavior, or lack thereof, that the host will often use to explain away their lack of productive activity.

Parasitic sociopaths in relationships are almost always domestic abusers—some physically; others manifest their abuse psychologically. But all use volatility, deception, and sophisticated gaslighting techniques to keep their target(s) off balance and walking on eggshells. Such behavior comes as easily to the sociopath as breathing.

Getting rid of a parasitic sociopath can be

somewhere between difficult and next-to impossible, especially if they have a means to exploit you on an ongoing basis (e.g. you've had kids together). Parasitic sociopaths have no conscience about using the kids as tools, regardless of the damage they will ultimately cause them, if they can provide leverage for the sociopath to continue to extort, manipulate, and torment you. Regrettably, they are often too smart to cross the lines that would get them removed from your life, either by jail or restraining order.

## 2. Covetous

It is not at all uncommon to envy another person, but a covetous sociopath is someone who takes jealousy to frightening, perverse, and ultimately destructive heights.

The covetous sociopath envies certain qualities in the person they choose to target, but because they cannot actually assume the success, beauty, youth, athleticism, charisma, or other quality they envy, they will settle for sabotaging, besmirching, manipulating, or otherwise hurting their target—for no other reason than it gives them pleasure. Here, pleasure lies in taking rather than having.

To the covetous sociopath, life is a game, one that has cheated them from the beginning. As a result, they must even the score by causing destruction in the lives of those who have "more." But while retribution is their defining motivation, those that they place in their crosshairs often have no idea they are even being targeted.

As dangerous as covetous sociopaths are to the livelihood, relationships, and reputation of those they target, they are among the most difficult to spot. Few decent people can imagine why someone would launch a targeted, often long-term vendetta against someone who in most cases has done nothing to hurt or even offend them. Such behavior lies in direct opposition to our veils of denial. As a result, we have a hard time seeing the warning signs, or believing them even when we do.

Commonly, the covetous sociopath will seduce or attempt to seduce their target, or manipulate them into embarrassing or compromising circumstances that the sociopath can use as leverage against them. If the sociopath is in a position of power or authority, they will almost always leverage that power to further their destructive aims, but they will almost never do so in a way that would allow others to spot their behavior for what it is and hold them to account.

Often, the actions taken by the covetous sociopath are so outlandish, and so gratuitously mean, that we or those we confide in simply refuse to believe they were intentional, or even that they happened at all. In this way, the covetous sociopath's true nature is concealed.

Coworkers and colleagues will often provide the sociopath with positive recommendations in an attempt to avoid being targeted themselves, and this provides the covetous sociopath with even greater cover.

3. **Sadistic**
This category is the one that most people think about when they hear the term *psychopath* or *sociopath*. This is the serial killer or serial rapist—the Ted Bundys of the world—who fundamentally take pleasure in the physical suffering of, and domination over, their victims. Luckily, sadistic sociopaths are the least common of the three.

The key is to understand that while most sociopaths can be categorized according to one of the above "types," all may share qualities of the other two. Covetous sociopaths are definitively sadistic, in my mind; they just don't typically manifest their pleasure in hurting others violently, or at least not murderously. Sadistic sociopaths may exhibit many of the same qualities as a parasitic sociopath in their daily lives, and certainly they may be motivated in their target selection in similar ways to a covetous sociopath.

The common threads for all three types of sociopaths described above include their fundamental lack of conscience and their incredible capacity for deception and manipulation. All will try to isolate their targets or at least undermine their relationships behind their back. All love to play mind games and manipulate their targets and circumstances to give them leverage and control. All are so good at deception that you will continuously second guess your radar, even when you have direct evidence of what and who they are and what they are doing to you. All view life as a game, and the people in it as nothing but pawns to be played. All carefully and meticulously select and groom their targets, often over long periods of time. And all view conscience as weakness.

## *How to Spot the Wolves*

On the positive side, just as all sociopaths share certain qualities and characteristics, so too do they share certain reliable indicators that you are indeed dealing with one.

### *Charm*

First described by Hervey M. Cleckley in the 1941 classic *The Mask of Sanity*,[63] superficial charm is one of the most universal characteristics of the sociopath. Much like a good salesperson, the sociopath uses charm to build rapport, make a connection, reduce your inhibitions, lower your defenses, and even build attraction.

As with the body language indicators, context is very important in the case of charm. If someone is trying to be overly friendly to you in the context of trying to sell you a car, that's one thing. If someone is using charm as a mechanism for breaking down your psychological defenses

---

63    Cleckley, Hervey. *The Mask of Sanity: An Attempt to Clarify Some Issues About the So-Called Psychopathic Personality, Revised Edition.* Mosby Medical Library, 1982.

in a dating situation, that's a different dynamic entirely, and the stakes are of course significantly higher.

As Gavin de Becker states in his book *The Gift of Fear*,[64] the best way to address charm is to simply ask yourself the question, "Why is this person trying to charm me?" If you feel uncomfortable (at all) with someone who appears to be trying to charm you, the first step to disrupting the effort is to view that charm as a tactic to lower your defenses and treat it as you would any other "interview" (which we will address in depth in the next chapter).

One key to understanding charm, as it relates to socio-paths, is that it is always superficial. Meaning, it's an act. It doesn't persist. Much like the parasitic sociopath, once the goal has been achieved—be that getting you into bed, marriage, a business deal, etc. the façade will quickly fall away, or it will only emerge when it suits the sociopath. Often, you will be left wondering what you ever found so charming about this person in the first place...

*Deception*

In the event that you find yourself in a relationship with someone, at any level, and you begin to suspect trouble, one of the most universal indicators of a sociopath is deception. Okay, everyone lies. But the difference between a sociopath and the rest of us is that they almost make lying an art form. They lie continuously. About everything, big and small.

---

64   De Becker, Gavin. *The Gift of Fear: Survival Signals that Protect Us from Violence.* Bloomsbury Publishing PLC, 2000.

They might lie about being a doctor despite having no education beyond high school. They might lie about where they were yesterday, or what they were doing. They might even lie about something as inconsequential as what they had for breakfast.

You might ask yourself why they would lie about such unimportant things. The answer is that they take pleasure in it. It's as if their need to deceive and manipulate others is as fundamental as food, clothing, and shelter. Sociopaths even lie about things that could be easily disproven, simply because they really enjoy getting one over on people, and they just don't care.

Diane Downs not only lied—and continues to lie—about her heinous crimes against her children, but once behind bars freely admitted to cheating on her husband with at least ten lovers in one two-year time span.

Look for the duping delight. Look for signs of contempt when they think they are getting one over on you and trust your alarms when your radar warns you that something isn't right about what someone is saying or doing.

### The Pity Play

The final and often the most definitive indicator for you to internalize is also likely to be the one you will have the hardest time overcoming: the pity play. When a sociopath gets caught in a lie, or when they feel cornered, they will almost always resort to the pity play. They will try to appeal to the most fundamental emotion that makes you human: your empathy.

The sociopath will tell you how hard they have it, or how

bad their upbringing was. They will spin a web of lies that seems to provide rationale and justification for their actions, or that further reinforces the impression that they could not possibly be the person you are making them out to be. They will often simper and cry in Oscar-worthy performances. All of this is designed to play to your sense of pity.

Why? Because as a decent person—someone with a conscience—you will naturally feel bad for people who are suffering or having a hard time. You're going to fall under the veil of reciprocity: "If I were in trouble, I would want someone to show me some charity." Or you'll cling to the veil of normalcy and second-guess your earlier assessments and beliefs. Sociopaths use pity as the ultimate manipulative trump card.

They are so good at playing off others' sense of pity that even I—someone who has dedicated a whole career to understanding, spotting, and teaching others how to spot the warning indicators of Bad Guys—have fallen victim to their manipulations and pity plays. But as I tell my students, sometimes the best way to avoid stepping in dog shit is to accidentally step in it and then have to clean it off your shoe. Do that a couple times and you get really good at spotting and avoiding dog shit.

The reason I have spent some of our precious time together examining sociopaths is to teach you how to spot them, how to deny the opportunity for them to target you, and how to protect yourself from them, should you find yourself being targeted.

The key factor is that no matter who they are, where they come from, whether they were born without a conscience or their environment shaped them that way, none of them can completely mask the indicators that they intend to do you harm. It is in learning to read those indicators that you can keep yourself safe from them.

## *Clusters and Context*

Again, to get to the heart of a person's intent, a single indicator isn't enough. What we need is to recognize *clusters*. Clusters are exactly what they sound like: groups of indicators. But never forget that indicators are only as valuable as our understanding of the context under which they appear. If you see someone exhibiting a series of strange behaviors, you have to ask yourself: is what I'm seeing incongruent with my environment?

Let's say you meet someone in a bar. You're single. They say they're single as well. They're interested in you. A conversation ensues, and he or she appears very charming. It seems to be going well for a while, but then you get a bad vibe. You start to feel uncomfortable.

What could be causing this? It could be that you've picked up a nonverbal indicator that broadcasts this person's intent. Maybe, for a flash, you spotted an expression of contempt or duping delight. Maybe something he or she said just doesn't quite add up and even though you can't put your finger on it, you just feel this person is not really being honest. This cluster of indicators may not be conscious, but collectively they might trigger your radar.

Now, let's return to the situation I described earlier in this chapter as happening in a place of worship. You're sitting and watching as everyone in the audience is raising their hands in praise. But there near the back of the group is a man with a thousand-mile stare. He's pale. Sweating. He's still in his seat, fists clenched, while everyone else is up and singing. At first glance, that might seem like a pretty obvious cluster, one that would indicate that this man is plotting to hurt the worshippers in this building.

The *context* of the situation matters. In a situation such as this, just asking "hey buddy, are you okay...?" is often the easiest way to evaluate what's actually going on. Maybe the person really is feeling unwell and needs medical help? If the person is in a dark place mentally and contemplating harming himself, or others, this simple human outreach may be all that's needed to defuse that ticking time bomb. And tactically speaking, you are now close enough to respond should your inquiry trigger an attack that was preplanned and already imminent.

The situation is similar in a work setting. Imagine a coworker or employee who is demonstrating a marked change in their behavior, dress, or mannerisms. Where the person is usually well groomed, maybe he or she starts coming to work disheveled. Where generally polite and genial, he or she now seems surly or withdrawn. Where before they seemed fine with the routine demands of work, now even small things seem to bother him or her a whole lot more than they should. All of these clusters indicate stress, but you cannot assume the cause or help matters until you understand the context.

Again, just reaching out can make all the difference. Maybe you will discover that his spouse is having a health issue and he's extremely stressed. Maybe he's just looking for someone to let him know they care or for a chance to vent. Maybe she's experiencing trouble at home, or even domestic abuse, and she doesn't know where to turn or what to do. On the other side of the coin, someone could respond to your outreach with something like: "I've taken so much abuse from this place and I'm not gonna take it anymore!" This leakage could be a critical indicator of someone on the descent pathway to violence that we described in detail in chapter 8.

Telling the difference between clusters that indicate garden variety stress versus leakage that might indicate impending violent behavior is considerably easier with people we know than with total strangers. We see our family, friends, classmates, or coworkers every day, and as such, we develop a baseline for expected behavior; in much the same way, our radar develops a baseline for environments. When people deviate from that baseline, we pick up on it quickly, giving us a chance to further assess whether the change is significant or not.

In any situation, if your radar alarms you to danger—Pay Attention! If you read limbic indicators, threat displays, or evidence you may be dealing with a dangerous person— leave. The best way to deny opportunity once you've identified someone who may want to do you harm is to get away from them.

If you can't deny further opportunity, then you are likely going to have to deter that threat as it progresses into the "I" of TIME.

## CHAPTER 10

# Deter: Managing the "I" of TIME

IMAGINE THAT YOU'VE been charged with protecting a high-profile client. You've been equipped with all the tools of the trade, you know how Bad Guys operate, and you've been trained in the principles of personal protection, weapons, tactics, and close protection tradecraft. But in this particular case, the client you're tasked with protecting is being actively targeted by a known threat. And by the way, since the Bad Guy gets to choose the time, the place, and the method of attack, the element of surprise will be working against you.

One more thing: the historical data tells us that, overwhelmingly, attacks on public figures are over in just five seconds.[65] This means that from the moment you recognize

---

65  *Just 2 Seconds: Using Time and Space to Defeat Assassins.* Gavin de Becker, Tom Taylor, and Jeff Marquart. Gavin de Becker Center for the Study and Reduction of Violence. July 1, 2008.

the attack for what it is, right up until the conclusion of the event takes just five seconds. You have five seconds to dictate whether the Bad Guy succeeds or you stop him. That's it.

Oh, by the way, if you recall from chapter 3, you're going to burn at least the first half second going through the S.A.F.E. process, as your mind analyzes the stimuli, forms a plan, and begins to execute a response. So in a perfect world, you actually only have about four-and-a-half seconds to get into motion and save your client or stop the threat once you recognize the attack for what it is. And that's being very generous, as we haven't accounted for the element of surprise.

Given all that, what do you think are your chances of success?

Most people answer, "Not very good…" This answer is often followed by some variation of the question "Who the hell would do a job like this?"

In reality, the only reason it looks like the Bad Guy holds all the cards is because most people consider the situation

---

With this book, de Becker, Taylor, and Marquart provide research on a subject that previously had relatively little empirical data: attacks on public figures. One of the most interesting conclusions they reached from their analysis of attacks where the outcomes are known is that if you string together the total elapsed time of all the assassinations in known history into a single event, that combined event would amount to less than thirty minutes in collective human history. The majority of attacks took only five seconds to complete.

from the wrong perspective. Here's the correct perspective: the stopwatch isn't racing against the protectors; it's racing against the Bad Guy.

You see, in the mind of the Bad Guy, he only has one chance to pull off his mission. One chance to get it right, or he gets stopped. Maybe he gets hurt, or caught, or killed. Whatever the case, the target escapes, and he fails in his mission. To the Bad Guy, the notion of failure is ever present, and this fear (or lack thereof) is what ultimately determines whether or not he launches an attack.[66]

But don't feel bad. Almost everyone arrives at similar feelings of powerlessness when I ask the question about the fictional scenario above. This is the crux of the myth of helplessness to which we've all been conditioned. It comes from the erroneous belief that you are incapable of defending yourself. It suggests to you that the Bad Guy holds all the cards—the physical upper hand (whether he is bigger, younger, stronger, or armed); the opportunity to choose the time and place; or the element of surprise. That Bad Guy has total control of the situation.

The reality is that *you* control the most important situational factors. You just have to understand what those factors are and then consciously never relinquish control of them. By understanding and accepting your own power, deterrence is not only possible; it's *probable*.

---

66    Ibid.

## *What is Deterrence?*

Most people have an idea of what *deterrence* means, but I'd like to give you my simple working definition. At its essence, deterrence is about creating fear in the mind of the adversary. But to create fear in the mind of a Bad Guy, we need to know what they're afraid of.

If you recall, in chapter 5 we examined the three distinct types of Bad Guys—Professionals, Predators, and Potentials—and we defined that regardless of their specific motivation (whether they're mission oriented, driven by situational factors, or opportunistic by nature), all are afraid of the same fundamental outcome: failure.

To a terrorist or assassin, failure might mean getting stopped before they can complete their mission. For a predator, it might mean getting hurt or killed. For a Potential Bad Guy, it might mean going to jail, getting hurt, or ending up dead. In the moment, we can't be certain of exactly what they are afraid of, but we don't need to be. The notion of failure equates universally to whatever specific thing they might be fearing. A hard target always represents a greater probability of failure, even if the Bad Guy feels that he has advantages.

As you've seen throughout this book, this fear of failure, and thereby the fear of a hard target, underpins every lesson. It is why Bad Guys are so careful in selecting their prey. It's why they interview targets to validate their selection. And it's why the TIME-Line of Violence is so observable and predictable and why violence is ultimately never random.

Fundamentally, no matter what the brand of violence, or which level of Bad Guy we are dealing with, he knows the stakes (for him) and must be sure that his target and/or the situational factors won't give him too much trouble. He needs a soft target, and he fears a hard target.

Now, most decent people don't typically spend time thinking about how to create fear in others. In fact, most of us do exactly the opposite. We invest considerable time and energy to behave in ways that would reduce fear and make others more comfortable around us, not less so.

Generally, decent people try to be sensitive to the way in which their body language and words impact the people around them. Most try actively not to offend or disrespect those they are interacting with. And in many ways, this infrastructure of courtesy is what enables all of us to function as a civilization. Without rules by which to behave and treat each other, people would have very little ability to trust, collaborate, and cooperate toward goals.

Indecent people (or Bad Guys), on the other hand, violate these rules regularly. It is often in the violation of these rules that Bad Guys deliberately test you. And it is through this violation of rules that you can recognize and manage the I of TIME.

## *Understanding the I of TIME*

For Professional Bad Guys, the I of TIME represents Intelligence gathering. This takes the form of grooming, planning, training, surveilling, testing, rehearsing, and ultimately validating their target and intended method of attack.

245

For Predatory and Potential Bad Guys, the I of TIME takes the form of what we refer to as an "Interview." The interview serves to validate the target and method of attack, similar to the intelligence process of a Professional Bad Guy. The key differences are that interviews are much more common, they happen more quickly, they are generally more direct, and they may bring more immediate consequences.

The hard reality is that when you recognize the indicators of the I of TIME, you have already been selected as a potential target and are now being evaluated to confirm that target selection. Will you make a soft target, or are you too much of a hard target to attack?

While this does make interview management extremely important, it does not mean that if you fail to manage an interview perfectly, it will *always* lead to an attack. Nor does it mean that an interview always *immediately* precedes an attack. Sometimes, Bad Guys conduct interviews just for practice, with no intention of committing to an attack. Others may conduct an interview at one time and then wait or plan for a more opportune time or location to launch an attack. How you manage an interview can have consequences hours, days, or even weeks later.

Lisa, a twenty-one-year-old college student, illustrated this dynamic while attending one of my self-defense classes several years ago. One Friday evening, Lisa was waiting for her boyfriend to pick her up outside her off-campus apartment building when she noticed a car driving by unusually slowly. She knew it wasn't her boyfriend's car, but the vehicle's unusual speed and movement drew her attention. Lisa then saw the driver and reported, "a chill ran down my spine." She didn't recognize the middle-aged man driving the car, but the intense look he gave her instantly made her feel fear, and she locked his face into her memory.

As the car turned the corner Lisa's fear receded, and she went back to waiting for her ride, but in the back of her mind she kept thinking *I hope I don't see that guy again.*

A few moments later, the same car rounded the corner in another slow drive by, the driver giving that same disturbing look. Lisa, again feeling a chilling fear, turned away to avoid eye contact and pulled out her cell phone to call her boyfriend to ask how far away he was. As it turned out he was right around the corner, and shortly after the disturbing car once again rounded the corner, her boyfriend picked Lisa up.

When Lisa told her boyfriend about the disturbing situation, he teased her about "overreacting" and said that she had nothing to worry about because he would protect her. After a couple of days, Lisa began to believe that her boyfriend was probably right. She had overreacted and had nothing to worry about.

One week later, on a Friday, Lisa was once again waiting outside her apartment for her boyfriend to pick her up to go to dinner. Her first thought was *I hope I don't see that guy again,* but she immediately dismissed it as an irrational fear. Until, that is, she saw the same guy—this time on foot—surreptitiously standing across the street and staring right at her. Lisa's radar screamed at her, and she ducked back into her apartment building's secured foyer, this time calling 911 instead of her boyfriend. Wanting to describe him thoroughly to the 911 operator, she looked right at the man as she made the call. During the call, he gave her one final look and walked away. The police showed up hours later, but Lisa never saw the guy again.

Was this an interview or a threat display, as discussed in chapter 9? Well, it was both. The predatory gaze that Lisa immediately picked up on during the first drive by was the initial threat display—that first warning sign that she may be being targeted. Her radar correctly and effectively alarmed based on the Bad Guy's limbic indicators, warning Lisa that she was in the presence of danger.

When the driver took a second pass, the situation progressed to the interview phase. Did Lisa's turning away from danger at that moment present her as a soft target? Perhaps.

When she saw the Bad Guy a third time, this time in a position to physically intercept her if she hadn't seen him, the interview dynamic was clearly (at least in my mind) progressing toward a method of attack. Because Lisa was paying attention, she was able to spot the Bad Guy and interrupt the pattern of the interview from progressing by making eye contact as she called for help. In other words, she simply had to demonstrate to the Bad Guy that she was aware of him and doing something about it. This was enough to raise his fear of failure to the point where he left her alone.

The other takeaway message of this story is that Lisa's awareness and quick thinking—and *not* the "protection" of her boyfriend—are what prevented this interview from advancing to something more dangerous. I'm confident that this experience, coupled with the training Lisa received from me afterwards, ensures that she will remain a hard target and will not be easily victimized in the future.

The line between the Deny and Deter stages can easily blur. This is because the same indicators that alert you to trouble in the first place are present during the interview phase. And while there are some key differences, drawing a hard line between the two is simply not necessary.

Denying opportunity relates to the steps you take in general to recognize and avoid trouble. Deterrence relates to your actions and behavior once you believe you are in danger and may be being targeted. Whether your alarm comes as a result of a limbic indicator, a threat display, or some combination, you have to TRUST YOUR RADAR. That alarm is the first and most vital warning sign that you may be being targeted, and that you are likely going to have to respond to manage an interview.

## Street Smarts

Early in my close protection career, the firm I worked with was engaged to provide executive protection for the director of a national telecommunications company's local call center. The call center employed several thousand people and was in the midst of a contentious attempt to unionize the employees.

Anonymous threats were made against leadership. Given the severity of the threats and surrounding behavior, the company decided to engage protective services. However, due to the delicacy of the situation, they wanted security to be covert. So I was given a cover story as a young

(I was only thirty at the time), up-and-coming manager of a call center in Florida that was expected to face a similar unionization process in the coming year. I was introduced to this unionizing call center under the guise of a need to shadow their director to learn how to help manage the process in my "own" call center.

I had actually lived and worked in that part of Florida, and so I was intimately familiar with the area. I studied up on the company and my fictitious role, and even bought sweater vests and clothing intended to strategically soften and reduce my physical profile so I wouldn't draw a lot of attention (I was a pretty big, fit, and physically imposing guy). The only people who knew my actual role were the director herself, the human resources director, and the senior leadership of the organization that had engaged us. With my preparations in place, I felt confident that I could pull off the ruse. Plus, I was too young and inexperienced to know any better.

One hundred percent of the management team—supervisors, managers, and executives at every level—bought my story. They were convinced that I was who I said I was, and they never really questioned any of the details of my story. It was amusing to see how some among the management would uncomfortably maneuver themselves to figure out if my presence somehow posed a threat to their position.

It was a very different story, though, with some of the call center employees, many of whom had grown up in tough neighborhoods. I would routinely notice some of these employees carefully watching me, and when the chance arose, they would ask probing questions about who I was and what I was doing there. I could clearly see in their eyes that they doubted my cover story.

After a week or so, I ended up in a conversation with a small group of the wary employees, and one looked at me slyly and said, "You don't work here. You're a cop, aren't you?"

I denied it, of course, playing it off with something like "Heck no! I could never be a cop. That stuff scares me…"

This deflected the issue in the moment, but I doubted that they believed me. A couple of days later I ran into the same small group of employees, and the same individual approached me again. This time, she declared, "You're definitely a cop."

Now this opinion seemed to be shared by a number of the call center employees I had noticed watching me from time to time.

I never admitted anything, however, and eventually the detail came to a safe conclusion. But at the time, I was astonished at how accurately some employees were able to see right through my act, while others bought it hook, line, and sinker. This experience led me to two very important conclusions: first, I was definitely not suited to undercover work, espionage, or anything that involved deception; second, just as a Bad Guy cannot conceal his true intent from you indefinitely, neither can you totally pretend to be something you are not—at least not in the case of seasoned observers of human behavior.

The suspicious employees who saw right through my cover, every one of them, had grown up in some tough parts of town, and as a result, demonstrated significant *street smarts.* Street smarts is defined as the experience and knowledge necessary to deal with the potential dangers of life in an urban environment. In many ways, all of the skills we've been developing throughout this book are elements of street smarts.

If you're not conscious of your body language, and sometimes even when you are, the subtleties of your eyes and facial expression, or how you might unconsciously stand, walk, and move, will betray whether you are a soft or a hard target, often regardless of how you want to be perceived. Ever notice how veterans and police tend to walk differently than others? Ever notice how people in positions of authority or influence tend to exude a certain level of personal power? The same goes for those who lack confidence, or who feel insecure in a situation.

Bad Guys generally have significant street smarts, and as a result, they are superb at reading people. They pick up on subtle cues when selecting their targets, much in the same manner that those suspicious call center employees saw through my act. Their radar may very well have been accurate, but the other key piece to note here is that they required a fair amount of time and observation before they formulated their belief that I wasn't who I said I was. A Bad Guy needs similar time and observation, and that can only come through an interview. This is why the critical inflection point is your ability to project the right body language and "hard target" messaging during the interview.

In a perfect world, you have both the willingness and the ability to respond—you are, in fact, a hard target and therefore don't have to pretend. But even if you don't have the physical skills, tools, or ability, you can still display yourself as a hard target well enough (and for long enough) to disrupt most interviews and deter most threats. You can "fake it till you make it," as they say, and I'm going to show you how. You can do this, no matter who you are or what your background and experience. And you can do this even if you're scared to death about everything you've learned in this chapter so far.

## Dog Language

Previously in this book, we've explored how to read people for the purpose of tuning your ability to recognize danger and interpret a Bad Guy's intent. Now we want to explore this from the reverse perspective: how to manage and project your own nonverbal signals, such that if a Bad Guy interviews you, all he sees is a hard target.

In his bestselling books and popular TV show "The Dog Whisperer," celebrated dog trainer Cesar Millan says that owning and raising well-behaved dogs requires you to become the "pack leader," otherwise referred to as the "alpha."[67] Millan explains that the alpha energy of any species is always calm yet assertive. When you see a dog or group of dogs making a scene—barking and leaping, and generally behaving in a frenzied, out-of-control

---

67   See, for example, Millan, Cesar. "The Real Top Dog." cesarsway.com/the-real-top-dog/

fashion—that is not an indication of dominance; it is an indication of their *lack of confidence*.

A true alpha, meanwhile, views this kind of behavior as beneath it. As the other dogs in the pack yap away, the alpha calmly watches. If the alpha has to take action, then it does so decisively and dispassionately, making a quick behavioral correction before reverting to a calm/assertive posture. Put another way, the alpha *responds* rather than *reacts*.

The interesting thing is that being an alpha has very little to do with size. Perhaps you've seen a small dog dominate much larger dogs just through the force of their personality. As the saying goes, "It's not the size of the dog in the fight; it's the size of the fight in the dog." The same is true with people. You don't have to be big to be powerful, or even to be seen as an alpha.

In this way, as we consider the interview management tactics to come, keep in mind that it is not aggressiveness but rather a calm and assertive demeanor that will most clearly demonstrate to the Bad Guy that you are in control and not to be messed with. To do this, you need to display confidence even when you may be unsure of the situation or your ability to respond.

In furtherance of this goal, I'm going to show you some very simple, easy-to-remember nonverbal tactics that will help you manage interviews confidently, reduce your fear, and project calm assertiveness, all while minimizing the possibility of escalation toward physical confrontation.

*The Power Stance*

If you are forced to manage an interview that you can't *just leave*, you must begin by controlling the distance.

But we also have to imagine a scenario where the Bad Guy has already compromised your distance. In this scenario, if you back up (but can't escape)—or worse, if you turn away as if it's not happening—then you will look like a soft target and invite further problems. On the other hand, if you stand your ground, then you're still within critical distance and are therefore vulnerable. Meanwhile, if you advance on him, then you risk creating an escalation.

So…what are we to do?

This is where you can use a technique I call the "Secret Service Stance," or when I teach it to children, the "Power Stance." The stance looks like this:

I call it the Secret Service Stance because this is one of the go-to stances for close protection professionals.

To assemble the stance from the ground up, imagine you're riding a bicycle and you have a foot balanced on each pedal as you stand up. This will give you the ideal spacing between your feet from front to back and side to side. But while your foot spacing is important, the key aspect of the Secret Service Stance is in your hands. You'll want to steeple your fingers and bring them up to your midline, with your hands slightly above your elbows. Your fingertips touch, with your palms apart and your thumbs pointed upward in what is referred to as a "high thumb display."

The reason close protection professionals (as well as politicians and business leaders) use this posture is because it's the most powerful way the human body can display itself. Compared to having your arms crossed, or hands on hips, the Secret Service Stance projects calm, assertive confidence and authority without arrogance or other potentially negative nonverbal signals. This is true even if you are, in reality, quite scared.

In an interview, the Secret Service Stance masks your fear and says to the Bad Guy, "I know exactly what's going on here and I'm putting my lunchbox down. What do you want?"

Like flipping on a light switch, dropping one foot back into your Secret Service Stance becomes your physical trigger to activate yourself and mentally snap from "normal" mode into "tactical" mode. This helps facilitate a laser focus on managing the danger at hand. Further, by positioning your feet appropriately and bringing your hands to your midline and above your elbows, you've coiled yourself, greatly reducing reaction time should you need to take explosive physical action—whether offensively or defensively.

Taking this stance will often cause other people to unconsciously back away from you, yielding to more appropriate personal boundaries, particularly if the person was merely being inappropriate rather than threatening.

One of the reasons I find the Secret Service Stance so effective is that it not only displays confidence and authority when you need it most; it actually makes you *feel* more confident and assertive. If you're scared or feeling insecure, go to your Secret Service Stance. As world-famous peak performance coach and personal improvement icon Anthony Robbins says, "Motion creates emotion. Changing your physiology changes your mental state..."[68]

This can be a huge benefit in a job interview, during a negotiation, while public speaking, asking someone out on a date, or almost any other circumstance that makes you anxious or scared. It can even be used while seated, simply by steepling the fingers. Think of how Hollywood often depicts the CEO or mob boss leaning back in his seat with his hands steepled under his chin.

Obviously, this is a fairly low-key move. As such, if it fails to accomplish distance control, or if you need a more immediate pattern-interrupt to someone's attempt to penetrate critical distance, you will likely need to escalate to the next tactic.

---

68  https://www.tonyrobbins.com/mind-meaning/are-you-stuck/

*The Stop Sign*

If the Secret Service Stance fails to establish distance control, or if the situation demands that you get yourself out of critical distance immediately, then you have no choice but to create your own space. But how do you do so without displaying yourself as a soft target or escalating the situation?

Now we introduce the Stop Sign.

The Stop Sign can be projected with one hand or two hands, and can be presented at high or low "volume," depending on the situation, just by changing the elevation of your hands. The Stop Sign can be an incredibly powerful pattern-interrupt during an interview when you still have an opportunity to leave or escape, and also in interviews where that opportunity has been closed off.

Think of the Secret Service Stance and the Stop Sign in the same way as a boxer putting up his guard. You're making yourself ready and able to physically respond should you need to. But unlike the unmistakable body language of putting up your dukes—which says, unequivocally, "Talking is over!"—using a Stop Sign is defensive and nonthreatening and allows you to continue talking if necessary. Additionally, it clearly communicates to any nearby bystanders *exactly* what is going on. Even if they aren't close enough to hear what is happening, the Secret Service Stance and Stop Sign clearly communicate that you are the defender, and the Bad Guy is the aggressor.

Bear in mind that the Stop Sign requires your arm or arms to be extended. You do *not* want your Stop Sign too close to you, because if it gets too close to you, the message changes from "Get away from me!" to "I surrender!"

This is why I never want your hands to be in the middle, as the nonverbal messaging becomes too ambiguous. "Please back away from me" winds up looking too much like "Please don't hurt me."

259

When you use the Stop Sign correctly, the only appropriate response from the Bad Guy is to back up and give you space. He may back up angrily, but as long as he gives you space it doesn't matter what he says or how he feels. If he complies, you have established significantly more control of the distance, and thereby significantly more control of the whole situation. However, just because he complies doesn't mean you are out of danger. You still need to keep your guard up, but you've definitively taken a step in the right direction.

On the flip side, if he advances on your upraised Stop Sign, you and everyone else who sees the situation will instantly see the threat for what it is. This situation isn't going to be deterred, and you're going to have to switch from talking to touching. The only thing you don't know precisely is how hard you're going to have to touch. Don't worry, we'll address defensive responses (in a non-terrifying way, I promise) in chapter 11.

One final word on the Stop Sign: it represents a universal, unequivocal, and nonverbal "No." So, if you're dealing with an interview in a more social scenario, such as in a bar, nightclub, or on a date, and the person is simply not listening to you when you say "no" verbally, you can use the Stop Sign to reinforce your message calmly, assertively, and unequivocally. If the person still refuses to accept your "no," they are clearly not interested in what you want—only in what *they* want—and you are likely going to have to take some further action.

As we'll examine later in this chapter, the best response is always just to leave, but if you can't outright escape, much the same as with a Bad Guy approaching your upraised hands on the street, you are likely going to need to go from talking to touching in some fashion.

*The Listener's Pose*
While it's rare, there are interviews that occur in which your distance is compromised but you can't just leave or even increase your distance without potentially escalating the situation. An example of this might be a work scenario where you're engaging with an employee or customer who's upset, maybe even yelling and gesticulating with their hands, yet it's your responsibility as the manager to defuse the situation. Even a low volume Stop Sign might be seen as too aggressive, and because your distance is already compromised, the Secret Service Stance presents your hands too low to improve your defensive reaction time. This is where the Listener's Pose is particularly valuable.

In a calm, neutral way, you bring your lead hand to your face, bracing your lead arm elbow with your other hand, kind of like the famous statue "The Thinker." The unmistakable nonverbal message is that you are listening intently and trying to understand what someone is saying. This is particularly powerful, as in any conflict that you are trying to defuse, one of the most important aspects is that the other person feels like they are being heard and taken seriously.

In reality, though, while you are in fact listening, the Listener's Pose serves as a guard, much in the same way as that boxer keeping his hands up. Your lead arm is covering your solar plexus, throat, and chin—effectively protecting your centerline—and if the Bad Guy lunges at you, takes a swing at you, or pulls a weapon, your arm is already in position to deflect attacks or strike first should the situation demand.

The Listener's Pose can also serve as a nonverbal duress signal to team members or family members around you, provided these people have had similar training. When I train protection teams, and even managerial teams, I explain that the Secret Service Stance is a nonverbal duress signal that alerts everyone to the fact that there is a potential problem, but the Listener's Pose is more like a 911 call. It says, "I'm busy managing the interview and can't break to ask someone to call the police." If you're a bystander in this kind of scenario, it's better to err on the side of caution and call the police than to try to get them there after the violence erupts. It's easier, after all, to thank them for responding even though you managed to defuse the situation internally than it is to wait for violence to erupt.

One question that often arises in managing an interview is: "When does an attempt to disengage come across as weakness and invite escalation?" Think about dealing with a bully in grade school, for instance. As with most human dynamics, nuance plays a role. Even in cases such as school and work, where you may have to repeatedly see and interact with a potentially dangerous person, the rule remains: because all Bad Guys are afraid of a hard target, and all interviews ultimately share the same purpose (to test you and validate whether you are a hard or soft target) you can't go wrong with calm assertiveness and using the Secret Service Stance, the Stop Sign, or the Listener's Pose as the situation demands.

Beyond this primary rule, if you listen to your radar, it *will* give you an accurate, real-time assessment of whether you can disengage safely or if the situation is going to demand some greater level of response. I half-jokingly tell my clients that it's much like the Supreme Court definition of pornography: you'll know it when you see it.

What I can tell you from my own experience—as well as the collective experience of many of my clients, including law enforcement officers and security professionals who deal with confrontations all the time—is that if you manage an interview with the tools I'm suggesting above, you will generally be able to deter situations from escalating to violence.

Now, with those tools at your disposal, we can pivot to an examination of what an interview looks like—starting with the dynamics of a Bad Guy's approach.

## *Approach Dynamics*

While there are many nuances to an interview, the process generally takes one of two primary forms. The most common is some form of approach. The other is the form of being followed or inappropriately pursued. Either dynamic necessitates action on your part to deter the threat from escalating.

If you're uncomfortable with someone, and that person approaches you (in any way), treat it as an interview. This is the rule. That approach might be on the street by a stranger, or it might be by someone you know in a social setting. On the street, Predatory Bad Guys will often try to engage you conversationally as part of the approach: "Hey, do you have the time?" or "Can I ask you something?" or "What's the score (of the game)?" Sometimes the verbal engagement will take the form of "cat calling" or suggestive gestures or sounds.

Potential Bad Guys, meanwhile, often approach with a dirty look or a challenge statement, such as some variation of "What are you looking at?"

All approach dynamics are designed to do one thing: engage you in the interview. And the interview has one primary purpose: to determine whether you are a hard or soft target.

I know it sounds a bit harsh, but the same can be said of the attractive stranger offering to buy you a drink, or the charming coworker or classmate asking you out on a date. Of course, we can't go shutting everyone out all the time. This is why it's so important to know the difference between a normal interaction and a potentially dangerous approach. The key differentiator is: how does the approach make you feel? If it makes you uncomfortable, or it turns uncomfortable, be careful.

Any approach that makes you feel uncomfortable will naturally raise your alert level and trigger you to investigate further. This is when you perform a deep scan. During a deep scan, you look for incongruencies, body language and facial expressions, threat displays, and other warning signs that you've learned throughout this book. Even if you don't see any obvious threat displays, limbic indicators, weapons, or other discernable warning signs—all of which may be well masked—it's still best to trust your radar and keep your alertness raised. Do not fall into the veils of denial and pacify yourself that just because you can't articulate tangible evidence, "it's probably nothing" or that you are "overreacting."

This certainly doesn't mean you can't be kind to people, help strangers in need, or flirt with people you are attracted to; it simply means that you need to trust your radar. If you choose to engage with someone or a situation that makes you uncomfortable, then you're taking a risk. Do so while being fully aware. And take reasonable precautions to avoid putting yourself in situations you can't get yourself out of. Just make sure you're taking full responsibility for your actions.

For simplicity, I'm going to break down the most common approach dynamics that a Bad Guy will display during an interview. Along with each breakdown, I will present specific response options for managing each type of approach. Much like learning a language, I want you to think of the response techniques I'm presenting you as letters of the alphabet. I'm going to show you how to build some basic words and phrases with these letters, but once you understand these patterns, you'll be able to form your own sentences to address whatever situation you're faced with in the real world.

*Approach Type 1: Just Leave*

As a general recommendation, should a stranger approach you, particularly if they are triggering your radar, *just leave*. Don't engage with the interview. Don't even slow down. Just leave.

This first response is the most effective and is also the simplest. If you can avoid the interview by just walking away, then do so. Keep moving, and simply don't respond. Let the Bad Guy know that you see him. Do this by looking at his face or chest, but don't make prolonged eye contact as that can be interpreted as an invitation for further engagement. Regardless of what he says, simply stay calm, ignore the verbal tactics, and keep moving.

However, if the approach happens too fast or too close to simply walk away from, you'll need a technique to "pattern-interrupt" the process of the interview—something that will create a pause to give you the opportunity to keep moving. This normally involves saying something, but what do you say?

In my experience, both as a security professional and as someone who has been approached numerous times by Bad Guys in the real world, the best way to verbally pattern-interrupt an interview and create the opportunity to keep moving is with a simple, catch-all statement:

"I'm sorry, I can't help you."

When you use this phrase, you essentially refuse to answer any question the Bad Guy might throw at you even before he has a chance to close in to critical distance. When coupled with a powerful nonverbal Stop Sign gesture (pictured again below), it is an incredibly effective way to show that you are aware of the interview dynamic, and that you are not going to be a soft target.

Consider all the ways that the above response, coupled with "I'm sorry, I can't help you," can effectively turn away an initial Approach from the Bad Guy.

Again, you can modulate the "volume" of the message simply by adjusting the volume of your voice and the elevation of your Stop Sign. The closer your hand is to face level, the louder the volume. Additionally, you can add a verbal "STOP" in advance, if needed. For example: "STOP! I CAN'T HELP YOU!" spoken loudly and directly, is a very effective deterrent to any further interview dynamics and will likely draw more attention to the interaction than the Bad Guy wants. When you use the nonverbal Stop Sign to reinforce your verbal tactic, any bystanders who see the incident will know exactly what's going on, even if they can't hear you or understand your language.

"Do you have the time?"
"I'm sorry, I can't help you."
"Excuse me, do you know the score?"
"I'm sorry, I can't help you."
"Do you have some change you can spare?"
"I'm sorry, I can't help you."
"Hey, can I talk to you for a second?"
"I'm sorry, I can't help you."

There's no predatory approach interview question that this simple statement can't deflect. If you keep moving and pattern-interrupt the approach in this manner you are sending a clear message that you have no intention of being interviewed, all in a manner that gives you control without disrespecting the Bad Guy.

This pattern-interrupt is so effective that, by itself, it's worth the price of this book. You are, after all, acknowledging him rather than ignoring him or giving him a dirty look (which, again, in the Bad Guy's mind, could be indicators that you are lacking confidence, or are challenging or disrespecting him). If you keep moving and deliver these words in a calm, assertive manner, then you have executed a polite and yet powerful pattern-interrupt—a most efficient way to disengage.

*Approach Type 2: When You Can't Leave*
One of the biggest challenges in managing interviews is that the Bad Guy gets to choose the time and place. And if they're good at interviewing, you might find yourself in a position where you can't swiftly and easily disengage. You may be with your young children or elderly parents, or you have your hands full of groceries, or you're otherwise encumbered and just can't leave quickly enough.

Or you could find yourself in a scenario where the Bad Guy is between you and the only exit, or retreat is not tactically viable, and you have to either back him down or peremptorily escalate to defensive measures.

Or it could be that what previously seemed like a benign social encounter with someone you knew suddenly makes you feel uncomfortable, but now you find yourself behind closed doors.

In any of these scenarios, this is when you must exert control over the most important situational factor in any confrontation: distance.

If you are forced to engage with an interview from close proximity, distance becomes your barometer of safety and the key indicator of whether you'll be able to manage the situation by talking or if you are going to need to touch in some fashion. Put another way, it will determine whether you can talk your way out of it or will have to fight your way out.

Let's not worry about the potential *fight* part of the equation yet. In the next chapter, I'll address the most important principles you need to know in the situations when talking turns to touching. But there is one principle to understand now: there are only two kinds of fighting in the world—fighting on your feet and fighting on the ground. Regardless of weapons, if you're rolling around on the ground with someone, whoever is in control of the position has control. On your feet, it's all about distance. Whoever controls the distance is in control of the entire dynamic. In an interview, how you respond to the Bad Guy's approach and attempt to get close to you can represent—all by itself—whether you are presenting as a hard or soft target.

So how close is too close?

Normal social distance is defined largely by situational factors, but the general rule we all understand intuitively is this: if you don't want to make someone uncomfortable, then keep your distance. For example, in some parts of the world, it's not uncommon for acquaintances to converse at distances much closer than is the norm in the United States. But regardless of culture, there is a noticeable sense of discomfort that comes when someone you do not trust gets too close.

There are exceptions, of course. Sometimes we're jammed in with strangers like sardines on a subway or at a concert. In these situations, we're usually not uncomfortable being this close to a stranger unless he begins engaging with us in a manner that sets off alarms. There is a huge difference, after all, between someone being forced

up against you because of the crowd and someone displaying behaviors that indicate he is trying to take advantage
of that proximity. When something like this occurs, our
natural reaction is to feel uncomfortable and to want to
create distance from the person whose proximity doesn't
fit the situation.

The thing is, Bad Guys love to invade your personal
space. Most of the time, this distance penetration is not so
aggressive or overt that you would immediately take it as a
threat and be forced to respond physically. Rather, they stop
right at the inappropriate social distance we colloquially
call "close-talking."

Close-talking distance is best defined as occurring at
about arm's reach—right inside the threshold of your invisible personal space bubble. All of us, universally, regardless
of culture or context, feel uncomfortable in close-talking
proximity with someone we don't trust because our limbic
system knows we are inside the half-second hardwired
reaction time gap discussed in chapter 3: Staying SAFE.
Distance literally equals time. When someone is within
arm's reach, it doesn't matter if you're a ninja; if that Bad
Guy wants to hit, stab, or tackle you, you will not have the
physiological reaction time necessary to respond. We call
this "critical distance" (in the parlance of the street, it's
"sucker distance").

The main reason that Bad Guys universally try to
engage you at critical distance in an interview—whether
the context is a stranger on the street or someone being
too friendly in a bar or nightclub—is *because* it makes you
uncomfortable. Your discomfort is a huge part of their

intent. In response, how you manage (or choose not to manage) that discomfort is very telling. It can cause you to slip into the veils of denial, as decent people don't like to be rude and certainly don't want to anger someone, plus it's probably nothing… right? Fall victim to this, and you will present as a soft target.

Or you can recognize the tactic for what it is, and when you feel uncomfortable about someone's proximity, *treat it as an interview*. When you are forced to engage with the interview at close proximity, understand that it really doesn't matter what you say; it only matters how you say it and what you do about it.

*Approach Type 3: Confrontational Management*
"Conflict resolution" is a popular term to describe a mechanism for people to negotiate resolutions in a dispute. I think of this as the "I'm okay; you're okay" kind of compromise.

*Confrontational management*, by contrast, addresses how you handle situations that, if mismanaged, could escalate to violence.

Confrontations of this sort include:

- Road rage
- Someone giving you a dirty look and approaching you with some variation of "What are you looking at?"
- A conflict occurring between others in which you (perhaps as a manager, schoolteacher, parent, or security professional) decide to intervene

By our earlier definition, we classify the primary instigators of these dynamics as Potential Bad Guys, not because they're bad people, or even necessarily predisposed to violence the way a Professional or Predatory Bad Guy might be, but rather because there is the distinct potential for violence to occur. Potential Bad Guy scenarios are driven primarily by situational factors: maybe the guy just lost his job, or his girlfriend just dumped him, he's drunk or high, or maybe he feels slighted, disrespected, or upset for any variety of reasons. Functionally, you may be completely unaware of the situational factors that underlie the issue, but in the moment, for whatever reason, you find yourself either being targeted or obligated to intervene. Either way, you need to manage the situation carefully.

The good thing is that most situationally driven interviews are easily managed or defused, as it almost always takes two to tango. Take a road rage situation, for example. If someone gets road-ragey with you and you simply wave an apology and calmly-assertively refuse to engage with the interview, the overwhelming majority of the time, the situation will simply defuse. If you engage with it aggressively in return, the situation could easily escalate. Always remember that to truly control dynamics such as this, you must remain the alpha. Stay calm-assertive. Engaging with this situation is beneath you and a sign of weakness, not strength; and as an alpha, you simply don't need to prove yourself to anyone.

One of my clients shared a self-effacing story with me once. He was driving with his teenage son in the passenger seat when another driver cut him off in traffic. Both father and son had trained with me. My client lost his temper and proceeded to engage in high risk, back-and-forth, rage-driven driving with the driver of the other vehicle, who engaged him right back. This give-and-take went on for a couple of minutes until both cars ended up stopped in bottlenecked traffic.

My client, despite all his training and better judgment, threw the car in park and jumped out of the vehicle to angrily confront the driver stopped ahead of him. It turns out that this driver was another teenager. After yelling at the young man who was now scared out of his wits, my client returned to his car.

He explained to me that, the moment he saw the horrified look on his son's face, his anger evaporated and was replaced by a sense of shame. He realized not only how foolish and dangerous his behavior had been but what a terrible example it had set for his son. He apologized to his son for his behavior and discussed how inappropriately he had handled the situation on so many levels.

"What would Sam have done?" his son asked.

"Nothing," my client replied.

And that was exactly right. I wish I could say that I'm a paragon of perfection in this regard, but I can't. I still occasionally catch myself losing my temper or reacting rather than responding, but those times are few and far between nowadays. Being an alpha takes practice and steadfastness, but the mindset is worth cultivating—not only for managing interviews, but for managing all of the difficulties life throws at you. (And I do want to mention that my client above is one of the most truly exceptional people I've ever met, and his behavior was as anomalous as his humility in sharing the story. I've never once seen him lose his temper since.)

The same rules apply if you are interviewed by a Potential Bad Guy via some variation of "What are you looking at?" If you respond with "Not much. What are you looking at?" then you can expect the situation to go nowhere positive. As with the road rage scenario, or any other unwanted approach on the street, the easiest course of action is to just leave. Just take your ball and go home. If some verbal pattern-interrupt is needed you can use the "I can't help you" framework, with a wave or a low volume Stop Sign. Just remain calm-assertive. If you're an alpha, you don't need to prove yourself to anyone, and you can feel free to internalize walking away as doing him a favor rather than being cowed.

Unfortunately, many people let their ego or emotions get the better of them and engage with the interview right back—especially when pride (or alcohol) is involved. They are all too willing to go chest to chest and nose to nose with someone challenging them without a moment's regard for the implications.

In his book *Facing Violence: Preparing for the Unexpected*, former prison guard and expert on violence, Rory Miller, coined the term "the Monkey Dance" to describe this behavior.[69] I find this a very apt term to describe this type

---

69  *Facing Violence: Preparing for the Unexpected.* Rory Miller. YMAA Publication Center. May 1, 2011.

of interview. Most of us who've witnessed a confrontation escalating toward a fistfight have seen this behavior: loud verbal altercation, chest bumping, the combatants getting in each other's faces as they gesticulate aggressively. It looks a lot like two out-of-control monkeys.

We see this kind of behavior often in bar fights, on basketball courts, and on reality TV. In many ways, we see this behavior so often that it has become something of an unconscious go-to reaction for many men and women.

When you see this behavior in a Potential Bad Guy, doing the same thing yourself is the absolute last thing you want to do. First of all, this posture almost never deescalates a situation. Sure, there are times when the Bad Guy might back down, but it is just as likely that he will escalate even further. That is not a coin-flip scenario you want to get into. And if you're nose to nose with someone and the Bad Guy launches an attack, what do you think your chances are of responding? Remember that half-second reaction time gap? Yep, pretty slim. Not to mention how vulnerable you've made yourself by posturing in this ludicrous manner: you've presented some of the most vulnerable parts of your body—your centerline, with your face, throat, solar plexus, and groin—wide open to attack.

As with managing predatory interviews that you can't just leave, the Secret Service Stance and Stop Sign become your primary go-to processes to manage distance. Remaining calm-assertive is vital. Don't get sucked into the challenge. It's one thing if you need to fight back to defend yourself and create an opportunity to escape, and another thing entirely if you engage in the monkey dance and become "mutually combative" in the eyes of witnesses (and for that matter, the law). Engaging with the interview in such a manner could drastically alter your legal protections, and the consequences, should you have to touch someone in self-defense. For more on the legal considerations and realities, see chapter 11.

*Approach Type 4: Inappropriate Pursuits*
While the most common interviews involve an approach, sometimes a Bad Guy will engage in some kind of pursuit or surveillance of you. Sometimes this takes the overt form of following you to see if you are aware of their presence. Following you might also involve waiting for an opportune moment to launch an attack, such as you entering an area of mandatory travel. Professional Bad Guys use surveillance to gather intelligence on their targets, to learn their patterns and vulnerabilities in preparation for an attack. Sometimes, pursuit takes the form of harassing or stalking behavior.

As with an approach-style interview, we must understand the basic forms that an inappropriate pursuit takes so that we can recognize the patterns and disrupt them from escalating. In most pursuit-type interviews, simply recognizing the pursuit for what it is provides significant deterrent from further escalation, and at the minimum, it takes away the Bad Guy's element of surprise.

But in other situations, we need to consider hostile surveillance tactics.

## *Hostile Surveillance*

If you're walking down the street and think someone might be following you, and you don't normally think people are following you, then the first step is to trust your radar. You are likely being followed. But how can we be sure?

Say hello to TEDD, the acronym used in the intelligence community to refer to the aspects of Time, Environment, Distance, and Demeanor.

- *Time*
  In this case, "Time" refers to *instances* of contact. If you notice a stranger more than once, in different locations, the overwhelming odds are that it's not a coincidence—particularly if that person interacts with you and makes you uncomfortable.

  For example, if you see someone at the airport, then see him again at your hotel, this might not be directly indicative that he has been following you, but it should raise a red flag and warrant a deep scan. Again, situational factors are key. Lots of people go from airports to hotels, so this could well be happenstance. But depending on how he behaves once reaching the hotel, he could be following you.

  Is he ahead of you in line to check in? And does he then check into a room? Probably nothing.

  Does he just so happen to be behind you in line, and he doesn't have any luggage? Maybe something.

Remember the concept of the "bump" discussed in chapter 5? If he speaks to you in one or more locations, this should only heighten your awareness. If you randomly cross paths with him in a third location, you can almost completely rule out that this was a coincidence.

▸ *Environment*
There are of course circumstances where seeing the same person on multiple occasions simply means that you are here for the same reason and following the same logical pattern, and not that he is following you. As with everything in personal protection (and in life), context matters.

Maybe you saw him in the airport baggage claim, then at the hotel check-in, and then at a conference hosted in the hotel. As long as he is behaving in the context of how someone following this pattern would be expected to behave—gathering a bag at baggage claim, actually checking in to the hotel, wearing a lanyard for the conference—you have less reason to worry. But if he is not behaving as you would expect most people to behave in those settings, and you keep running into him, look for other indicators or accomplices.

The classic example is the beach. If you go to the beach for the day, you're likely bringing a bag full of sunscreen, towels, a book; you might have a cooler full of food and beverages; maybe you brought beach chairs, an umbrella, or a surfboard. You're almost definitely wearing a swimming suit, or at least some clothing suitable for a hot day under the sun. This is what people who go to the beach do, and this is what they bring and wear.

So if you happen to notice someone on the beach staring at you, and that person is wearing a polo shirt, jeans, and some heavy boots, that should strike a note of concern. This person isn't dressed for the beach, nor is he using the environment for its general purpose. He didn't bring any beach-related items with him. Even if he takes his boots off and rolls up his jeans to make it look like he's trying to enjoy the environment, he clearly didn't plan to come here—at least not initially. If he is also engaged in scanning behavior, and if his gaze keeps returning to you, then you may have trouble.

▸ *Distance*
Bad Guys usually aren't successful because they're particularly good at what they do; rather, they're successful because the good guys have no idea what to look for and fail to spot (or listen to) the obvious warning signs.

From the perspective of a competent observer, Bad Guys are always telegraphing or leaking their intent, and they're usually not that good when it comes to surveillance tactics. When they look for a target, they always telegraph. When they follow that target, they usually follow too closely because they don't want to lose their target.

Just as we discussed earlier regarding proximity during an interview, if someone is too close, there is a reason.

▸ *Demeanor*

Demeanor is the tipping point. If he is exhibiting the signs that you would expect a normal person to exhibit—mostly, that he doesn't seem agitated or particularly focused on you or the people around you—then it may be nothing.

However, the lack of professionalism demonstrated by most Bad Guys manifests itself most frequently in what the intelligence community refers to as *burn syndrome*. Burn syndrome is where the surveillant believes you have spotted him—that his cover is blown and that he has been "made" or "burned."

Your radar will frequently pick up on these limbic indicators. Why is he behaving strangely? Is he just a little too vigilant right now? Is he looking at me with an abnormal frequency or intensity? Is he agitated in a way that doesn't fit the circumstances? In the end, Bad Guys, even if they are generally experienced, always telegraph their intentions, and that telegraphing most readily exhibits itself in their demeanor.

## *What to Do If You're Being Followed*

If you believe that someone is following you, one thing I don't recommend is to confront him. If you call out a Bad Guy for following you, you may actually precipitate an attack right then and there.

Further, there could be reasons that this person is following you that are unrelated to an intent to harm. If you are a business traveler overseas, for instance, some countries' intelligence agencies make a point of surveilling business travelers. You definitely do not want to confront them, or even show that you know about their presence (for more information on this subject, check out my book *The Traveler's Guide to Personal Security*).

Generally, my recommendation is to defeat the surveillance simply by losing your pursuer.

### ON FOOT

If you're on foot, there are two key steps to losing someone who is following you.

*Step 1: Validate the pursuit.*
In the security and intelligence community, we refer to this first step as a *surveillance detection route* (SDR). An SDR can be very sophisticated, involving multiple protection specialists or counter-surveillance teams, or it can be as straightforward as making a few simple maneuvers and seeing if your pursuer is still there. For our purposes here, we'll stick with the simple processes you can easily

remember and execute on your own.

If you're on foot and think you're being followed, the easiest way to validate the pursuit is to simply cross a street and then surreptitiously watch to see if the person following you does the same thing.

Now, if he crosses too, that does not necessarily confirm your suspicion. The confirmation comes later—not too soon, but sometime in the next minute or two—when you cross back to the original side of the street. This time, if he crosses back again, you can be almost certain that you are being followed.

*Step 2: Lose the pursuit.*
Once you have confirmation, what do you do next? Ideally, find a building that has a central entry point but multiple exit routes, such as a restaurant or hotel.

Let's say you choose a restaurant. When you enter, your pursuer will likely pause and wait a few minutes before following you in. This way, they won't seem so obvious. When they arrive, the first thing they will likely do is post up at the bar (or at least somewhere that they can try to reacquire you visually). By that time, you will have already exited the building through a side exit or even through the kitchen. Every restaurant in the world has at least one secondary exit through the kitchen. They need it so they can take out the trash, accept food deliveries, or allow their staff to take breaks outside without having to pass through the main restaurant and front door.

Most people don't consider the kitchen as a potential entry and exit point for the same reason they don't think of backstage at a concert or show as a potential escape route: if you aren't a member of the show or of the kitchen staff, those areas are considered off-limits.

When your pursuer enters the restaurant and doesn't immediately see you, he might think you're in the restroom, and he'll wait to visually reacquire you. Ultimately, by the time he realizes that something is wrong, you will be long gone. This is what my firm calls creating an "Exiting Problem."

Hotels, given their general entry points in the lobby and multiple exits elsewhere, make for strong candidates to create an Exiting Problem for the Bad Guy as well. In any case, if you enter the building and exit immediately, you will have created a considerable amount of distance between you—and distance equals time.

Even the most sophisticated criminal cartels rarely have the manpower or technical expertise to conduct surveillance operations properly, which almost always involves multiple operatives, and possibly sophisticated technology such as aerial reconnaissance assets. In order to know where you've gone, a surveillance team would need to deploy to the entire perimeter of the building from the moment you enter it, and even then, there's no guarantee of their success if you move quickly.

### In a Vehicle

If you're in a car, there are two different tactics based on similar principles.

*Step 1: Run the Crazy Ivan.*

Whether you're driving or are a passenger in a cab or rideshare, if you think someone is following you, the easiest strategy can be drawn from the 1990 classic film *The Hunt for Red October*. In the movie, the Russian submarine *Red October* randomly executes a 360-degree turn to check if they are being pursued in their sonar blind spot. The pursuing sub, the *USS Dallas* calls the maneuver the "Crazy Ivan."

In the real world, the Crazy Ivan is a simpler matter: you make three or more consecutive right turns, essentially circling a city block. If someone is still following you after three consecutive right turns, there is almost no chance that this someone isn't following you intentionally.

*Step 2: Transfer from vehicle to foot without warning.*

Whether you are driving or in a cab or rideshare, the best way to defeat a pursuit is to make a sudden and unexpected change. Without warning, stop the car (or have your driver stop the car) in a safe spot near a location that can create an exiting problem for your pursuer.

You suddenly getting out of the car will leave the Bad Guys disoriented and disorganized. They might not be able to deploy quickly enough to pursue you on foot. They may have trouble parking their car quickly enough to catch up. And even if they manage to keep after you on foot, you are likely to lose them when you enter that restaurant or hotel and immediately exit through a different door.

Whether you're on foot or in a vehicle, once you have evaded your pursuer, what should you do?

*Step 3: Abandon predictable routines.*

The first thing you'll be wondering is: where do you go? Do you go back home? If you're overseas, maybe you should go back to your hotel? The answer to both is, "Probably not, but if you have to, then *be careful!*" Why? Because if you've lost the Bad Guys, where are they most logically going to go next? They're going to try to intercept you in a predictable area of mandatory travel.

The minute they lose you, they'll be on the phone to their other team members to set up stationary surveillance at your hotel or on your home street so that someone will be there waiting to reacquire you.

This is one of the reasons that I tell my clients to always have the essentials on their person when they're traveling. Never go anywhere without everything you would need to either get to an embassy or out of the country. Have your passport, a sufficient amount of cash, and a go bag filled with the essentials you would need to survive a day or two if you had to move quickly. In any situation like this, just forget about anything you might have left at the hotel. Your favorite jeans can be replaced. You can buy another book to read at the airport. There is nothing back there more important than your life.

If you need to go home, do so carefully, staying on your guard when entering areas of mandatory travel.

## Stalkers and Inappropriate Pursuers

Social dynamics are complicated, to say the least—particularly when you find yourself in a relationship that you need to exit. But those complexities can seem to increase exponentially if you find yourself being stalked or pursued in an inappropriate manner. This is an unfortunate reality for one out of six American women in today's world.[70]

For the purposes of this chapter, we won't be doing a deep dive into every aspect of stalking, intimate partner violence, and inappropriate behavior. Rather, we will focus on the critical tactics you need to deter or escape from someone who makes you uncomfortable or who refuses to hear you when you say "No." This could be someone you just met, or someone you've dated or even have a relationship with. The issue is, if you've made the decision to end the interaction, and they aren't hearing you, then you need to recognize that this dynamic could become potentially dangerous if it's not managed appropriately.

Inappropriate pursuit behavior can run the gamut from someone being overly persistent, to invasive and intrusive stalking behaviors, all the way to "If I can't have you, no one can" threats. The key is, when someone's behavior begins to make you uncomfortable, or they refuse to hear you when you say "No," you need to pattern-interrupt the process to deter further unwanted behavior as early as possible. Surprisingly, the response for any of the above pursuit types is fundamentally the same: you must make a clear, direct, and unequivocal refusal or rejection and then disengage from further contact or communication entirely.

I know this may seem harsh. The social veil and the veil

---

of reciprocity, in particular, will want to reject this strategy in favor of "letting someone down easily." After all, you don't want to hurt anyone's feelings, right? The trouble is, persistence does not demonstrate love; it only demonstrates persistence. And when someone refuses to hear your "No," they are telling you they aren't interested in what you want—only what they want. Like water inexorably finding the path of least resistance downhill, any response other than a clear, direct, and unequivocal rejection will be willfully misinterpreted and will invite further persistent behavior. Being clear, direct, and unequivocal in this interaction is not only tactically appropriate; it is in fact the kindest response you can have. Like ripping off a band aid swiftly, it may sting for a moment, but it prevents the issue from lingering and festering.

*"I'm not interested, and I never will be."*
So what does a clear, direct, and unequivocal refusal or rejection sound like?

"I'm not interested in you, and I never will be."

That's it. Say it once, and say it firmly. You can empower the statement even more by adding "I've decided" to the start. "I've decided. I'm not interested in you, and I never will be." This places the power squarely and solely in your hands. It is your decision. No one else's opinion matters.

Notice that this statement isn't qualified in any way. It doesn't contain any modifiers like "…right now." Adding a subtle time stamp like that can leave the pursuer the opportunity to think that you might eventually come around if they're just persistent or patient.

Once the refusal or rejection has been made, it is vital that you disengage from further interaction. Whether you are breaking off contact with someone you just met or breaking off a long-term relationship, if you've decided to end it and they refuse to hear or accept your decision, your next step is to disengage from any further contact or interaction. Obviously, the more complex the relationship, the more complex the disengagement strategy becomes. In the matter of a divorce and custody battle, breaking off all contact may be impossible, but the principle remains. If you cannot disengage totally, only engage when required to do so, and refuse to engage in anything beyond what is necessary.

Engagement feeds the fire. Non-engagement lets it burn out and dissipate—eventually. This is true even though the beginning stages of a non-engagement strategy often play out in a way that make it seem like the strategy is backfiring. Often, the Bad Guy initially pursues harder. Failing to reach you directly, he attempts to reach out to proxies such as mutual friends, family members, or coworkers. He maybe even escalates his behavior from pursuit to threats.

When the pursuer is a sociopath, these manipulations can be very troubling. They are intended to be. He wants to get a reaction from you. Don't fall for it! This progression is nearly as predictable as the TIME-line of Violence itself. All of it represents different moments of what is effectively an ongoing and protracted I of TIME. Sometimes it will feel as though the pursuit itself is the Method of Attack, especially if it takes the form of harassing and intrusive behaviors, but we will reserve that phase and your corresponding ability to respond for chapter 11 and the action-oriented domain of physical defense.

In this regard, deterrence is achieved by denying the Bad Guy the fuel with which he feeds his fire: your interaction.

In the case of breaking off a long-term relationship, use the framework of the clear, direct, and unequivocal statement to craft the message as you see fit. For example: "I've decided that I no longer want to be in a relationship with you, and I am certain I will never again in the future. I intend to file for divorce/see other people/etc., and I suggest you do the same."

As before, the situation may get worse before it gets better, but historically, non-engagement remains the best overall strategy to defuse and deter even complex situations from escalating. Even when you are stuck dealing with a potentially sociopathic ex who uses your kids as pawns in their game, remaining calm-assertive, and carefully modulating any required engagements to just the facts and just what's necessary is almost always the safest course of action—both physically and psychologically.

*"But I want him to stop! I want him to pay!"*
Most victims of inappropriate pursuit, stalking, or abuse justifiably feel a sense of righteous indignation about the dynamics. Most want the pursuer to simply stop, but many want them to pay for the pain they have caused. I understand. And I can certainly relate. After all, why should the victim be the one who needs to modify their lifestyle or behavior? Shouldn't the police or the government be able to intervene and make the pursuer stop? Shouldn't a stalker

or abuser have to pay for the damage they've caused?

Unfortunately, especially when dealing with this particular breed of Bad Guy, justice and security are often mutually exclusive.

As author and speaker Wayne Dyer said, "Never underestimate your power to change yourself, and never overestimate your power to change others." The cold, hard reality is that the only factors the victim fully controls in this equation are their own attitudes and actions. Even attempting to modify the behavior of a pursuer via legal interventions, threats, or other confrontational actions rarely results in positive behavior modification. Typically, it only serves the Bad Guy by adding fuel to his fire. To the pursuer, power and control is the mission, and when they realize they can get you to dance to their tune they feel as if they are succeeding.

From this perspective, interventions of any kind—especially legal interventions—are the height of folly, as you will almost never feel that justice has been served, nor will you feel safer. Mostly, you will just feel tied to your pursuer. This is a result that serves him, not you.

As the Talmud says, "To live well is the best revenge." Without belittling (in any way, shape, or form) the emotions and trauma that a pursuit victim might feel, I always recommend that you try to look past the emotions and analyze the situation from a calm-assertive perspective. What is your real objective? The real objective is not to punish someone, no matter how much they might deserve it: it is to get away; to be able to live your life in peace, without having to deal with this person ever again.

*Interventions*

Sometimes, legal interventions are warranted and may serve to deter further bad behavior. As a general rule, if you can criminally prosecute someone for an act of violence, and it's a path you want to go down, I recommend doing so. Especially if there is a strong likelihood of him being incarcerated as a result. However, the most common legal intervention sought by those being pursued, harassed, or actively abused in an exploitation cycle is to seek help from the police.

Sometimes—particularly if you live in a community with a smaller local police force—the police will speak with and try to warn the offenders from continuing pursuit. But typically, the default law enforcement recommendation is for the victim to seek a restraining order, or what some states call a Personal Protective Order or Protection from Abuse Order.

This occurs for two main reasons:

1.  **It's how police are trained.**
    Functionally, the police can't do much about the situation (except threaten the pursuer with legal consequences) until a law has been broken. Filing a restraining order is the simplest way for them to create an environment where the Bad Guy has to break a law in order to see his target again, and once he does, the police can intervene.

2.  **There's some measure of fatigue involved.**
    Whether they want to admit it or not, many police become exhausted dealing with domestic

abuse cases, especially when the victim seeks help, only to turn on the police in favor of their abuser once intervention is attempted. This dynamic happens quite often. So, law enforcement officers often use the restraining order as a validation step for the victim to demonstrate that they are actually serious about their desire to disengage from the abusive relationship.

In some cases, a warning by the police, or a restraining order and the resulting threat of criminal prosecution, can deter further bad behavior. But somewhere between half and two-thirds of the time, these warnings or protective orders are outright ignored or violated. All too often—at least 21% of the time, by one study— these interventions can escalate the situation to violence.[71] Ultimately, you never want to forget that a restraining order is a paper tiger. It seems to have teeth, but in reality it depends on the Bad Guy's willingness to modify his behavior. This is especially true because the penalties for violation of most restraining orders do not rise above the misdemeanor level, meaning that those violations will not typically remove the offender from society, or from the possibility of getting to or harming you.

From a threat-assessment perspective, the key is not to reflexively seek law enforcement intervention or a

---

71   https://www.domesticshelters.org/resources/statistics/law-enforce-
     ment-and-domestic-violence#.Vvm7FXomQQN

restraining order; it is to carefully evaluate whether doing so would be more likely to deter or to escalate the situation, and to evaluate it as one part of a more comprehensive safety plan to arrive at your ultimate objective of getting away.

Assessing whether a restraining order will be effective, or if it might exacerbate the situation, is something many victims are not equipped—emotionally or tactically—to do without help. My recommendation is to seek professional counsel from those who can objectively evaluate the factors of your situation and who have experience dealing with these matters. A good place to start is the National Domestic Violence Hotline (https://www.thehotline.org). This organization can not only help you develop a safety plan and then provide assistance; they can help you locate local resources, including shelters, should you need a way to escape.

*In the Extreme*
No matter what the situation, just because someone wants to hurt you doesn't mean they can. Ultimately, you are the final arbiter in the equation, and there are always situational factors you can control.

If you believe your pursuer intends to physically harm you, the best defense is, once again, to avoid contact entirely. To control this factor in the most extreme cases may require you to escape to a secure shelter or even relocate out of town entirely. Sometimes, this even involves changing your identity, abandoning your previous life, and literally disappearing, like in the witness protection program.

Before you throw this book across the room, please understand that I know how extreme, difficult, and invasive a suggestion this is. And I also recognize how fundamentally unfair it is that this may be the best strategy. But avoidance and escape are almost always preferable to living in constant fear of violence—particularly if you have kids to consider and do not have the financial resources to hire 24/7 close protection.

This is not a strategy I like to recommend, nor is it one I've had to recommend more than a few times in my career, but it is a strategy nonetheless. And while I know that it can feel as though the cure is worse than the disease, I mention it to demonstrate that even in the worst case scenario, you always have some options.

At the end of the day, however, whatever course of action you take in an effort to deter the Bad Guy, you are responsible for your own protection and must make those critical decisions. If avoidance fails, and you must take physical action to defend yourself and your loved ones, you have the power to do so. But first you must be both willing and able.

# CHAPTER 11

# Defend: When Violence is the Answer

For seven years after my discharge from the Marines, I worked as a close protection specialist and, when not on assignment, I taught a sophisticated system of self-defense. The system addressed situations as varied as one-on-one scenarios, multiple opponents, weapon disarms, and just about everything in between. It was light years beyond anything I'd ever encountered before, despite having trained in multiple martial arts disciplines, collegiate wrestling, and a variety of practical self-defense systems.

But one day, I had a client share an experience with me that changed my perspective and forced me to reevaluate not only what I was teaching but how I was teaching it.

Jim was an executive at a commercial real estate firm and had been training with me privately for a couple of years. He was well into the training, having begun to learn techniques and processes to defend against some genuinely complex scenarios. He also happened to be a pretty tough guy—certainly no pushover, physically or mentally. One day, when he arrived for his session, I noticed that his body language was off. His head was hanging, and he looked a little dejected as he came into the training studio.

"What's going on?" I asked.

"I got into this confrontation the other day," he explained. "This guy was in my face, you know, yelling and gesticulating with his hands. I kept my cool and stood my ground, but the whole time, I'm thinking to myself, *This thing could get physical really fast*, and honestly, I wasn't sure what I was supposed to do… Should I move first? If so, what should I do? Throw a knee strike or a kick? Or should I grab him and try to do a joint lock or a takedown? What if he moves first? How am I going to manage it?"

The more he thought about potential options, the more his mind reeled. At the moment of truth, instead of having purpose and direction, he experienced only confusion. He didn't know what his priorities were in the moment, or how to achieve them.

Ultimately, the confrontation resolved without any violence, and while Jim was glad it didn't escalate, he was very unhappy with how he felt about it afterward. He had this sense that he had somehow failed in his training.

In reality, it was his training that had failed him. He had certainly trained hard and learned how to execute a variety of techniques at a highly competent level, but when the moment of truth arrived he still froze—not because he didn't have any options, but because he had *too many* options. He found himself suffering from paralysis by analysis. Regardless of his level of physical competency, I had failed to achieve the most critical objective of training with him: the ability to think and make decisions under pressure—specifically, to know what to do and when to do it, not just *how* to do it.

This forced me to critically reexamine and evolve the physical skillsets and teaching methodologies I was using. I needed to find a way to achieve balance between the technical skills and the mindset. More specifically, I wanted to ensure that my clients always knew not just how to defend themselves but also what their priorities were at any moment along the continuum of conflict. The new training had to teach them how to recognize danger in advance, manage interviews, and know unequivocally, if they had to take physical action, what that action should be.

I needed my clients to develop an internal navigation system from which they could become problem solvers, even under the effects of Red Zone adrenaline stress, all within a framework that is technically, legally, and morally viable in the real world. To meet all these needs, it occurred to me that the system of decision making had to be as simple and intuitive as driving a car.

I never again wanted one of my clients to say to me, "I didn't know what to do..."

## *What This Chapter is About*

With respect to all the authors who've come before me and attempted to teach physical skills via books, it seems to me that this is functionally impossible with anything but the most basic stances or principles. This medium simply makes it incredibly difficult to learn dynamic skills in a way that will be practically effective.

This is not to say that you can't learn critical strategies or principles; it's just a reality that no matter how I may try, how thoroughly I may write about each technique, and how hard you study, a book simply isn't a viable medium for imparting physical skillsets or for conditioning your nervous system to use those skills under pressure. Any attempt to do so, knowing that I can't achieve the right outcomes, would, to me, lack integrity.

So instead, what I'm going to provide you in this chapter is something that I believe to be far more valuable, something that will serve you far better: I'm going to teach you what I've learned over a lifetime of practicing and teaching personal protection skills and tactics. Specifically, I'm going to impart the criteria by which you can discern what works, what doesn't, and most importantly, understand *why* they work or don't work. These criteria will help you competently and confidently select the right training, skills, and tools to meet your specific and personal goals. Whether you're a complete novice, a law enforcement officer, a professional soldier, or an experienced martial arts practitioner, this perspective will better enable you to define (and refine) the skills and tools you need to manage violence in the real world.

Since we are not born with the skills to defend ourselves, everybody fundamentally needs training in how to respond to violence. A quick caveat to go with that: for some people and some circumstances, defensive tools or force multipliers such as firearms may be the best option. Again, I'm taking an agnostic stance on the subject of weapons. But if you do choose to defend yourself in this way, training is the essential first step.

So, let's turn to the subject of training.

## *The Renaissance of Personal Protection*

There's no question that we're living in interesting times. From a personal security standpoint, unprecedented advancements in technology and communications have ushered in what I think of as a renaissance in training and tactics.

In 1993, Art Davie and Brazilian martial artist Rorion Gracie introduced us all to the Ultimate Fighting Championship, or UFC as it's known today. Of course, this wasn't the first time such a competition existed. The idea of Mixed Martial Arts (MMA), combining grappling and stand-up fighting, has existed in different forms and at different periods throughout history, going all the way back to the ancient Greek Olympic version of MMA called Pankration. Pankration likely resembled what we see in today's modern MMA, combining striking and grappling in a type of no-holds-barred competition (except that it was done in the nude...I know, right?).

But prior to 1993, martial arts were generally clois-tered into very specific traditional styles: Karate, Tai Kwon Do, Kung Fu, Judo, etc. The practitioners of these traditional arts rarely crossed over into exploring other styles, and even their competitive matches followed rules designed to further their specific style and keep others out.

Many martial artists viewed their style much as some people view religion; they thought that their way was the right one and the only one, and that everyone else was wrong.

In the 1960s and early '70s, Bruce Lee become famous, not just through his movies, but as a pioneer in the martial arts. He veered away from the prevailing insular type of thinking and was one of the very few martial artists who openly explored, experimented with, and taught styles and tactics from varied martial arts disciplines. He wanted to be guided only by what worked, instead of what was traditional.

Lee viewed the field of martial arts as a "classical mess" and railed against doing things in a certain way just because it was the way it had always been done. And he was largely hated, attacked, and condemned for his beliefs by many of the leaders in the martial arts world. But Bruce Lee's courage, skills, and scientific approach laid the foundation for every martial artist and personal security trainer in today's world—a foundation that calls for us to explore, experiment, and collaborate to advance ourselves and the field. In many respects, he paved the way.[72]

As Victor Hugo said, "there's nothing more powerful than an idea whose time has come." Two decades after Lee's

---

72  There were of course others, both known and unknown, who similarly went against the grain, but for the purpose of this section, I have chosen to mention only Bruce Lee, as he was undeniably the most influential of his day. I mean no disrespect in omitting any other worthy pioneers, and please forgive me for doing so for the purpose of brevity.

death, the UFC changed everything. Advertised originally as the ultimate experiment to see which martial arts style was superior, early UFC events pitted stand-up fighters against grapplers, throwing divergent styles against each other to see which emerged superior.

Since those early experiments, modern MMA has evolved. Rules were set in place, as were weight classes. Athletes naturally gravitated to a combination of skillsets designed to address both stand-up and ground fighting capabilities. If you wanted to be a fighter, MMA was the way.

In the early '90s, self-defense training was generally an offshoot of traditional martial arts styles, and trainers geared it almost exclusively toward women. Most self-defense tactics were, by today's standards, simply ineffective. Back then, most people thought of self-defense as foot stomps and eye pokes. Part of the problem was the general lack of codified, scientific understanding of how the body performs under the effects of survival-level adrenaline. And what little was known was rarely incorporated into training methodologies.

With the advent of the Internet and the communications age, things changed. For the first time in modern history, physical techniques and strategies were able to be tested and evaluated objectively by many people. The science of physiological human performance was studied and codified and began to be incorporated into training methods. Finally, practical knowledge of criminal psychology and data, coupled with thousands of real-world attacks caught on film and widely shared and evaluated through social media, allowed experts on violence to begin to develop training methods centered on data rather than tradition. This led to the emergence and expansion of what the industry termed "practical martial arts." These more practical approaches to defense were designed to address violence and self-defense in the real world, not just to make you the best *fighter*.

In many ways, this book is a culmination of the knowledge and lessons learned through this renaissance of personal protection techniques and tradecraft—specifically, the more practical side of the equation—in an effort to make this critical knowledge more readily available.

Collectively, this renaissance has been a boon to anyone wanting to learn how to protect themselves. The problem is that only the *dynamics* have changed; the fundamental challenge of finding competent instruction remains. Many of the same old mentalities and belief systems persist today, and while easy access to information benefits everyone and everything, such easy access has caused the industry to become flooded with good advice and also some very bad advice, and with competent instructors as well as irresponsible ones.

Nowadays, you can't throw a stick without it hitting someone who calls themselves an expert on personal protection. Given the sheer number of choices and competing opinions, it's often difficult for people to separate the wheat from the chaff. The matter becomes all the more difficult when you know less about the subject than you would prefer. When that's the case, anyone who knows even a little, or even just anyone with strong opinions, can seem to know a lot.

This is why this chapter seeks a more effective way to think about training: so you can be more discerning as you navigate these treacherous waters.

## *Vertical, Not Horizontal*

After my experience with Jim, I realized that the problem with every martial art and self-defense system I'd ever learned, including the system I had been teaching, was that they were "horizontal" by nature.

Let me explain.

Every martial art and self-defense system, for various reasons, presents a variety of techniques that you can deploy against a variety of stimuli. What this means is that you typically learn multiple techniques, or solutions, to the same problem. For example, you might be taught four or five solutions to respond to a simple attack like a right-hand punch. You could learn response options to block it, or redirect it, or counter it, or evade it, or any combination of the above, in any number of ways.

Assuming that all the options are equally practical, if you have to choose from options A, B, C, D, or E at the critical moment of the attack, then you simply have too many options to choose from. Having too many options creates a decision-making dilemma that can easily lead to the type of analysis paralysis that Jim experienced.

The primary reason most systems teach this way lies in the general approach to teaching martial arts. The common approach is to teach a variety of skills or options with the expectation that you will then evaluate which ones work

305

best for you and focus only on the skillsets you prefer to keep in your personal skills matrix.

The problem with this basic theory is that your ability to discern and retain only what works for you versus what doesn't is highly dependent on experience, and often on athletic ability. This means that for you to evaluate and determine which skills work "for you," you need sufficient experience attempting to use those skills, and under the specific circumstances where you would have to use them (e.g. in competition, or during an attack on the street). This of course assumes that all of the skills you've been taught have efficacy in the first place (many simply do not).

Well, if you don't intend to get into a bunch of street fights to see what works and what doesn't, how are you supposed to legitimately figure out which skills you're going to rely on for self-defense? This is obviously a nonstarter for people simply looking to learn how to protect themselves, and no single person is likely to find themselves in, let alone survive, enough real-world experiences to evaluate skillsets objectively.

The solution that most martial arts land on, as a result, is sparring, where you can theoretically test your skills in a controlled, purely athletic environment. While I believe there can be great value in sparring if done right, sparring brings with it a plethora of other complications and issues.

First, implicit in the notion of sparring is that we can now only choose techniques and targets that, by nature, are safe enough to use while still minimizing risk of serious injury to you and your partner. This limits the tools you practice with to striking or grappling techniques, or a combination of both in the case of MMA. In addition, you must scrupulously avoid targeting some of the most vulnerable parts of the body for safety's sake. And of course, it becomes almost impossible to address real-world issues, such as weapons and multiple opponents, within these limits.

Despite all this, if you are mentally willing and physically able to engage in sparring practice long term, you can develop better reflexes, skills, and experience to effectively become a competent fighter. When done right, this isn't a bad thing. The problem is that this process is simply not feasible for the vast majority of those just looking to learn how to defend themselves. And even under the best of circumstances, it takes considerable time, often years.

On top of this, the biggest limitation is that by its very nature, the act of sparring is competitive. On the one hand, competitive training provides the laboratory in which you can test your skills, and yourself, under pressure and become better desensitized to the stress of violence. On the other hand, it means that your skills need to continually expand as your opponents learn your tricks and tactics. This forces a never-ending "arms race" of skill building.

Put another way, competitive training, by its nature, forces your skills matrix and corresponding decision making to become even more "horizontal."

The inherent complexities and stress associated with real-world violence, as we know from chapter 4, are different than competitive stress. As a result, they require a different approach—one that I have come to think of as "vertical" by nature.

In a vertical system, there is no confusion. Any one stimulus is responded to via a single, carefully selected, and reflexively trained response. One stimulus, one response. Simple. Let's call it Plan A. When you're faced with that stimulus, your brain doesn't need to filter through a slew of possible responses to somehow choose the best one; you simply respond immediately with Plan A. To allow for problem solving, if Plan A doesn't work, then we have a Plan B. But if Plan B doesn't work, we don't go to Plan C, D, or E; we revert to Plan A.

The skills you choose to absorb into your self-defense toolbox must be simple enough to work in the Red Zone of stress, and then, obviously, they must be effective. The skills must also become a matter of unconscious competence, meaning that you can use them automatically. If all of this is true, then the vertical approach will streamline your tactical responses so that you can still think and make decisions strategically during the heat of the moment.

In a perfect world, you arrive at a system that looks like a funnel, whereby you actually codify a wide range of attack stimuli and funnel them into a carefully selected handful of response protocols which are simple enough to work in the real world, allow for adaptation and problem solving, and can be trained enough to become reflexive and be retained long term, even if you've been out of training for a while.

The basis for this approach is a scientific principle called Hick's Law (sometimes referred to as the Hick-Hyman Law), named after psychologists William Edmund Hick and Ray Hyman. In a nutshell, the study that led to this law examined an individual's reaction time relative to the number of stimuli they had to choose from.[73] Unsurprisingly, the more choices a person faces, the longer it will take that person to make a decision. This applies in any setting or circumstance, but when it comes to the layer of split-second, crisis-level decision making needed in a violent altercation (along with all the stress that accompanies), suddenly it becomes extremely important to avoid cluttering your mind with too many options.

Tony Blauer, one of the world's leading authorities on personal security, defensive tactics, and scenario-based training, bases his approach on the human physiological response to danger and attack stimuli. It was Blauer who first introduced me to Hick's Law and the notion that the best self-defense response is often the one that reduces the user's choices to a minimum. In keeping with Hick's Law, any number of options greater than two will slow you down dramatically and functionally create critical failure points in your response continuum. In the face of real-world, life-and-death decision points, you need a vertical, binary approach.

## What Are You Training For?

Understanding the difference between horizontal and vertical approaches is critical, but only in so much as it relates to your ultimate training objectives. If you want

---

73   Hick, W. E. "On the rate of gain of information." *Quarterly Journal of Experimental Psychology.* 4(4:1): 11-26, 1952.

to be a competitive boxer or UFC fighter, you will need a much larger, more complex toolbox. You will also need more extensive training to be capable of prioritizing and deciding which tools to use and when to use them within a broad horizontal matrix that you will encounter within the ring or the cage. But if you want to be able to defend yourself on the street, and you have little or no interest in competing with anyone, you likely don't need to commit years of practice to rigorous martial arts training, sparring, and competition.

Make no mistake, you need training. Everyone does. But your training must be specific to the environment you need to perform in. If you're training for self-defense in the real world, then there are no controls or expectations. Weapons and multiple adversaries, and other complicating factors, may be present; you may have your family with you; or there may be significant unknown factors or the fog of war; and legal consequences for your actions are ever present.

This dimension of training demands that you be very careful with what skills you decide to rely on, and you need a vertical decision-making process not just to perform, but to avoid critical pitfalls.

If you are going to train, you therefore first have to decide what, specifically, you are training for.

*The Three Types of Defensive Training*

1. **Self-defense**
   Even though the real world presents the most complicated and stressful dimensions of violence,

real-world self-defense is often the easiest to accomplish. This is because the central objective of self-defense is simple: to escape.

The ideal self-defense training will teach you how to recognize danger, give you a simple tree of options to avoid it, and then (as a last resort, if violence becomes the only answer) provide you with functional, adaptable, simple techniques to create an opportunity to escape. Even if you have to fight your way out, your ultimate objective should always be the same.

It's not about defeating an opponent, or being the toughest fighter, or subduing the Bad Guy until the police arrive. It's about creating the time and opportunity for you to get to safety. As a former CIA field agent I worked with once said, "I'm convinced that running is the world's most underrated self-defense technique." If you're able to run away from a conflict, then you have won.

Escape is often the easiest objective to achieve, because, as we've discussed throughout this book, most Bad Guys fundamentally need a soft target to succeed. They need a target who cannot or will not fight back. If you swiftly and competently respond to an attack, the vast majority of Bad Guys will realize that they have selected the wrong target and will want nothing more than to escape themselves.

Even if your opponent is bigger, faster, and stronger than you, if he wants to go one way and you want to go the other, escape becomes a fairly easily achieved objective.

2. **Defensive Tactics**

The term Defensive Tactics generally refers to the realm of law enforcement. The key difference between self-defense as it exists for private citizens and defensive tactics as it applies to law enforcement is that the goal changes from escape to apprehension.

The problem here is obvious: if a Bad Guy wants to escape, and a police officer is trying to stop him, then we have the potential for a much higher level of violence to ensue. The mere presence of a law enforcement officer brings with it the threat of apprehension itself, which often leads to extreme violent reactions even during what seem like relatively benign police interactions, such as traffic stops. This dynamic in itself means that police officers must have a higher level of training and capacity, both mentally and physically.

The ability to recognize pre-attack indicators that could presage an ambush becomes even more critical. Similarly important are the physical skills, stamina, and will to restrain and subdue someone who doesn't want to be restrained.

3. **Combatives**

Here we arrive at basically every Hollywood depiction of hand-to-hand fighting. Think of any action movie you've ever seen, from Jason Bourne to 007, or John Wick. What you're seeing is a well-trained Good Guy going against (a) well-trained Bad Guy(s), and neither side intends to back down. The fight will continue until one of the combatants utterly defeats the other.

This is exactly the same manifestation of violence we see in the realm of combat sports such as wrestling, boxing, and martial arts. Two well-trained competitors duking it out, and no one is going to surrender. In this environment, your goal is to defeat your opponent.

Does this manifestation of violence occur in the real world? Sure it does. Though it is extremely rare.

For all the reasons explained throughout this book, real-world violence almost never becomes competitive. Even when dealing with Professional Bad Guys or the situational volatility of a Potential Bad Guy, competitive violence is unusual. Bad Guys are very careful in the selection of their prey and the circumstances under which they execute an attack. This is expressly to ensure that the situation does not *become* competitive.

On one level, there's simply too much risk and potential for failure if the Bad Guy chooses a target who is willing and able to fight back in a competitive fashion. But on a deeper level, I would argue that the basic character and qualities necessary to become competitive at any level of violence—the grit, resilience, discipline, humility, and dedication necessary to engage in training—are fundamentally lacking in most Bad Guys' psychology. Remember, all criminal violence exists on the character-disordered side of the Teeter Totter of Personal Responsibility discussed in chapter 8.

This does not mean, of course, that you don't find Bad Guys who are physically tough or capable of committing horrendous acts of violence. What it means is that even the physically toughest Bad Guys are usually still psychologically brittle and therefore incapable of standing up to a willing and able responder. This is why even the biggest, toughest Bad Guys rely on careful target selection and strategies and tactics designed to give them an advantage—such as the element of surprise, or force multipliers like weapons. Again, they just want to ensure that the fight does not *become* competitive.

Does this mean that it's impossible to ever find yourself in a competitive fistfight on the street? No. What it means is that if you get into a competitive fight with someone on the street, almost always, it was a scenario that you chose to engage in. Usually, if you make this choice, you owe it all to your ego. It's like two college kids in a bar "taking it outside." They're only doing this for their own sense of pride. Regardless of the controls or expectations (or lack thereof), this is not a self-defense situation; it is by definition a mutually combative, competitive fight that you willingly participated in. This type of behavior, as we will discuss in detail in a moment, also brings with it significant legal implications.

The only place you frequently see competitive dynamics apply to real-world violence is in the realm of warfighting. Not always, but sometimes. Sometimes you have well-trained, dedicated, and highly motivated troops on both sides of a conflict, and neither side is going to back down. Both sides employ every conceivable tactic and strategy to defeat their adversaries and win.

But even in examining warfare as a context for the need for combative training, sustained competitive engagements are extremely rare, and close quarters, hand-to-hand fighting is rarer still. Historically speaking, whenever one side gains a dominant advantage, or appears to do so, the other side typically retreats. Additionally, modern warfare technologies have made hand-to-hand combat on the battlefield far less common than it used to be.

If you have to fight—whether at the macro level of war or the micro level of two people duking it out—it's always better to hold a position of advantage, whether that be the high ground, the element of surprise, or the overwhelming force to avoid the conflict becoming competitive.

This is simple logic, as competitive fights ensure that both sides suffer.

Sun Tzu's *The Art of War*, written some 2,500 years ago, is filled with this fundamental wisdom.[74] At the pinnacle of *The Art of War*, we find the precept: "the greatest victory is that which requires no battle." But if you have to fight, one of the core dictates is to always leave your adversary an escape route. You never want to fully encircle an enemy force, because if you leave them no escape route the enemy may fight to the death out of desperation, much like a cornered animal. But if you give them an exit, and you have the advantage, they will almost always take it—allowing you to more safely and easily destroy them as they flee, if that is indeed the objective.

If you are a professional soldier, I would argue that you need a combative toolbox, because you could run into a fanatical or well-trained adversary, and you will need the skills, stamina, will, and tools to prevail if the fighting becomes hand to hand.

Modern MMA training can be a solid foundation for this approach. As a fighting system, MMA has proven itself effective against trained and competitive opponents. But remember that MMA is only part of the equation, because you

---

74    Sun Tzu, translated by Thomas Cleary. *The Art of War*. Shambhala, 2005.

still need to address real-world dynamics such as weapons and multiple opponents—the elements of violence that occur outside of the controls and expectations inherent in a controlled competitive environment. And because your tools must still be viable under the effects of Red Zone adrenaline, I would advocate that you still need to refine and focus your MMA skills into a vertical approach designed for the real world. Just practicing MMA or other competitive martial arts systems will not do this for you.

However, the biggest issue with training in an exclusively competitive fashion is that you begin to assume that every encounter is going to become competitive and will therefore require significant force. And for citizens as well as law enforcement, this could come with serious legal consequences...

## *The Legal Implications*

Using force, or deadly force, in the real world is like walking a minefield, and any training you choose *must* be capable of helping you understand and navigate such dangerous terrain. This is why any training you choose must be more than just tactically sound. It must also be legally and morally sound.

With that in mind, it would be virtually impossible to try to educate you fully on the legalities of the use of force within the confines of this chapter. The subject could easily span an entire book.[75] But to leave this critical facet of personal protection unaddressed would be a disservice. My goal is to provide you with at least enough capacity to be able to make educated decisions about your own training.

Just to remove all doubt, let me be clear about what my objective with this section is and what it is not. My objective is *not* to do a deep dive into all aspects of the laws pertaining to self-defense, their nuances, interpretations, and precedents, nor am I going to evaluate a series of case studies. My objective, rather, is to give you a foundational understanding of the principles that govern the use of force, so that you can discern whether the systems, tactics, techniques, and tools you may choose to train in are legally appropriate for your personal security needs. This section in no way provides legal advice. It is designed merely as a measuring tool for selecting the training that is legally appropriate and is right for you.

Let's begin with the basics. On TV, you often see people claiming that they acted in "self-defense." The idea of self-defense is a simple and universally understood notion that if the circumstances are appropriate, a person has a right to protect themselves from grievous harm. I have

---

75   There are numerous resources designed to provide a deeper understanding of this subject matter. Two books I highly recommend exploring: *In the Gravest Extreme: The Role of the Firearm in Personal Protection*, by Massad Ayoob (one of my mentors) (Police Bookshelf, 1980), and *The Laws of Self-Defense Principles* by Andrew Branca, Perfect Paperback, 2020.

always found that the law as it relates to self-defense, especially in the United States, is founded on great wisdom, born of many generations of people wrestling with the question of what is right and what is wrong and attempting to come to grips with how people should fundamentally treat each other.

Simply speaking, the law does not like it when people touch each other—or more directly, try to harm each other unlawfully. Attempts to kill each other, successful or otherwise, are obviously frowned upon as well. So, because the law doesn't like it when people touch each other, what this means is that if someone attacks you and you respond with some level of force to protect yourself, the perspective of the law is that both parties are fundamentally in the wrong. However, logic and the wisdom of the law recognize that if someone tries to hurt you, you may be justified in using force to protect yourself. This principle of *justification* is the mechanism by which one can claim self-defense.

There are numerous factors that go into determining whether you are in fact justified in your actions. The most important factor to understand is that there are two distinct levels of force under the law: Force and Deadly Force. Force refers to violence directed against a person, or the threat of force used to compel. Deadly force is defined as force that is intended to cause, or that carries a substantial risk of causing, death or serious bodily injury.

Consider this scenario: someone assaults you by grabbing you by the shirt and pushing you up against a wall. As your mind hits the analysis phase of the SAFE process, you flash back to a memory of some martial arts instructor on YouTube demonstrating a technique to respond to just such an attack. In response, you do what he did: you take your thumb and jam it into your attacker's eye. Could the technique work to create an opportunity to escape? Possibly. But what level of force have you used? Force or deadly force?

Believing that there is virtually no way the attacker is going to die from such a response, most people say "Force." But we have to remember that deadly force includes force that can cause "serious bodily injury." It is in this gray area that a lot of confusion—and legal problems—can arise.

The legal definition of *serious bodily injury* is "bodily injury which involves—(a) a substantial risk of death; (b) protracted and obvious disfigurement; or (c) protracted loss or impairment of the function of a bodily member, organ, or mental faculty."[76] If we are evaluating our example based on the definition above, then jamming your thumb into someone's eye could be considered use of deadly force. And this isn't because you could have killed him (death would have been a considerably unlikely outcome), but because you could have disfigured or maimed him such that he could lose the function of that bodily organ. In other words, you could blind him, and so this could be construed as deadly force.

Most reasonable and prudent people evaluating this case of use of force would likely feel the same. Incidentally, this is what is known as the Reasonable Person standard of law.

76    21 U.S. Code § 802(25).

Simply put, would an otherwise reasonable and prudent person have acted the same way, in the same situation, knowing what the defendant (you) knew? If you asked a group of otherwise reasonable and prudent people—like, say, a jury of twelve of your peers—"If I jam my thumb into someone's eye, could that person at least suffer serious bodily injury?" and they say "Yeah…" then guess what level of force that is?

You got it: deadly force.

Why is this important? Yes, you were attacked; but if your choice of technique to defend yourself crosses the line from the use of force into the use of deadly force, and that amount of force is considered excessive according to the reasonable person standard of law, then your actions may no longer be considered justified under the law, and you could lose your legal protections.

But you were attacked! Can't you use any means necessary to defend yourself? No. You can't. Under the law, private citizens can only use an equal (or proportionate) amount of force to what is brought against them by their attacker. If you are faced with the threat of force, you cannot and should not respond with techniques or tools that would constitute deadly force. This means you shouldn't shoot someone with a firearm, hit him in the head with a baseball bat, stab him with a knife, run him over with your car, or anything else that could reasonably pose substantial risk of death or serious bodily injury.

The generally accepted principle is that private citizens can use whatever force is necessary to stop or escape the threat, but not deadly force. The only time you are legally allowed to use deadly force is when you are defending yourself, or another, from the threat of deadly force. This is the essence of proportionality.

Police are given a greater degree of latitude when they need to use force while in their official capacity, like when they are making an arrest. But, interestingly, the standard for when deadly force is justified is virtually the same both for law enforcement and for private citizens.

When it comes to self-defense, the four most universally accepted conditions where deadly force is justified are if you are defending yourself, or another, from the imminent threat of death, serious bodily injury, rape, or kidnapping, and you have no other choice. Once again, your justification will be examined against a number of conditions, including:

- ▸ Could you have avoided the situation or retreated safely instead of resorting to a violent response?
- ▸ What led to the incident, and did you provoke it or contribute to its escalation?
- ▸ Were you in jeopardy? Meaning, would another reasonable person have similarly viewed the threat as imminent and necessitating an immediate response?
- ▸ Where did the incident take place—in your home, on the street, etc.?
- ▸ Did you stop the violence when the threat ceased?

As you can see, using force in the real world comes with many considerations, implications, and consequences. Almost universally at this point, my clients ask two very logical questions:

1. What if the Bad Guy is much bigger or stronger than me?
2. How in the world am I supposed to figure all of this out in the heat of the moment?

Let's address these one at a time.

The question of size and strength emerges logically, and quite frequently, from my more diminutive or elderly clients. Size, strength, and physical capacity are obviously all important factors in one's ability to defend oneself, and anyone telling you otherwise is simply misleading you.

As it applies to the law, there is a protective concept that takes this into consideration. It's called "Disparity of Force." Common disparity of force considerations include: an attacker with an overwhelming size or strength differential; significant age disparity, such as a twenty-something attacking a seventy-year-old; infirmity, such as the defender having physical impairments; disparity of training, such as one party having advanced combat training or competitive fighting experience; or multiple attackers.

The law often takes these factors into consideration in determining whether a defender is justified in resorting to deadly force to stop an unarmed attacker. So, if we take our previous scenario and add the context that it's a 6'3", 285-pound man grabbing a 120-pound woman by the shirt and pushing her up against a wall, she may very well be considered justified in using a deadly force technique, such as jamming her thumb in his eye or using a defensive tool such as a firearm.

The second question, "How in the world am I supposed to figure all of this out in the heat of the moment?" is another matter entirely. There is one simple answer: training.

I said *simple*, not *easy*.

The legal implications of using force or deadly force, even in self-defense, are significant, and this complexity means that you must plan for and define your responses in advance. Whatever training you choose must not only give you the skills to protect yourself from the initial attack but also protect you from the legal battle that may ensue. Ultimately, you and only you will be held accountable for your actions, and that accountability begins by ensuring that the tactics you learn will be legally compliant. This is a huge part of why your choice of training is so important.

Several years ago, I received a call from an acquaintance who was a young MMA competitor and instructor. He'd gotten into a bar fight and was facing some serious legal consequences, and he wanted my help as an expert witness pertaining to Use of Force. When we discussed what happened, he explained that a verbal altercation led to the other guy throwing a punch at his face. He deflected the punch, then reflexively grabbed the other guy behind the neck with both hands and drove his knee into his face. When his opponent fell to the ground, my acquaintance automatically straddled him and proceeded to throw a few more punches while on top of his downed opponent.

These tactics and techniques are fairly standard maneuvers in the realm of Mixed Martial Arts and full-contact combatives. My acquaintance certainly "won" the "fight." But it was quite obvious, when considering the reasonable person standard, that his actions, and the serious injuries his opponent suffered, exceeded proportionality. My acquaintance did what he was trained to do, and as a result he faced lifechanging consequences far exceeding the danger he initially faced. There was little I could do to help him.

Once again, as first quoted in chapter 3, "We don't rise to the occasion; we fall to the level of our training." Archilochus's 2,500-year-old statement applies not just to our ability to respond but to our attitudes and ability to think and make decisions under pressure. This is why it's so important to select the right training, and to select it for the right reasons. If you train for combative arts, where you are expecting every fight to be a significant competitive engagement, then, in a Bad Guy situation, you may quite easily use more force than necessary or persist after the threat has been reasonably stopped.

Many martial arts, and even some self-defense systems, teach the idea of meeting aggression with greater aggression. Some teach responding to virtually any attack with counterattacks that could cause serious bodily injury. Many do this because they don't know any better. Others do it because they just don't care about the legalities. I can't tell you how often I've heard the cliché "I'd rather be tried by twelve than carried by six," spoken by supposedly professional instructors. While I certainly agree that your first priority should be to survive, those who flippantly make such declarations are in fact loudly proclaiming that they just don't get it. I doubt anyone who would say something like this has ever had to face violence in the real world, because if they had had to deal with the legal consequences they would never be so flippant with the lives of those they are teaching.

Be careful whose opinions and advice you take regarding your safety and your training for personal security. Too much is at stake to take this lightly.

Let me be clear: I'm not suggesting that you shouldn't practice combative arts, or that you should avoid learning deadly force tactics. I'm merely saying that if you do so, make sure you understand when they're appropriate. If you find yourself fighting for your life like Anthony Smith did, as discussed in chapter 4, you may need deadly force responses to keep you or your loved ones alive. In such extremes, nothing less may suffice. But what's far more important is understanding how to avoid trouble in the first place—to actively deny and deter threats so that you don't need to resort to defense. And if you do need to defend yourself, it's critical to have trained yourself how to do so within a framework that is not only tactically but legally and morally sound.

## *The Moral Implications*

The legal and the moral generally coincide, but to be clear, *morality* is understanding the difference between what is right and what is wrong. Most people I teach have little desire to hurt anyone, even if they may be legally justified in doing so. This, in many ways, is what it means to be a decent person. *Primum non nocere* ("First, do no harm"). So simple. So basic. It's the foundation of the Golden Rule ("Do unto others as you would have done to you").

But there may come a time when you must protect yourself or those you love; and to do so, you may need to use violence. An important byproduct of any training program should be to desensitize you to violence, at least to a certain a degree. Not just so that you aren't overwhelmed by it, but so that you can commit violence if you absolutely need to.

Good training will not only provide the physical skillsets you need but will systematically build your emotional muscle to be able to think and perform in high-stress situations and desensitize you to doing violence if you need to protect yourself or another. One positive aspect of the killer culture we live in, as discussed in chapter 7 (if you can think of it as a positive), is that you are likely already significantly desensitized to violence. Between movies, TV, video games, and the evening news, you are likely already more capable of doing violence than were previous generations. This is only a positive as long as you remain a person of character, driven by conscience, and who takes firm responsibility for your life and actions.

I've spent a lifetime immersed in the subject of violence—studying it, learning how to do it, and teaching how to defend against it. As a result, I have systematically become so conditioned to the stress and desensitization necessary to perform during extreme crises that I know I would not hesitate to do violence if needed to protect those I love, those I'm charged to protect, or the innocent. Yet I have absolutely no desire to harm anyone.

To me, this is the essence of Living Ready. To be peaceful is not to be helpless; it is to have the capacity to do violence if need be, but to never do so inappropriately.

To achieve this balance, you must clearly decide what you are training for. If you are training for self-defense, do so with purpose and direction. However, if you choose to train in combative arts, realize that you will have a broader, more horizontal toolbox. To remain legally and morally responsible, you must decide on and condition the strategies and tactics you will need for real-world application versus sparring or competition. If you are in law enforcement or are a professional warfighter, this applies to you especially.

I have personally practiced competitive martial arts and combative styles my whole life. I enjoy the physical and mental pursuit and the challenges that such training brings. I also appreciate the art and science of modern MMA and how effective such arts are. I also feel that having this background better prepares me for any eventuality of violence, but the tactics I rely on for the real world, and that I teach my clients professionally, are vertical, simple, practical, and of course, legally and morally sound.

## *Defensive Tools and Force Multipliers*

Self-defense tools are quite common, from pepper spray to stun guns, to firearms and knives, to everyday items like flashlights or pens that can be used to increase or enhance your capacity to deliver force.

Pepper spray can be a valuable tool to deter an aggressor, to disrupt an attack, and to sufficiently create an opportunity to escape. Advantages of pepper spray include its nonlethal nature, its potential effectiveness against more than one opponent (including dogs and other animals), and the fact that it allows for a degree of stand-off distance from the opponent. The primary downside of pepper spray is that it does not incapacitate; it only disrupts. Additionally, if it's not already in your hand, it can be hard to access when needed. There are also places where you won't be allowed to carry it (past security in an airport, at event venues, in certain public places both abroad and in the US, etc.). Critically, it can also affect you, especially if you find yourself in confined or enclosed spaces, and it can be used against you if taken away by your attacker. For all of these reasons, pepper spray should be considered a complement to unarmed self-defense training, not a replacement for it.

Stun guns are a whole other matter. First of all, they simply *do not work* to incapacitate people as you see on TV or in movies. This is fiction. The way a stun gun works is to send an electrical current through the body on contact. This electrical current causes the muscles to contract. The contraction is exceedingly painful, but on contact, as the muscles contract, an opponent will reflexively pull away just as when touching a hot stove. The problem with this is threefold: first, the only thing a stun gun does is to cause momentary pain rather than disruption or incapacitation; second, the pain the attacker experiences can sometimes cause an escalation of violence; and finally, you need to be within contact distance to even achieve this effect. For these reasons, I see stun guns as entirely ineffective—merely the illusion of security.

The one exception is the Taser, which is a type of stun gun in common use for law enforcement. The company makes civilian versions that are legally permitted in most states (check your state's laws before owning). The difference between a Taser and a more common stun gun is that a Taser fires barbed prongs into an opponent to deliver the charge. If you are successful in hitting the opponent with both prongs, the Taser will run a current of electricity for a predetermined amount of time which can in fact cause immobilization. Civilian Tasers run for up to thirty seconds—enough time to allow you to set the Taser on the ground and get away. They shoot up to fifteen feet, giving you good distance control. And when successfully used, they can be very effective.

Limitations include having only one shot, and the fact that clothing, movement, and stress all make it difficult to hit the opponent successfully. Additionally, as you can't fly or travel internationally with a Taser, once again, you should consider it a complement to unarmed self-defense training, not a replacement.

"Improvised" weapons, such as tactical flashlights or pens, may be designed to be used as impact weapons. These can be very powerful force multipliers. Similar to a hammer, the tool is designed to localize striking force to maximize effect. Tools such as these are generally innocuous and multi-purpose. Everyone can use a pen, and you may have need of a flashlight in your daily life. They are easy to carry and can generally travel with you anywhere in the world, including on airplanes, with one critical exception: most "tactical pens"—yes, this is a thing—are designed incorrectly in my opinion. Most are designed to turn your pen into an ice pick, meaning that they come to an acute point or are sharp enough to stab. This makes a "stabby" tactical pen that is illegal to carry on an airplane and in many international locations. And in fact, the design drastically reduces its effectiveness as a defensive tool.

The general principle of improvised weapons is to bluntly strike vulnerable nervous-system areas of the body in a manner that can cause temporary incapacitation (at least when it's done right). When you stab with a pointy tactical pen, you lose this nervous-system-disruption effect. As the tissues separate, you virtually eliminate the localization of force intended, and you simultaneously elevate your own response to deadly force.

It should be noted that even a blunt instrument designed to enhance force while minimizing damage can still cause serious bodily injury if used to target extremely vulnerable areas such as the eyes or throat. As such, training and discretion are essential to understanding not only how to use these types of tools properly but also how to avoid using them in a manner that might be excessive for the situation.

One of the key advantages of improvised tools is that if they fall into the hands of an adversary who doesn't have specialized training, the tool is functionally meaningless. I highly recommend tactical pens for their utility and defensive capability—so much so that I hold two patents on a tool called the ResponsePen, which can be carried on your keychain for ready access and incorporates a glass break feature if you ever need to escape or rescue someone from an automobile. As with Tasers and pepper spray, the tool is not a substitute for training, but the better the tool, the less perfect you have to be.

Finally, let's talk about guns.

If I can respectfully set aside the often visceral political and emotional reactions people have with regard to guns, I will say this: from my perspective, a gun is just a tool. Nothing more and nothing less. In the right hands and under the right circumstances, it can be a very powerful tool for self-defense. And for many, the gun is a vital self-defense tool. But more than for any other force multiplier, *owning guns and using them responsibly requires training*.

The importance of taking this responsibility cannot be overstated. If you are new to guns and want to learn, then please, *learn before you buy*. Understand that you *must* have a secure means to store your gun and prevent unauthorized access. Even if you live alone, or have no children in your home, you *must* take the right precautions to prevent that gun from falling into the wrong hands. Keeping it in your nightstand, or on top of your bookshelf, or under your pillow is simply *not* acceptable and never has been.

There are many inexpensive solutions that allow for rapid access for authorized users in an emergency while still keeping unauthorized users' hands off. All these solutions are far less expensive than the cost of your gun falling into the wrong hands. Learn what the right solution is for you, invest in it, and *use* it.

Beyond the fundamental issue of safe storage, you must understand and live by four universally accepted safety principles (or laws, as I like to think of them):

1. **All firearms are always loaded:** Treat every gun as if it was loaded at all times, no matter what.

Think and *believe* every time the gun is handled: *it could fire.*

2. **Never let the muzzle cover anything you are not willing to destroy:** Be conscious of the direction your muzzle is pointed at all times. This includes at yourself and any other person, animal, or property.

3. **Keep your finger off the trigger until your sights are on the target and you have made the decision to fire:** Pay attention to what you are doing while handling a firearm. Your finger should never contact the trigger, or enter the trigger guard, until you are sure of your target, your sights are aligned on target, and you have *decided* to fire.

4. **Be sure of your target and your surroundings:** Pay attention to what is going on in front of, around, and beyond your target. *You* are responsible for the terminal resting place of every bullet you fire, intentional or not.[77]

---

77    Cooper, Jeff. "Mid-Winter." *Jeff Cooper's Commentaries, Vol. 6, No. 2.* 1998. http://dvc.org.uk/jeff/jeff6_2.html

### *You must understand these laws—and live by them.*

Carrying a gun, whether as a law enforcement officer or a private citizen, requires significantly more training. Many states that issue concealed carry permits or allow for open carry (something I never recommend for anyone other than uniformed law enforcement or military, due to the tactical and social problems it presents) do not have a requirement for training. This means that it is up to you to do the right thing. And to be clear, learning safe gun handling, ownership, and concealed carry only scratches the surface of what it takes to become competent to use a gun as a defensive tool.

One of the most foolish statements I periodically hear is "I don't need self-defense training because I carry a gun." The notion that a gun is the end-all-be-all of self-defense is ludicrous. And I've had people say this to me while they're *not even carrying a gun!*

"So if you're not carrying a gun and someone attacked you right now, how would you handle it?" I will ask them.

Setting aside the foolishness of this statement, let alone the legal and moral implications of this mindset, practically speaking, you simply can't carry a gun everywhere. There are numerous places, cities, and states in the United States where guns are prohibited. Not to mention virtually all international locations. So, if a gun is the only tool in your toolbox, then you are willfully exposing yourself to the potential for harm during those times when you can't carry.

Then there's that famous Abraham Maslow quote: "If the only tool you have is a hammer, you tend to see every problem as a nail." If a gun is your only self-defense plan, you have now set yourself up to where every solution is a deadly force solution, despite the reality that gun-related self-defense is only tactically and legally justifiable in a very small percentage of circumstances.

Finally, there's the moral question. Presuming you've trained sufficiently to become capable of using a gun as a defensive tool, are you willing to do so?

Let me be clear: I'm not trying to discourage you from owning or carrying a gun for self-defense. I just want you to have a clear understanding of the implications and responsibilities inherent in doing so, and the only way to fully understand this dimension is to invest in the right training.

## *How to Select the Right Training*

Like any industry, the personal protection industry is a "let the buyer beware" market, one that comes with certain myths and propaganda. One of the most common myths is that "ninety percent of all fights are going to end up on the ground." Unquestionably, defense from the ground is vital, but in all my years of studying this dimension of human behavior, I have yet to find any true substantiation for this percentage or assumption. What I believe is that this myth is the result of some very good marketing, particularly for the grappling arts.

The trouble is that most propaganda like this is based on opinions rather than fact, and the challenge is that just about everyone who has ever taken a class or watched YouTube videos has an opinion. I often joke that if you put three personal security trainers in a room, somehow you'll end up with five opinions. This is not unlike the fitness industry, or the diet industry, or any host of other industries rife with considerable propaganda and multiple possible viable solutions.

To me, the bottom line is this: when it comes to selecting training, you must be able to make educated decisions. That is the purpose of this chapter. Every industry has its share of hucksters and amateurs posing as experts, but for whatever reason, the self-defense industry is particularly overrun with both. A huge part of the problem is that there aren't many formal certifications that a person can point to and prove that they are in fact an expert in the field. If you want to be a doctor, you have to go through medical school and a rigorous residency. If you want to be a lawyer, you have to go to law school and pass the bar before you receive your credentials to practice law. In the self-defense industry, meanwhile, people who have simply taken a weekend class will sometimes claim they're an expert equipped to provide safety advice to other people.

Just as you would exercise care in selecting a surgeon, you probably want to exercise care in selecting who you're going to rely on for lifesaving techniques and advice. As Mark Twain once said: "Be careful about reading health books. You may die of a misprint."

Even if someone can present to you that they have earned a black belt or some other credential or certification, you still have to ask whether their teachings are

DEFEND: WHEN VIOLENCE IS THE ANSWER

applicable to your specific situation—or for that matter, to a noncombative, real-world scenario. They might be able to teach you good techniques, but if these are not part of a comprehensive process for avoiding and deescalating trouble, and if they're not legally sound, then what good is it to you? Even if it comes from a credentialed expert, bad advice is still bad advice.

Most problems have many possible solutions, and while there are many opinions as to which techniques are best for a certain situation, I would like to give you my criteria for gauging whether a particular move or technique is sound. Bear in mind, like virtually all "rules," these may not be able to be applied to every technique or process, but I have found it helpful to have parameters for defining what works versus what may not. I call these the Four Ss.

1. **State**

   The techniques must be able to do the job they are intended for regardless of the "state" of the Bad Guy. Whether he is drunk, high, angry, big, strong, aggressive, sane, or crazy.

2. **Strength**

   The techniques must be usable and effective regardless of your physical strengths. If a one-hundred-pound woman can't make it work against a three-hundred-pound Bad Guy, then the technique may be problematic.

3. **Spectrum**

The techniques must be versatile enough to work throughout the full spectrum of potential situations, from one-on-one assaults to armed encounters to multiple aggressors. What you don't want are techniques that work for only one type of attack (say, an unarmed attack) that if you accidentally use against an armed opponent will get you killed or completely compromise your damage control.

4. **Stress**

The techniques must work under extreme stress. This means the tactics must be simple and gross motor enough that they remain effective even in the Red Zone of adrenaline.

## *A New Language*

I know I've hit you with a lot of information in this chapter, so if I may summarize, the first step to selecting the right training is to decide what your objective is.

If you're looking for self-defense or defensive tactics, make sure the techniques and strategies are simple, practical, and as vertically integrated as possible.

If you're going for combatives or martial arts, understand that you will still need your own core vertical process that you can confidently rely on in the real world.

Sometimes you have to make the best of what training is available. Use the guidance of this chapter to define for yourself which techniques you will choose to keep and which to discard.

Ensure that whatever you are being taught is tactically, legally, and morally sound, and always decide for yourself which strategies are right for you.

Ensure that your techniques meet the Four Ss if possible, or at least understand which ones may not, and why.

Ensure that your training addresses both skillset and mindset.

Ideally, your training will address the full spectrum of threats you may face, including armed encounters; but at the minimum, it should address the most common issues you may face.

If you're integrating defensive tools, understand their capabilities, limits, and legal implications, and then train appropriately.

Remember that *all* skills are perishable, and for any skillsets to be ready when you need them, you must periodically revisit training and practice.

Lastly, be patient with yourself. This is an important one. Learning defensive skills is much like learning a new language. First you learn the basic alphabet. Then, you form simple words...CAT, RAT, BAT (techniques that meet the Four Ss will provide connective threads that make them easy to learn, retain, and use, just like words that all end with the same sounds and letters).

As you progress, you will learn to form bigger words, the basic rules of grammar, and eventually sentences and paragraphs. Finally, once you become fluent, you can even bend the rules of grammar to suit your needs, but when in doubt, the framework is firmly ingrained for you to fall back on.

## *You Are Never Helpless*

The most damaging part of the myth of helplessness and the myth of randomness is that they convince so many people that they are incapable of protecting themselves. Even as you read this book designed to empower you against the dangers around you, the natural tendency is to fall back into fear. Countless times, I have had clients confess to me, after the first session or first week of a training program, that the lessons they have learned initially made them more apprehensive. This is natural. Once you know how Bad Guys think and operate, you begin to see the Bad Guys more readily. You see the world with new eyes, and this can be frightening.

In response to this fear, too many resort to the security blanket of the veils of denial. There is a comfort in this, but ultimately it is a lie. A save now, pay later scheme. The veils of denial leave you vulnerable and more likely to be overwhelmed should you be faced with real danger. But the real tragedy is that the discomfort of facing reality often causes many to give up the effort of learning how to protect themselves right when they're on the cusp of true empowerment. This reflexive pulling back is never more prevalent than in those who have been victimized previously. The simple act of engaging in defensive training brings the victimization back to the forefront of their minds. It happened, and preparing oneself to prevent something similar in the future initially brings with it profound feelings of helplessness.

*Do not stop!*

As Winston Churchill famously said, "If you're going through hell, keep going." I promise you that if you persist in taking personal responsibility for your own protection, you *will* emerge empowered: stronger, more resilient, and more powerful than you ever imagined. You will be able to live life on your own terms, and what once caused feelings of powerlessness and victimization will become fuel for the engine of your life.

In a dangerous world, you have two choices. You can either pull the veils of denial back over your eyes and return to the myths of helplessness and randomness, or you can choose to become dangerous yourself, own your personal security, master this step on the hierarchy of self-actualization, and Live Ready.

It is my sincere hope that you will choose the latter.

# CHAPTER 12

# Safe Spaces

I SHOULD OPEN this chapter about protecting the physical spaces we occupy by admitting that there is only so far that most people are willing and able to go when it comes to the question of personal security. We can only prepare for bad things and Bad Guys so much, so the tendency is to unconsciously fall back into the myths of helplessness and randomness and just go about your business hoping that nothing bad ever happens to you.

Of course it is important for us to recognize that there must be a balance. On the one hand, we don't want to become so paranoid about the world around us that we think only of self-protection, and quality of life suffers. On the other, we do not want to fall back into denial and the kind of complacency that could lead to victimization. So how do we find the balance?

Whether we're talking personal security or institutional security, the real problem isn't a lack of balance; it's a lack of direction.

When designing and constructing a building, architects and engineers follow a well-developed playbook. For instance, the fire code and the Americans with Disabilities Act mandate guidelines that shape a large number of design and build decisions for any facility. There is good reason for this: Those guidelines ensure equal access for all people, and just as importantly, they keep everyone safe. And the measures are remarkably effective. For example, when you look at commercial buildings, the fire code has been honed over the years to the point that it has become remarkably rare for a fire to result in injury or death.

In contrast, as workplace violence, mass shooting incidents, and individual personal attacks increase in frequency, there is still no universally agreed upon *security code* for organizations or individuals to follow. Institutionally, there are certainly plenty of security firms that claim to have the solution to active shooters and violence, but there is still no codified standard for security "experts" or their processes. As we discussed in the previous chapter, for individuals like you who want to learn to protect themselves, it will sometimes feel like you can't throw a stick without hitting someone claiming to be a self-defense or firearms "expert."

This chapter introduces a simple process—a word that holds great meaning for me and my firm—for helping you systematically navigate your priorities to improve your personal security in a logical and holistic manner. It is a process that my firm pioneered and has spent nearly three decades implementing to protect people and teach them how to protect themselves, their families, their homes, and their workplaces.

While the problem of security is multifaceted and complex, the solutions are relatively simple, and whether we're talking about security in the workplace or the security of your family and home, the process is universal and can be organized into four deliberate steps.

Some of this is elementary, but just as I've learned never to assume the Bad Guys are idiots, I've learned never to assume the Good Guys know even the basics...

## *Step 1: Assess*

"Efforts and purpose are not enough without courage and direction."—PRESIDENT JOHN F. KENNEDY

When my firm is tasked with protecting someone, or with improving the security profile of an organization, our first step is to comprehensively evaluate the risks and vulnerabilities associated with the specific case. Typically, this relates to the physical vulnerabilities of buildings, campuses, homes, and the like. This "vulnerability assessment" is designed to identify soft areas that a Bad Guy might try to exploit to gain access or cause harm to the site, its occupants, or their operations.

To get there, we examine and test the physical site through the lens of someone who would want to do harm. We run through the crisis response plan (if one exists), and we gauge the readiness level of the people inside in the face of threats that are known and that we can predict. In preparing this assessment, we begin to formulate a blueprint to systematically close any security gaps and, in so doing, make the location a much harder target.

While "vulnerability assessments" like these relate to places, risk assessment relates to people. On a personal level, risk assessment is a matter of asking the right questions. Most people don't pause and take a look at their environments and lifestyles through the lens of whether they might in fact be vulnerable to the kinds of tactics Bad Guys employ. Are there vulnerabilities in your life? If so, what are they, and what are the risk factors that you can mitigate? What are your safety goals and how can you implement them without having a negative impact on your life? As with identity theft, many people know the problem exists, but few actually take steps to deny the opportunity because 1) they don't really understand the gravity of such an event's impact, and 2) these things only happen to other people.

Most people don't ask these questions for a simple reason: there's a certain amount of bubble wrap that society has put around us to help insulate the question of safety from the forefront of our minds. Laws, seatbelts, security measures in public settings—these can help us stay safe, but they can also help us become complacent about our personal responsibility to keep ourselves safe.

At home, to take the appropriate level of responsibility into your own hands, you might conduct your own vulnerability assessment. Evaluate your home from the perspective of a Bad Guy. Ask the kinds of questions he might ask:

- ▸ How would I gain access if I wanted to?
- ▸ What are the weak points and the blind spots?
- ▸ Are there natural areas where I could observe or surveil you, your property, and your comings and goings?
- ▸ Do you have a security system and do you use it?
- ▸ Can I see if the security system is armed or disarmed from the outside? (Sometimes the little red or green light on the security panel is visible through a window, as we saw with Ben and Lauren in chapter 5.)
- ▸ What is the estimated police response time?[78]
- ▸ How hard would it be to break into your home?
- ▸ Do you have a plan in place in the event of an intrusion? If you do, does your family all know and rehearse the plan?
- ▸ Could I gain entry by kicking in a back door with little or no visibility from the neighbors?
- ▸ What about entering through a window or a glass door?
- ▸ Do you lock your doors at night, or sleep with the doors unlocked and the windows open?
- ▸ When your kids are playing in the backyard, is the front of the house kept locked, or could someone just walk right in?
- ▸ Do you have designated safe areas in your home that could further delay contact with an intruder?

---

78  This may vary greatly, depending on where you live.

Some of these things might seem obvious at first, but it's shocking how often people overlook them—or how good a Bad Guy can be at exploiting those moments when, for instance, you forget to lock the door. Do you know why a Bad Guy chooses a specific car to steal? More often than not, it's because the owner left the doors open and the keys inside.

In any case, these are just a few of the questions that a Bad Guy might ask to gauge whether to target you or your home. For a more comprehensive self-evaluation, my firm's website offers a self-assessment survey.[79] For now, the idea is to consider the basics, and to apply the knowledge you have gained from this book to your environment. We must think like a Bad Guy and then follow through with the Deny, Deter, Defend continuum for every space in which we regularly spend our time.

The assessment begins with the perimeter—the property line, fences, and exterior walls of the space in question. Think like a Bad Guy and consider the vulnerabilities in this perimeter and how they might be exploited.

Next, consider what we call the "hard line" of the space in question. This includes all the walls, windows, and doors. How would a Bad Guy assess these elements? Would he see opportunities for entry, whether by surprise or by force?

Finally, consider the safe areas within the space. Is there a place where, in the event of an attack, you can fall back and delay contact with the Bad Guy?

---

79   www.LiveReadySolutions.com

From a Deny, Deter, Defend perspective, we deny opportunity by doing things like keeping our doors locked, utilizing quality perimeter security, and having strong protocols to minimize opportunity and to know what to do in the event we are concerned about an attack at home or in the workplace. Deterring threats is a matter of having visible security like fences, cameras, reinforced windows, and so on—physical signs that this space would make for a hard target. Defend is then a matter of ensuring that you, your family, and your coworkers are well trained in their response to any threat, and simply put, they know what to do and how to do it.

In the workplace, it's always good to have an independent third party evaluate your risks and make recommendations, but that should not stop you from doing the same thing internally.

Whether utilizing a vulnerability assessment on a personal level or a professional level, the resulting blueprint serves as your plan on how to respond to and shore up vulnerabilities, prioritize the actions you will take to enhance your personal security, and identify the best way to allocate your resources to keep yourself and your loved ones safe. The best part about this document is that working through it will help give you peace of mind that if any threats arise, you will be better prepared to meet them. At the same time, we must also avoid letting this document contribute to complacency. We can't make this a one-and-done situation. The plan must be revisited, updated, and improved as you work through the other three steps in the process. Think of the report as a living document you can revisit and amend periodically to ensure that your plans are always current and adapted to your changing security needs.

## Step 2: Plan

> "In preparing for battle, I have always found that plans are useless, but planning is indispensable."—PRESIDENT DWIGHT D. EISENHOWER

If I have demonstrated nothing else in this book so far, it should be that the time to prepare for a crisis is not during the crisis; it is *now*. Regardless of your plans, it is also important to make sure that they remain adaptable. You must be able to adjust and improvise as the circumstance requires. This goes for both institutional crisis response plans and family emergency plans.

As a case in point, consider that New York City had never actually planned for the specific kind of attack it faced during 9/11, let alone the possibility that the World Trade Center could collapse. In fact, the World Trade Center was considered one of the safest, hardest targets in the city—so much so that the city's Emergency Management Operations Center was located on the twenty-third floor of 7 World Trade Center and was rendered unusable due to the attack. The reason the city's emergency response capabilities were so swift and competent wasn't just due to the resilience typical of New Yorkers and Americans in general; it was because they had methodically planned for every other conceivable possible crisis, and had the ability to rapidly adjust, adapt, and improvise even to unanticipated

SAFE SPACES

dynamics like someone flying a commercial airliner into the side of a building.

The Occupational Safety and Health Administration (OSHA) recommends that all businesses have a crisis response plan, and in today's world, any business with employees that doesn't have a competent and comprehensive plan is putting themselves and their people at risk. The same recommendation applies for you and your family, with what is commonly referred to as a family emergency plan. When preparing your own crisis response plan, the key is simplicity, and to think it through in an objective way.

At Platte Canyon High School in 2006, a gunman took seven female students hostage, and the disjointed response from the school and police led to the shooting death of Emily Keyes. Emily's parents, John-Michael and Ellen, responded by founding a nonprofit called the I Love U Guys Foundation. John-Michael and Ellen were not security professionals, but they poured themselves into the subject to determine what, if anything, could be done to improve the security and crisis response plans of American schools. They attended countless conferences and symposiums about school safety, hosted roundtables with security experts, and convened with hundreds of school administrators, parents, students, and first responders in search of answers.

What they discovered is something that I have also witnessed in working with dozens of schools on their own crisis response plans: there just isn't a universal plan for schools to follow. In my experience, some school districts don't even implement the same plan in each individual school within

351

the district. But as the I Love U Guys Foundation puts it, there is "a lack of clear, distinct, common language between first responders, students, and staff."[80]

This exploration led to one of the very few good things to ever come out of a school shooting: the I Love U Guys Foundation released what they refer to as the Standard Response Protocol (SRP). It is, in a nutshell, a vertical response system designed to help administrators, teachers, students, and first responders to react quickly and effectively to any threat with a total of four possible actions. Put simply, based on the threat, the order can be given to go into "Lockout," "Lockdown," "Evacuate," or "Shelter."

A lockout is ordered whenever the threat is occurring outside the building. The response is to get everyone inside as quickly as possible and then lock down the hard-line doors and windows.

A lockdown is ordered when the threat is inside the building. This is the order that happens when an armed Bad Guy or active shooter has been discovered inside a school, workplace, or other public setting. The response is for everyone to retreat into the nearest classroom, office, or room with a lockable door. There, they barricade themselves in, keep quiet, and stay out of sight—effectively retreating to a safe area that can delay contact with the Bad Guy until help arrives.

"Evacuate" calls for everyone to flee the building and get to the nearest safe location. Ideally, the evacuation plan

---

80   https://iloveuguys.org/About.html#A-Little-History

will have been rehearsed regularly to ensure that the order can be carried out in an orderly fashion. While it might be best for a school to use a lockdown in the event of an active shooter (to "clear the decks," as it were), an evacuation is typically used only in the event of something like a fire. In other locations, such as your home or workplace, evacuation may also apply as an option to a violent threat. It simply depends on the location and availability of safe areas.

Finally, "shelter" is the order in response to a natural danger like a tornado or earthquake, or a hazmat situation where there is no violent threat, but everyone is safest inside.

As a security professional, I could not give a system higher marks than I give this one. The foundation set out to codify the language used in schools in response to threats, and they have done far more than this. Their work has also illuminated an All-Hazards model for schools. I advocate for you to consider a similar All-Hazards model, one that can be adapted to your specific situation and circumstances, but using this concept that provides a logical, vertical process of determining responsibilities and priorities, regardless of the nature of the crisis—anything from a natural disaster to a terrorist attack or home invasion.

Now, while the threats to a school and to your home might not always be similar, the same logic can be applied. The question remains, how do you respond when the threat is outside the home versus inside? How do you know when to lock down your hard line versus evacuate? And what do you do in the event of a tornado, a fire, or threat from hazardous materials?

From a workplace perspective, matters become slightly

more specific to individual organizations. A retail environment is likely to require different response plans than office complexes. If you're in a high rise, you might need different evacuation procedures than if you're in a factory. So the answers on how to construct your plan will vary. But whatever the result looks like, it will be most effective if it is as vertical as the SRP.

When thinking about my home, I imagine the SRP process as "Get Home," "Stay Home," "Get Out," and "Get Down." If the threat is outside, get home and ensure that everyone is where they need to be in order to stay safe. If there is an ongoing problem like a natural disaster or a pandemic, we need to stay home. In this scenario, it's important to be prepared for those times when we can't get out of the house for food, water, and supplies. "Get out" refers to those times when our home environment is compromised and we have to evacuate. Having a go kit and a plan on where we might go to stay safe is essential in these scenarios. "Get down" refers to those times when we need to take shelter in the event of a storm, earthquake, or intruder—generally retreating to a safe area.

Whatever terminology you use, the key is to think through these scenarios. Ask yourself, "What do I want my family to do in the event of an incident?" If, for instance, you experience a home invasion, how do you want your family to respond, and what, specifically, do you want them to do to get through the situation safely? This may vary depending on where you live, whether in a rural area or a big city, as results on how long it will take for help to arrive may swing considerably.

If you're targeted for attack on the street, what is going to be your recourse?

If you're going out at night—whether on a date, to a party, or just out on the town—what will you be taking with you if a situation arises where you need to defend yourself or handle any other emergency? Should you have any kind of protective instruments on you, whether an improvised weapon like a response pen or pepper spray? What about a flashlight? What is your communications plan? Do you have any means to contact help beyond your cell phone?

It is always best practice to consider what you know about your companions. If you're going to a party or meeting up for a date, for instance, how well do you know the people you're going with? What happens if you get drunk? Or if they do? How will you get yourself home if you need to? If something happens that you don't approve of, how are you going to handle or get out of the situation?

From a family perspective, the biggest question to ask is: what is your family emergency response plan? If there is a major disruption to civil services, what will you do to protect yourself, the people you love, and your home? If you have to stay inside for an extended period, do you have enough food in your house? Do you have enough water to survive a prolonged need to Stay Home? Do you have a proper first aid kit, or better yet, a trauma kit? Does everyone in the family know how to use it?

Do you have the ability to protect yourself and your family, should Bad Guys try to get into your house? If something terrible happens that threatens to destabilize the country, does your communications plan cover how you will get your children home from school? What if your children are in college in another state or country? Do you have a plan for the next pandemic?

If you don't have the answers to these questions, do not worry. Just sit down with your family and loved ones and start planning. Ninety-five percent of bodyguarding is advanced planning to avoid predictable trouble and emergency planning in the event of the unexpected. Approach your home safety and security in the same forward-thinking manner.

The final measure for your preparation step is to make sure to keep your plans updated. Too often, people will prepare once but then fail to revisit that preparation and adjust on a regular basis as needs change.

## Step 3: Prepare

"Strong fences make good neighbors." —Proverbs

The old saying that your home is your castle tends to provide a false sense of confidence, at least from a security perspective. Actual castles were designed specifically with security and fortification in mind. The story was similar with the "fortress" design of older school buildings and massive industrial complexes. The goal was fortification—like a storm shelter or bomb shelter—even if that fortification sacrificed some measure of aesthetic appeal.

Modern buildings, however—from corporate campuses to retail locations to residential homes, and yes, even schools—tend to skew toward more open spaces and floor plans, many entrances and exits, and plenty of windows and natural light. While these environments are generally more inviting and inspiring, they do tend to be more difficult to secure. Openness creates vulnerability.

This is why the third step, once you understand your vulnerabilities and have defined your plan for managing emergencies, is to determine how to secure your environments. In many cases, these security measures rely on technologies such as door locks and access-control systems, fences, gates, alarm systems, cameras, and surveillance technologies. So, before we continue with the subject of preparation, I should add the caveat that technology is a challenging subject to cover, particularly in a book. I can (and will) share information about how to think about some of the more general technologies available today, but certain elements of the discussion are likely to become dated quickly. For this reason, the primary focus of this segment will be on the principles that are more likely to stand the test of time.

The other piece at play is that some technologies can be somewhat regional in nature. For instance, one solution to shoring up potential weak points in a facility is to use hurricane glass, which is for obvious reasons far more resistant to breaking and shattering than standard glass. This is all well and good if you live in a tropical area, where providers of hurricane glass are more common. But if you're like me and live in a place like Pittsburgh, hurricane glass is far more costly and less readily available. Here, we might retrofit glass with bars, but who really wants to live in a cage? Embassy film or laminates are also available for reinforcing glass without changing opacity. In the years to come, this technology is quite likely to change and advance beyond anything that we could currently imagine. The key is to recognize that glass is often the greatest vulnerability in the hard line and needs to be thought through.

In the simplest sense, your home, and nearly every work environment (with retail being an exception), should have basic access control such as locks. Ideally, you will also have a means by which you can automatically go into lockdown and limit access in an emergency. Alarm systems are always beneficial. But there are technology considerations that most people aren't even aware of. If embassy film is within the budget, I highly recommend it in most circumstances. Analytic cameras—an emerging technology that effectively means the camera itself will analyze unexpected or potentially threatening changes, like a person moving in a suspicious way, or a hint of smoke—can also boost your hard line and perimeter safety measures.

Cost is a factor, of course, but we also must consider the tradeoffs that come with any technology. Cameras reduce privacy, for instance. Alarm systems have a tendency to induce a false sense of total security, and many people simply don't use them. Anti-intrusion glass could make it more difficult for firefighters to respond quickly in the event of a fire.

When considering your preparations, it is essential that you do not overlook supplies. If you do need to stay home or shelter in place, do you have the food, water, and essentials necessary to remain comfortable for a prolonged period? If you need to evacuate, do you have a kit full of everything you need to do so quickly and effectively?

The bottom line is that the preparation step requires a close examination of your physical spaces and for you to ask and answer questions about its potential vulnerabilities. How secure are your locks? An almost universal recommendation for our clients is a set of programmable electronic door locks or deadbolts. These allow you and your family to access the door without keys, and most can be programmed to automatically lock after a minute if left unattended. This makes it easier to keep your hard line secured while still allowing everyone who needs access to enter and exit without the risk of accidentally locking themselves out. Many of these door locks can be tied to your security system, allowing you to remotely lock or unlock doors through your phone if needed, and you can add temporary codes to give access to nonfamily members for a period of time, so you never have to give anyone your primary code.

Of course, security must be applied to the access code. How many people know this code, and do any of them pose a potential threat? Do you have an alarm system? Does everyone in your family know how to use it? What is the response time for the security company, and for the local police? Relative to that, what is your response time to get geared up and ready to respond to a threat if you had to personally?

Should you have cameras positioned at the primary entrances? How do you protect your doors from forced intrusion? Should you be using embassy film or laminates on your glass? Do you have a saferoom in your house? If not, where are the locations you could go in the event of a threat that would be safest? If you intend to build one, what is the best way to construct a saferoom to delay contact from intruders for as long as possible?

As mentioned in Step 1, the physical security of your home, workplace, or any other building or environment you may occupy is a function of three distinct and separate lines of defense: the perimeter, hard line, and safe areas. The following is a detailed breakdown of what your preparation strategies might look like for each component.

*Perimeter*

The first line of defense consists of the exterior aspects of the environment in question, from the property line to the spaces that reside outside the exterior walls of the structure, including street fronts, driveways or parking areas, outdoor entertainment spaces, and green spaces. Reducing threats to the perimeter is a matter of installing or upgrading surveillance cameras, adequate and automated lighting, fences, gates, and architecturally designed natural barriers.

Yes, this means installing cameras, but it also means knowing where to install them based on what purpose you intend for them to serve. Are they meant to be a deterrent to break-ins? If so, you may want to keep them as visible as possible. If you don't think they will work as a deterrent, perhaps you could rely instead on more discreet, less expensive camera systems that function mostly as early detection systems. Any camera of course comes with the added benefit of providing evidence after the fact, but our goal here is to prevent and avoid violence so we don't wind up having to manage it.

*Hard line*

The hard line represents the exterior of buildings, including walls, windows, and doors. This is the most critical aspect of securing any environment, as improving security around the hard line includes managing access for visitors and occupants, as well as glass mitigation. What measures do you have in place to ensure that a Bad Guy will have a harder time breaching your home's hard line?

Okay, you have door locks and reinforced windows, but consider the surrounding environment. Is there enough cover to provide an intruder opportunity to pry open a window or wrench open a door without being spotted? Are there more vulnerable doors or windows in a more difficult to access portion of the house?

Put simply, when sizing up the hard line of your house, you have to think like a Bad Guy. If you were trying to penetrate this space, how would you do it? Would you try to kick in the front door that is visible to the neighbors, or would you try to go in through the cellar doors secured with nothing more than a flimsy padlock?

Now, as with everything in security, there is a balance to achieve, and it is based on personal preference. You want to keep yourself and your loved ones safe, but at the same time you don't want to feel like you're locking yourself into a prison. You also don't want to have everything so reinforced that it becomes more difficult than it needs to be to get out of the house in the event of an emergency or fire. Each situation is different. It's just a matter of asking the right questions and finding your comfort zone.

*Safe Areas*

Just like we can't control whether a Bad Guy decides to target us personally, we can't guarantee that he won't also select our home for attack. Even with the most advanced exterior security systems in place, it is possible for an intrusion or incident to occur.

In these scenarios, it is important to have spaces that allow for damage control and response capability. Defining and hardening safe areas inside your home will essentially allow for lockdowns in the event of a breach or an attempted breach. The objective of a safe area is not necessarily to secure you and your loved ones from all harm for an indeterminate amount of time, but rather to delay contact with an intruder long enough for the professional lifeguards to arrive.

As a practical matter, not all areas of your home or workplace can be made into safe areas. There are, however, some simple, universal strategies. The key to a saferoom is its ability to delay contact with an intruder or threat. A reinforced door, or even just a solid-core door reinforced with a lockdown device that makes it very difficult to kick in or breach, is a must. An alternative egress route is a plus, but often not a necessity. Communications are also essential, and simple things like an old cell phone that doesn't even have an active phone number can still call 911. Just keep it plugged in in the saferoom and you'll have a means to call for help if you are locking down.

Trauma kits, flashlights, defensive tools, body armor, and so on are all beneficial depending on your needs, emergency plan, and training. The key is to think through the use of the safe area—paying special attention to the amount of time you think you might have to hole up there—and plan accordingly.

In an office or school, medical and trauma kits are a must, as are lockdown kits that provide necessities like food bars, water, a portable toilet, toiletries, and a privacy curtain. These items can help people manage what could be potentially hours-long lockdowns while law enforcement clears the building.

## *Step 4: Practice*

"No plan survives contact."—MILITARY MAXIM

Of course, the final step to the plan is to remember that we can never be content to rely on technology alone. You can spend all the money in the world on smoke detectors, gas masks, and fire evacuation ladders that your child keeps in her bedroom, but if you don't actually test and train with these devices, how will you know that they will help in an emergency? We can't fall into that illusion of security trap.

Once you have all the planning in place, practice is absolutely essential. At home, introduce your family emergency plan to your loved ones and make sure that everyone is fully aware of what to do in the event of a variety of emergencies.

Does your family know what to do if there's a fire? How does everyone respond to a break-in? What do you do if you lose the ability to communicate with each other? Will everyone know what to do and where to go?

Planning and training are essential, but drills and rehearsals are where the rubber meets the road, where you and your loved ones can objectively test and evaluate the efficacy of your plans, tools, and strategies and help you define corrective actions. The goal of rehearsal is to ensure that everyone involved continually improves, and that you adapt security measures to meet any newly identified challenges.

From the moment the rehearsal begins, you should be measuring whether everyone knows where to go, who to call, and what to do. You ensure that security systems and measures are working properly. For instance, if you have left a phone in your safe area specifically for the purpose of calling law enforcement, is that phone working? Are the batteries charged? Is the charger functional? How about your flashlights? Are they in working order? Do you have everything you need in your trauma kit? Are all your lockdown materials fresh and usable? If you lose power and still have to shelter for a long period, do you have the means to cook a meal? If you have body armor or gas masks on hand, how quickly can you get to them, are they functional, do they fit, do you know how to put them on, and how long does it take you to do so?

All the gear and all the training in the world won't help if you don't practice. Rehearsing emergency procedures at home might sound over the top to some, but it is the only way to effectively evaluate how your plans and training would work in a real-world situation. There is no such thing as a crisis response plan that is perfect on first draft. There are always kinks to work out. When it comes to preparedness, testing efficacy, and identifying areas of improvement, these exercises are invaluable.

## *Building Fluency*

I like to think of self-defense training, personal protection, and crisis management as similar to learning a language. The trick is to start with the broadest, simplest lessons and then build your fluency with repetition and practice.

Learning a language starts by memorizing the alphabet, then applying those letters to form the simplest words. Often, you will learn these words in patterns designed to simplify the process. Eventually you progress to where you can form bigger, more complex words before moving on to simple sentences, followed by the basic rules of grammar. You will know you have achieved a higher level of fluency once you have figured out how to bend these grammar rules to suit the situation.

We see this progression at play anytime we attempt to learn a foreign language. At first, it seems as if everyone speaking that language is speaking with head-spinning speed. But the more you learn, the slower they seem to be talking. It's not that they have slowed down; it's that your rate of comprehension has improved. The same is true with self-defense, personal protection, and crisis management. The more you train, the more your skills improve, and the more natural and second nature your response becomes. The more confidence you gain in your ability to protect yourself, your home, and your loved ones from harm, the less fear the threat of violence will induce.

## *Readiness Means to be Willing and Able*

One of the courses I have developed is called ASSERT, an acronym meaning "Active Shooter Survival, Escape, and Response Tactics." This class takes attendees on a journey through understanding why we freeze and how to overcome that physiological response; how to act and react in one of the modern world's most terrifying situations; and how to fight back when running and hiding are no longer options. Toward the end of the class, after we have gone through a variety of tactical options, including how to simply and practically disarm both handguns and long guns from a variety of perspectives and distances, I present a critical question: "What happens if the Bad Guy is twenty feet away?"

In this situation, you're clearly behind the eight ball. You have little element of surprise, and in fact surprise may be working against you. The reaction time gap is not as valuable because the Bad Guy is too far away for the delay to be meaningful. If there is nowhere to run or hide, the only way out is through the Bad Guy. What do you do?

The first thing is to grab something and throw it at him. A cell phone. A chair. A stapler from your desk. This will capture an element of surprise. As he startles and flinches, you will maximize your reaction time gap. If you close with him immediately following that throw, you'll get there in less than 1.5 seconds on average,[81] and if you know what to do when you get there, you'll have the maximum possible chance of success.

But when you see this demonstrated, or see it in your mind's eye, it sure looks and sounds like suicide, doesn't it? Even when we logically know that any option is better than no option, it's not enough to get our mind to buy in. So let's look a little deeper.

Let's imagine you're dealing with a terrorist with a bomb strapped to his chest. He only has to push a button with his thumb to blow up everyone in the room. In this scenario, you're armed with a handgun. You get one shot. Where do you need to put that bullet to stop him instantly, like shutting off a light?

Most people say "center mass," thinking the chest or heart. But even if you were to shoot him right in the heart or a major artery, mortally wounding him, he'll still have too much time. Remember the vasoconstriction caused by adrenaline? Every system in his body is going to be geared toward keeping him conscious and fighting. Physiologically, even when critically injured, he'll have between nine and sixty seconds before his brain deoxygenates and he collapses.

So, what if you shoot him in the hand or the thumb? Nope. He has another hand to push the button.

You guessed it… It has to be a head shot. More specifically, a shot to the brainstem, which can only be achieved

---

81    Green, Marc. *Roadway Human Factors: From Science to Application.* Lawyers & Judges Publishing Company, Incorporated. 2020.

from a facing position through an eye socket or the nasal cavity. I know that's a pretty hardcore thought, but I explain it in detail because, in this context, a shot like this is the only way to ensure instantaneous stoppage of a human being's motor function.

If you have never shot a handgun, then let me be the first to tell you that doing so accurately isn't nearly as easy as the movies and video games make it look. Beyond a distance of about three feet, it becomes very difficult to pull off a head shot, let alone a deliberate precision shot to an eye socket, even in a controlled setting such as a range, where the target isn't moving or fighting back.

Now let's flip the scenario completely around. Imagine that the Bad Guy is holding a gun. His heart is pounding. His hands are shaking. He's tunnel-visioned and having a hard time seeing and hearing what's going on around him. He has lost some or all of his fine motor skills to Red Zone adrenaline. Suddenly, someone like you throws a chair at his face and is moving and closing at high speed with the full intent of stopping him. In those 1.5 seconds, all he's going to see is his mission failing. His delicate fantasy of control will collapse like a house of cards, his psychology likely too brittle to adapt and overcome this resistance. This simply isn't the way this was supposed to go…

I'm not trying to suggest that this situation isn't dangerous, or that it's easy to handle, or that you can't get shot in the process. What I'm suggesting is that *you can't be stopped*—at least not easily. There's only one place that Bad Guy can put a bullet to stop you from getting to him, and that's a head shot. The likelihood of him pulling that off under these conditions is virtually nil.

This is not to belittle the implications of getting shot, or the trauma of dealing with a situation like this. What I'm suggesting is that you are far more powerful than you have been led to believe. You are fundamentally never helpless, even in the worst-case scenario—or what some might (erroneously) call a no-win situation.

Fighting back is not suicide. Suicide is *doing nothing*. Suicide is having your options taken from you by your limbic system and freezing into tonic immobility, where the decision on whether you live or die falls to the discretion of the Bad Guy.

As with much of self-defense in general, you often don't have to be bigger, stronger, or even better than the Bad Guy to survive this situation. You just have to be willing and able to take action.

As former Marine and self-defense expert John Farnam says, "Willingness is a state of mind. Readiness is a statement of fact." If you have made it this far in the book, you are well on your way toward readiness. The only piece left is willingness, and willingness is a *decision*.

That decision comes down to a very simple question: if the only thing standing between that Bad Guy and the people you love and care about most in this world is you, then is there anything on Earth that would stop you from getting to him? Is there anything more dangerous than a mother bear defending her cubs?

Willingness is a decision you can make right here, right now. The world is full of dangerous people, but the most dangerous person is someone who has both the willingness and readiness to protect what they love. The only one in the world who can prevent you from becoming that person is you.

# Nothing Worth Doing Is Absent of Risk

"There is no possible victory in defense. The sword is more important than the shield and skill is more important than either. The final weapon is the brain.

All else is supplemental."

—JOHN STEINBECK

WHEN I DECIDED to write this book, my goal was twofold. First, I wanted to impart the skillsets I've (often painfully) learned over the past two decades of protecting people and teaching them how to protect themselves. To provide you with an "operating system" for systematically applying these principles in your life.

The past twelve chapters have focused on building this operating system: how to recognize danger; understanding how Bad Guys think and select their targets; how to tune your radar and overcome denial; how to recognize and manage interviews and deter threats from escalating; how

371

to choose the right training for you; and finally, how to apply the Deny, Deter, Defend operating system to your daily life and to your physical spaces.

The second goal for this book was to help you achieve something far more elusive, yet every bit as important: to help build in you a "warrior" mindset. To enable you to think differently. To overcome the lies of the myths of helplessness and randomness. To help you take full responsibility for your own protection and circumstances, and to understand how truly powerful you are and can become.

But I've learned that this mindset isn't something that can be pursued. It is something that must *ensue*. It is a byproduct of knowing what to do and how to do it; of knowing what to look for and when to look; and, ultimately, of knowing that just because someone wants to hurt you, it doesn't mean they can. *You* are the final arbiter in the equation.

True personal power doesn't derive from wealth, or physical strength, or illusions of control; it comes from our capacity to choose our own responses.

Most people think that to survive you have to be strong, both physically and mentally. Isn't that what Charles Darwin meant when he said "survival of the fittest?" In reality, "It is not the strongest of the species that survives, nor the most intelligent. It is the one most adaptable to change." This quote, by Leon Megginson, Professor of Management and Marketing at Louisiana State University in 1963, nails it.

It's not the strong who survive; it's the most adaptable.

No matter how big and strong the oak tree, it will break if the storm is too great. In contrast, the palm tree bends with the wind. And not only does the palm tree stand tall again when the storm passes, but all the stress and pressure of the storm serve only to make it stronger, more flexible, and more resilient.

The same holds true for those who try to meet the difficulties and challenges of life with strength alone. They ultimately find themselves worn down, beat up, maybe even broken.

This doesn't mean you shouldn't strive to make yourself stronger; it means that you must not lose sight of the most important factor: adaptability. Adaptability means flexibility. The ability to bend and to flow no matter how great the storm.

Some of the toughest, most resilient people I've met were not the biggest, strongest, or most physically imposing people, and in contrast, some of the physically strongest and fittest were the least capable of adapting to changing circumstances. Emotionally, in many ways, they were the most brittle.

The adaptable were the people everyone turned to in times of trouble. They were leaders, not because they held a title or position, but because they always seemed cool headed, able to make good decisions under pressure, and supremely capable of managing difficulties that would crumble most people. The thing is, they were experiencing the same volatile and uncertain conditions as everyone else. They had their doubts and fears and insecurities just like everyone else too. They just had a different way of thinking and responding.

So how do you achieve this kind of adaptability and resilience? Simple. You practice.

Internalize the lessons contained in this book. Maybe choose a physical training program based on the guidance in chapter 11—or if you're already training, keep going! Become comfortable being uncomfortable. Then practice. Simple.

I said *simple*, not *easy*.

Yoga teacher K. Pattabhi Jois was famous for routinely responding to virtually any question with "Practice, and all is coming."

The right practice changes you. And that's one of the reasons so many find value in ongoing training, well beyond the basic skills they need to protect themselves and their families. It's because whether they're conscious of it or not, they know they're onto something: that regardless of how big, strong, fast, or skilled you are, ultimately, it's the emotional muscle you build that enables you to survive and thrive in this dangerous world.

Life is not about waiting for the lifeguards. It's not about constructing bunkers and living in fear. When you accept that the world is not without danger, that anything worth doing is not without risk, and that you can be your own lifeguard, that is when you conquer fear and live beyond uncertainty.

Ultimately, you become certain not in the outcomes but in your ability to meet whatever challenge may present itself. You become dangerous yourself and learn to Live Ready.

**SAM ROSENBERG** has made a career of protecting people and organizations and teaching them how to protect themselves. He served as an officer in the U.S. Marine Corps, and in the private sector as a close protection specialist for heads-of-state, dignitaries, celebrities, and CEOs. He is the author of *The Traveler's Guide to Personal Security* and *The Path of the Victor*, inventor of the Response Pen, and founder of LiveReady, an organization which provides comprehensive enterprise risk management, personal protection training, and close protection services for clients globally.